BUILD INFORMATION SYSTEM PYRAMID

ECOLOGY OF DATA WAREHOUSE

(second edition)

TAIWEI CHI

ISBN: 979-8-88640-947-5 (sc)
ISBN: 979-8-88640-948-2 (hc)
ISBN: 979-8-88640-949-9 (e)

One Galleria Blvd., Suite 1900, Metairie, LA 70001
1-888-421-2397

CONTENTS

ACKNOWLEDGEMENTS

The purpose of this book is to provide a comprehensive view of data warehouse architecture and help audience see through complex data warehouse environment. As well as understanding the fundamental concepts, principles, structures and to incorporate them into their data warehouse designs.

The works on many professionals, architects, scholars, writers, domestic and international as well as many current books, periodicals, articles, and news items, have been consulted in the preparation of this book. I gratefully acknowledge my indebtedness to the authors of all of them, thanks to those who gave me great helps. Also to all of them, and to all others who have aided me in the preparation of this book.

Figure 3 run

INTRODUCTION

THE TAO OF DATA WAREHOUSING

故善战者，立于不败之地，而不失敌之败也。
是故胜兵先胜而后求战，败兵先战而后求胜。
善用兵者，修道而保法，故能为胜败之政。
-- 孙子
"The skillful fighter puts himself into a position that makes defeat impossible. The losers engage battle first and then seek to win while the victorious strategist seeks battle only after the victory has already been won. Thus it is in his power to control success."
Sun Zi, The Art of War, ~450 BC

Figure 0-1 Sunz Sword Bronze Cross

Business competition is war. It's a life and death struggle in a cut-throat world where every move counts, mistakes can cost dearly, and winners cannibalize losers. The keys to survival and winning depends on how quickly we observe, learn, decide, and act to an ever-changing world. The magic wand outplaying in this game is nothing else but knowledge and awareness/foresight. The corporation that knows the most, and uses that knowledge to their advantage, prevails. Business leaders who plan efficiently for success will see an outcoming victory ahead of them before the campaign.

That's where Data Warehousing (DW) comes in.
In today's IT product market, as the economy world warmed and ice began to recede, new products sprouted, Data warehouse and Business Intelligence (BI) tools, like seeds carried by the wind or dropped by birds (product vendors) germinated and brought color to the once cold, barren BI lands. In time, the Management Information System (MIS) solely belong to IT professionals gave way to business end users, management, executives, and decision makers. Little by little, bare ground of Business Intelligence freed by the retreat of legacy systems, turned to blooming pastures for prosperity. This is the hot area of the information technologies – data warehouse.

A data warehouse is a superstructure for management information systems (MIS). It integrates the various operational data sources (ODS) through extract/transform/load (ETL) technology and forms a new platform - multilayered superstructure which, as a transformational powerhouse converts data into valuable information, followed by knowledge, and eventually wisdom - business intelligence (BI), it in turn supports management decision making (DSS).

Together these different types of components (ETL, facts, dimensions, cube, analytical tools) constitutes the data warehouse, forming one of the great business intelligence: decision support systems (DSS). This book is about the data warehouse. It begins with a few descriptions and definitions. What do we mean by 'data warehouse'? what does OLAP mean? Where are they to be used? How did they come to be the way they are?

Having framed the questions, the book provides some of the answers. These will take you on an excursion through chapter by chapter. The book explains how DW forms, how data flows through it, and what outcomes are like.

This book explores data warehousing on two levels: the fundamental technologies and architectural concepts, also the strategic implications of proper DW design. It lays the groundwork for future DW design and development as well as all manners of decision-supporting systems (DSS). This is essential, as many organizations find themselves undergoing integration while lacking reliable resources.

You'll notice a lot of attention given to architectural design, and star, snowflake model topology. Here comes the snowflake - the natural, miraculously awesome topology to aid us in model selection and design. That's because architecture comprises a central issue in information integration, and sets the tone for all subsidiary systems. Once a system is born, it will carry its original architectural characteristics throughout its entire lifespan, affecting everything from system complexity, extensibility, expandability, flexibility, and to its capacity of loading future new supercharged solutions and features.

Following the general data flow, take a journey in and out of DW; start from sources to ETL staging area, from DW fundamental frameworks to OLAP cubes and building the sound multi-layered, multi-section DW architecture – **our Great Pyramid in business intelligence world, is the subject of this book**.

You'll also find frequent references to Sun Zi, the ancient Chinese strategist and author of *The Art of War* in the 500 BC. We interweave his timeless teachings with technical concepts throughout the book because he helps us see the forest beyond the trees. It would be all too simple to become mired in the layers of technical requirements that make up data warehousing. But that's not really what DW is all about. The point of DW is to manage information for strategic benefits, always maintaining a focus on system goals, functionalities enhanced by extensibility, expandability and flexibility – in other words, a Big Picture perspective for relevance. No one offers better advice than Sun Zi for keeping our eyes on the ball – and reminding us that in every aspect of business, as in war, therefore, the ultimate goal is not production efficiency, excellent customer relations, faster IT or even product superiority, but corporate survival through competitive victory.

CHAPTER ONE

DATA WAREHOUSE - THE INFORMATION SUPERSTRUCTURE

Energy is bending a crossbow; decision is releasing of arrow.
—Sun Zi

Definition

What is data warehouse? Figuratively speaking, it is the library of knowledge that comes into play after an organization's crossbow has been bent, yet before the critical moment of decision, when the arrow is released. Technically speaking, it is a centralized database for collecting and extracting data from online transaction process (OLTP) database or operational data source (ODS), plus a resource for organizing that data into a spectacular structure with computed, aggregated and informative formats. This creates an integrated platform for intelligent answers, available to a wide audience and end-users. The DW therefore stands at the core of a corporation's information assets, serving as the architectural superstructure of the enterprise's information system.

Data warehouse emerges as an important part of today's computing realm and it really came a long way…

Evolution of computing – Tree of Life

Based on Darwin's theory of evolution:
Natural selection and random genetic drift are forever constant and dynamic parts of life. More than 99.9% of all species have become extinct since life began over 3.5 billon years ago. Evolution is more death than survival and over time this has shaped the branching structure in the tree of life.

Since the beginning of the human civilization, artificial selection – selective breedings have been used to produce plants, domestic animals, and products that possess functions or characteristics that fit human's interests. Computer technology has evolved the same way.

Market's needs and favors promote new products development in a human environment. The Evolutionary tree of life not only show true history tree in biology and animal kingdom but also show true history in computing technology. The computing, just like tree of life in biology world, sprouted, and developed through a branching pattern of the evolutionary tree.

Tree of life

These will take you on an excursion through time. For better understanding the origin of the data warehouse, it helps to know how the computing evolved, where they grew, when they come to live in history. You will see how those movements explain some otherwise rather curious facts about the distribution of the evolutionary branches as you explore the way computing technology move.

Figure 1-1 Tree of Life

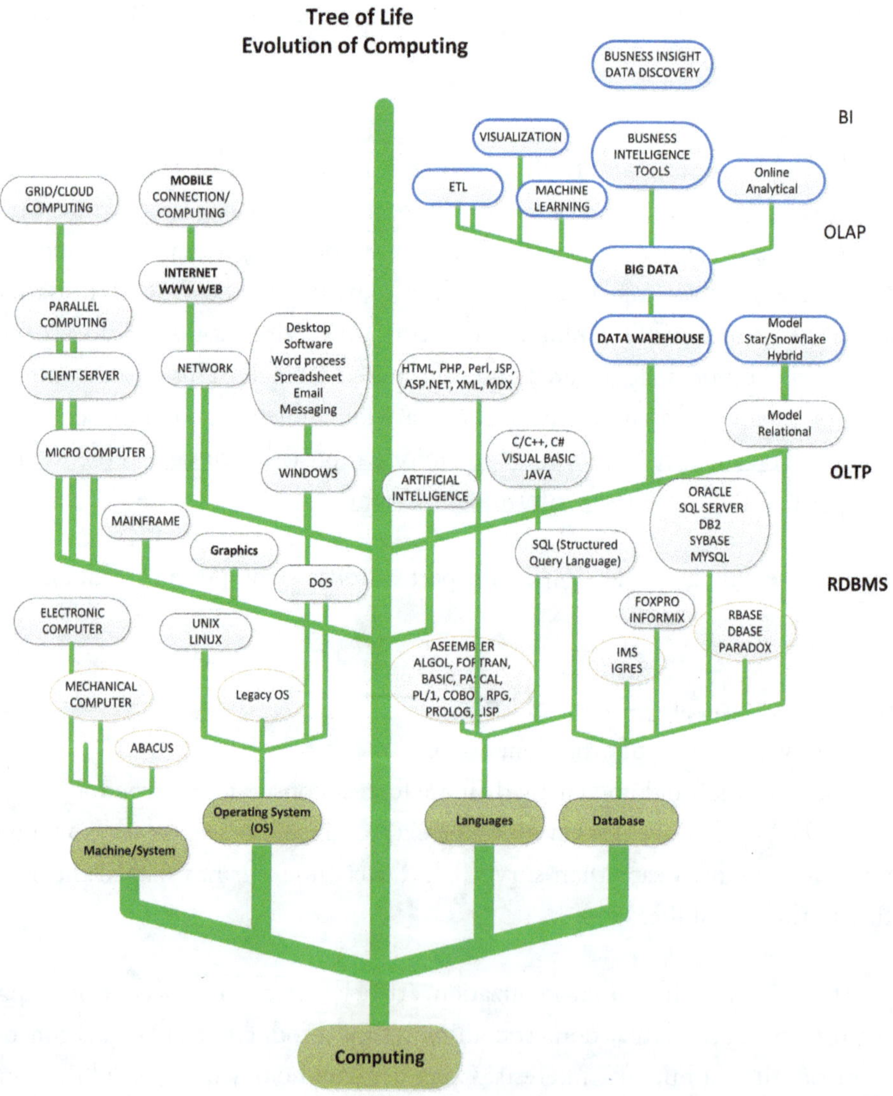

> *The victorious general makes many calculations in his temple before the battle is fought. The vanquished general makes but few. Thus do many calculations lead to victory, and few calculations to defeat; how much more no calculation at all! It is by attention to this point that one foresees who is likely to win or lose.*
>
> —Sun Zi

Data warehousing is the tool which modern businesses make calculations in their "temples" before embarking on any change. DW strikes at two major goals - integration and analysis. It does this by:

- Using ETL technology to capture and collect data from Operational Data Source (ODS)
- Combining and centralizing data from disparate and external sources
- Integrating data into an enterprise-wide centralized repository with a consistent format
- Presenting data in holistic views with a single, easily understood picture
- Relying on various techniques and methods to covert data into intelligent information
- Using advanced OLAP technology to produce and deliver analytical results to endusers
- Combining with internet technology, for interoperability among enterprises
- Serving as a central repository of historical data, so lessons learned effectively, the knowledge is retained. Armed with IT power, the organization is less vulnerable.
- Providing intelligent answers for management

For instance, DW and BI solution gives the CEO a view into corporation goals and objectives through executive dashboards, scorecards, and visualized overall corporation performance, meanwhile, different level of managers can drill down summary cubes into details and to find specific business performance by region, divisions and customer groups.

Specific characteristics distinguish the data warehouse from common databases. In a DW, information comes primarily from operational Online Transaction Process (OLTP) which can be converted into an Online Analytical Process (OLAP) system. It is fully integrated, and offers superior analytical capabilities.

According to **Bill Inmon**, known as the father of Data Warehousing, a data warehouse is a subject oriented, integrated, time-variant, nonvolatile information used to support the decision- making process.

Data Warehouse (OLAP)	Operational Database (OLTP)
Subject oriented	Process oriented
Analytical	Transactional
Integrated/centralized	Disparate
Invariable	Modifiable
Historic	Current only
Multi-dimensional	Relational
Star schema, snowflake or hybrid etc.	(3NF) normalized
Updated & refreshed in batches	Updated randomly
Used by endusers and decision-makers	Used by IT professionals

Note: Snowflake topology is the extension of star schema. The hybrid approach combines both multi-dimensional schema and relational (normal form) and thus in favorable case may have the advantages of both.

Why Data Warehousing?

If you know your opponents and know yourself, you need not fear the result of a hundred battles. If you know yourself but not your opponents, for every victory gained you will also suffer a defeat. If you know neither the opponents nor yourself, you will lose every time.

—Sun Zi

One might ask something like, "We already have plenty of databases to process our day-to-day work. Why would we need yet another system on top of everything else?"

It's true that organizations have immense amounts of data, gleaned from years of daily operation on many OLTP databases which were built by different vendors, for departmental specific purposes, but enterprise's data flows such as data flow of material, cash, and other financial transactions are housed in databases owned by different departments or branches in disparate systems and are presented in dissimilar terms, and do not correspond for a reliable snapshot of corporate health.

Because of this, valuable data remains unexploited despite its great potential for exploration, so businesses are prevented from taking full advantage of their information assets and the data that can be used to create the holistic views are often missing. Common sense tells us that data should be shareable throughout an enterprise. This means data must be collected and analyzed in a consistent way. The ability to analyze data enterprise-wide has been far too limited in traditional/operational database systems. Without an integrated system providing overall holistic view, the more you have, the less you see.

The arrival of data warehousing makes it possible to recover insight from vast sources of data, to find and to mine data resources in existing computer systems where they would have otherwise remained hidden and unused – and, as Sun Zi would say, know both the enemy and yourself.

DW - The parasitic plants rely on other organisms for suvival

A DW can be thought of as a **superstructure** built on top of operational data source (ODS). The nature of the DW is determined by the elements that comprise its base, namely the type of component ODS involved, the information they contain, and the ways in which they react with the DW.

> In nature, many wonderful creatures actually belong to 'parasites' or parasitic plants such as beautiful orchids and valuable sandalwood that rely on other organisms for energy and food supply.

Data that gets stored in a DW originated from the ODS. From there it takes an incredible journey through ETL processes, and is transformed into meaningful and insightful information. Like the parasitic plant which cannot photosynthesize, it takes nutrients from its host (other) plants or decayed organic matter. The same applies to DW; it relies on its ODS. DW itself cannot survive without ODS. In another figure of speech, DW is also like a tree living on its roots – ODS.

In particular cases, a type of DW is considered as grafted on rootstock-ODS.

The following picture shows that DW is like a majestic persimmon tree rooted on its soil – ODS, and an owl represent BI standing on top of it. The tree trunk acts as a natural pump that extracts water minerals, and nutrition necessary to give life to plants. Likewise, ETL does transporting data flow which fuels life and growth of DW.

Data Warehouse and Source Databases - From roots to tree top

Figure 1-2 Dw Tree

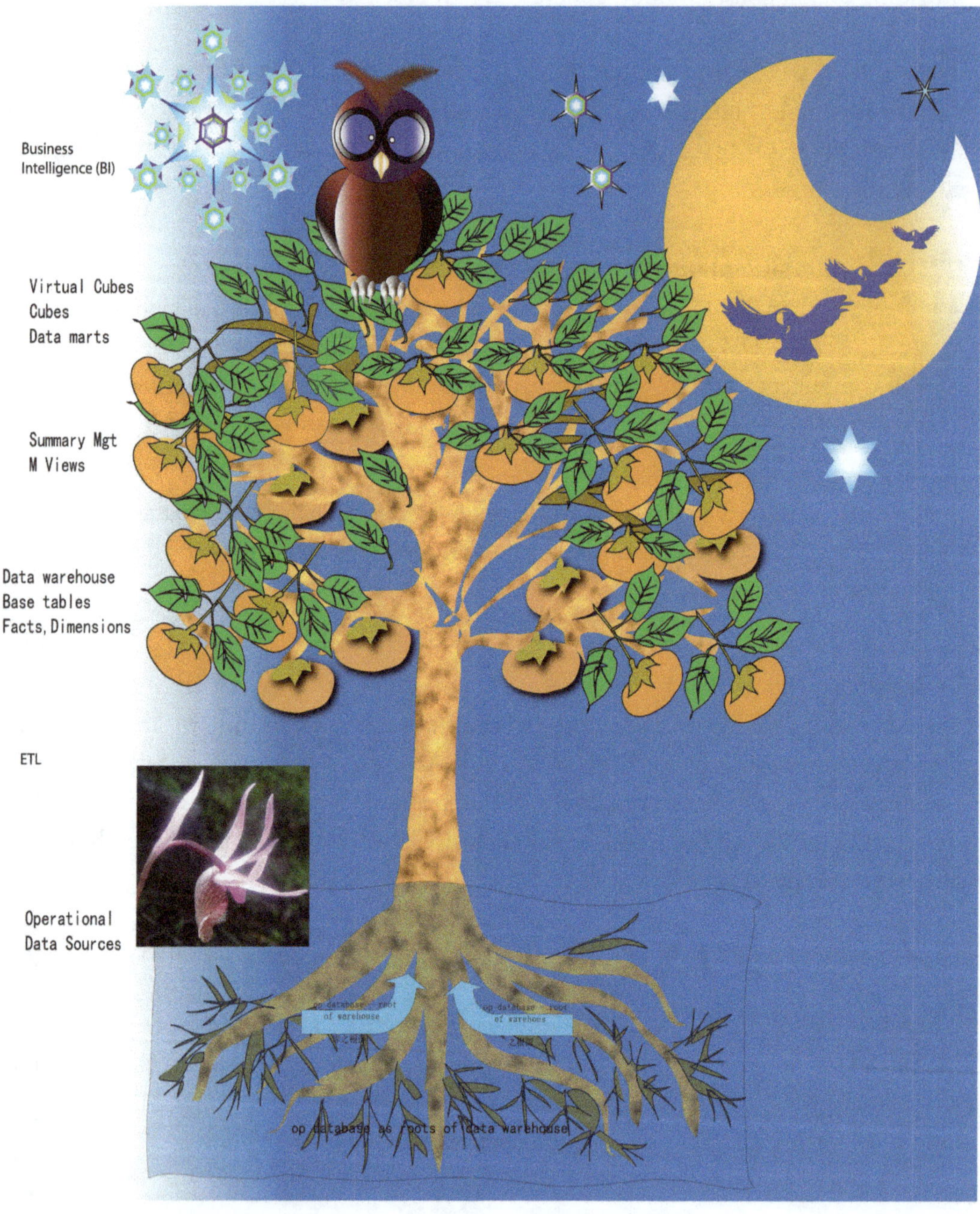

The Missing Link – Information Gaps

Before going further with this topic - DW structure, let's have a look at the typical basic business management system architecture that usually is a multi-layered, hierarchical structure with executive level at the top, managerial levels at the middle, operational level at the bottom.

- Top layer (Executive level): Strategic, executives making corporate-wide decisions and oversees business, market share and business goals.
- Upper layer (Managerial level): Strategic/Tactical, division heads creating strategies using available business intelligence in department levels or various business aspectives on business services, quality, costs and objectives.
- Middle layer (Managerial level): Tactical, mid-level managers making daily decisions: buying, selling, and resource planning; delivering services to meet requirements under guidelines and within quality and other constraints.
- Lower layer (Operational/Monitoring level): Task-oriented managers and staff implemented business transaction tasks.
- Base layer: Staff carrying out day-to-day production processes and business transaction tasks.

One would expect that the information would flow freely throughout the enterprise body (management hierarchies) that are heavily equipped with computer technologies without a hitch. In the typical OLTP-based systems, this may not be true. For instance, data flow, cash flow and material flow may be not integrated. They all reside on stand-alone systems. It's getting stuck here and there, thus here are enormous gaps between management hierarchies.

Figure 1-3 Dw None Tower

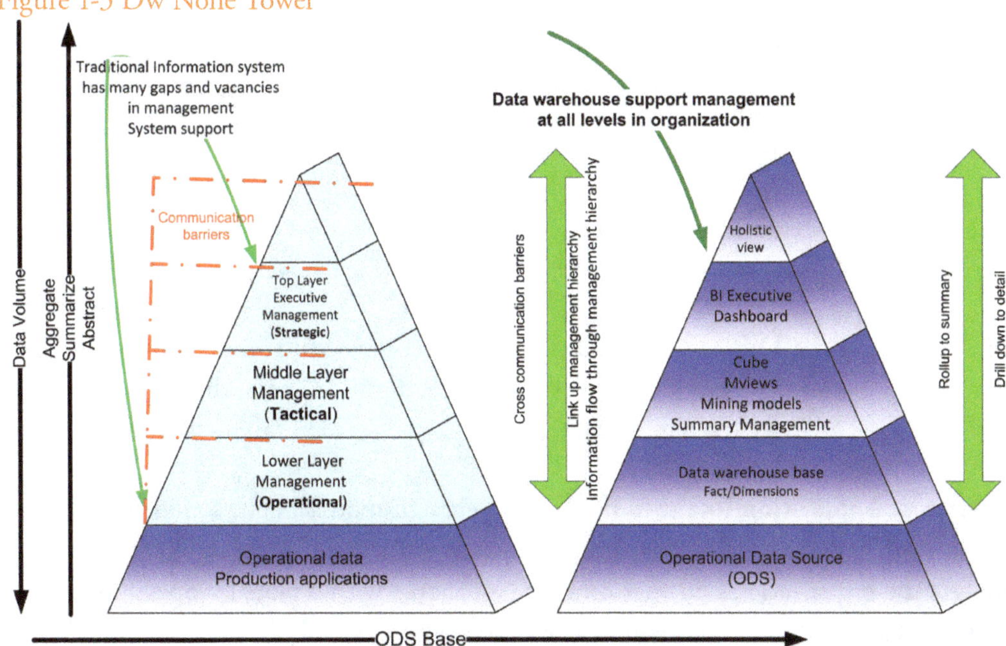

Bridging the gaps

Ideally, a Management Information System (MIS) should have the mechanism for integrating, interfacing and managing information on each management hierarchy /layer in a consistent way, and support efficient communications between management hierarchies. But the opposite is more frequently true. Bacause there are many gaps in Traditional MIS.

The gap lies between transactional data (provided by isolated database systems representing the efforts of the lower levels on the hierarchy) layer and the middle- and upper-tier management layers is so great, it is almost pale, empty void. It is so vacant in middle- and upper-tier management hierarchies, it takes a real data warehouse to do the job and fill the gaps.

Data warehouse (DW) and Business Intelligence (BI) solution added to fill the void with a summary management system/OLAP to support business management and decision-making. This solution works equally well in hierarchical, network and cluster-style management organizations structures. Instead of few, whole organization's **business community** gets support because this DW/BI is in place.

Data warehouse infrastructure – Basic components:

A platform for enterprise decision support

The data that has been transformed into meaningful information in the data warehouse through ETL processes has undergone further aggregations and calculations upward through the hierarchical paths. Finally, it is visualized in analyses, graphs, required listings, and so on that ultimately result in administrative actions.

Summary management – Aggregation/summarization of data based on hierarchical structure that forms the foundation of OLAP.

OLAP - When integrated with a data warehouse, vast amounts of data can be aggregated or summarized, thus providing the global perspective of the business scene quickly.

BI - leveraging the DW to help make business decisions and recommendations. Trend analysis and pattern recognition engines are deployed to help make these decisions along with statistical analysis and data mining tools.

Enterprise Application Integration - In an integrated approach, one can identify, extract, validate and gather data from disparate systems in order to define, compute, visualize and analyze the organization's key performance indicators with a global scope. This forms a central backbone for enterprise's information systems.

DW (BI solutions) fills the gaps between business decision-making support/management and business operation (transaction processing) systems. It also breaks management hierarchy barriers, by providing hierarchical information sharing and make information flowing efficiently. It breaks up bureaucratic gridlock, makes information flow from the bottom up; links management hierarchy system, and thus streamline information flow channeled through the management hierarchical boundaries. It has hierarchical analytical cubes, important objects built for management through OLAP systems. The primary benefits come from their ability to speed up the flow of information and to make it widely available to various endusers.

For a change of perspective, be able to look up, down and through

The goal, in other words, is that the business owner or executive should be able to rollup data and see the whole picture – Have a global view or ***birds eye view***. The regional managers or division directors should see their portion of the picture and a global point of view briefly which can help them be aware of the whole picture of the business performance and trend. Likewise, allowing them to drill down to detail – ***Eagle eye view***. Based on the role-based privileges each user has, information being shared broadly and flow quickly through the entire organization and reach to endusers to make better decisions and quickly, will push to the point of action.

Data Warehouse and OLAP Fill the Gap

Please refer to figure 1-3 DwNoneTower

CHAPTER TWO

ARCHITECTURE OF THE DATA WAREHOUSE

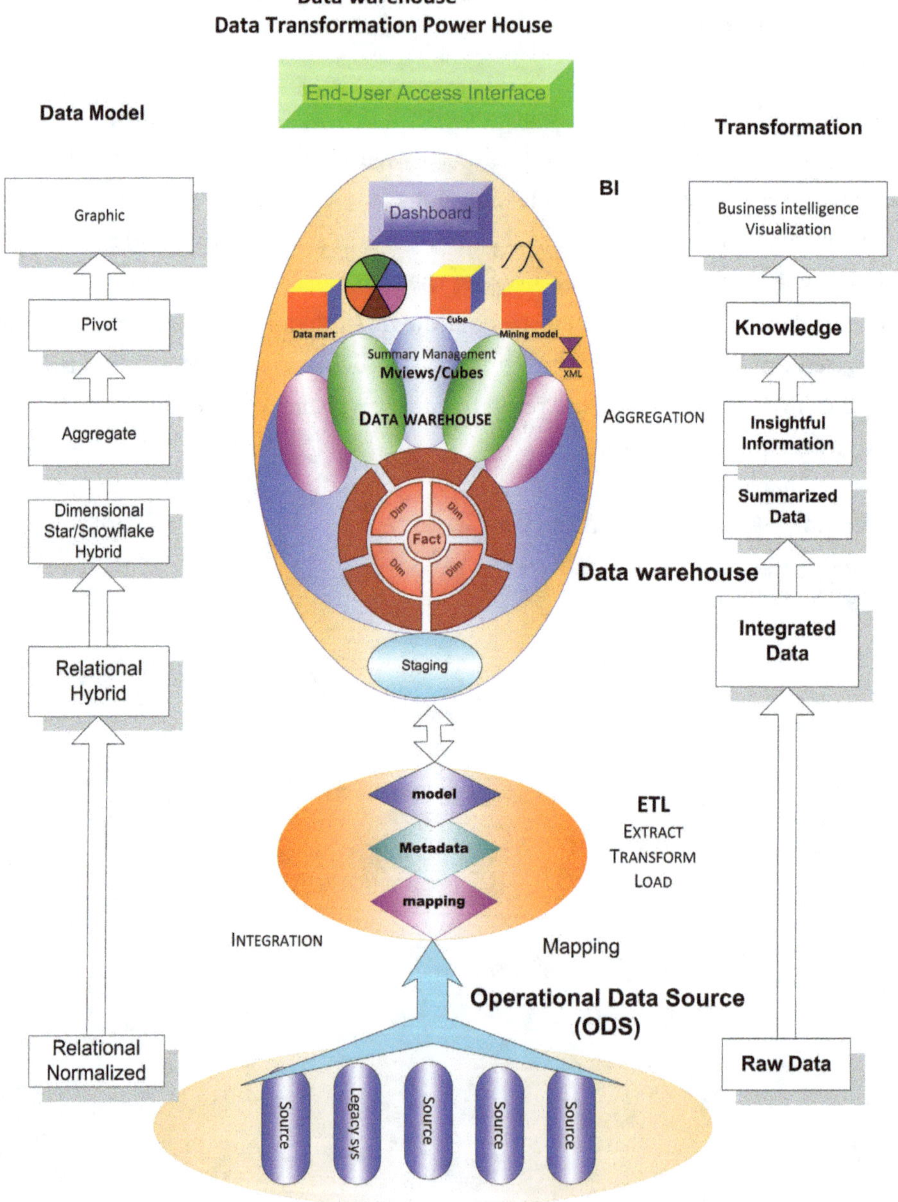

Figure 2-1 DwEnv

2.1 The Great Pyramid

The Great Pyramid, a rational structure designed and built by the ancient Egyptians is one of the seven wonders of the ancient world that is still standing today. These magnificent tombs of the Pharaohs carrie all of glories of ancient Egyptian culture which were built in superimposed layers—forming gigantic prisms that are unique in world architectures and mathematics on ultimate scale. Scholars believe that principles of the pyramid were held in secret at the highest priestly levels in ancient times for reasons concerned **with the centralization of power.**

Although their mathematics and architecture engineering may remain a mystery and people are still debating on what the true model of the Great Pyramid was. Its overall gigantic appearance clearly shows its architecture as built in superimposed layers.

So, what about superimposed structure used elsewhere, then... what is superiority of superimposed structure and what does it have to do with today's data warehouse?

Today's DW - superimposed layered architecture

Today's DW, modern style of information system pyramid is best enhanced by its superimposed layered architecture. Our DW model is somewhat similar to that of the great pyramid. It involved building/deploying layers containing various data objects; with each layer superimposed on top of another. Every layer serves a dual purpose: to rely on the supports of the underlying layers, and to simultaneously support its upper layers. In other words, each layer is developed from the components beneath it, and it in turn, serves as a foundation for the layers above itself. Another way of putting this is that every layer is a sublimation from its underlying layers and serves as a hotbed of its superimposed layer. Step by step, it soars high in the realm of BI wonder.

During the staggering stretches layered of the building processes, there are many variations in the layers of the DW. Each variation is to invest in the future layer with a different blend of objects with their own densities and textures. It was a process that may never have ceased until newborn BI began to emerge into the world. Like a multi-faceted gem, each jewel is like a layer that appears to be superimposed upon one another.

Transformation

As the DW layers built up over the course of several stages, data being compressed and cemented together are aggregating into summarized information from detailed data with their massive bulks. By the time the last layer was created, raw data had turned into informative, disparate data that had conformed and so on, creating the stacked layered DW we see today. It's tiered with ETL, staging area, core data (fact and dimension), cubes and dashboard, all rising up in new splendor – the great information system pyramid.

Before we go any futher, let's take a closer look at the relationships and transformations between the layers typically comprising a DW and its surrounding environment.

- Operational Data Source (ODS) is the base, the foundation of the entire DW environment. ODS can be considered as virtual in conceptual sense for some cases.
- Staging area serves as buffer zone between ODS and DW
- ETL (Extract-Transform-Load) takes data from sources (DW environment base layer) and transports it into the DW basic layer, where it stores fact/dimension tables - primary DW objects. Very often, a staging area between the source and target would be a necessary option.
- Data marts are derived from DW core elements as needed. A data mart is a segment of a DW that provides data for reporting and analysis on a section, business unit, department level, e.g. sales, payroll and, production.
- Farther up the pyramid, where the layers are formed with cube series as result of extensive aggregation or summarization operations against fact/dimension tables. It is this summary management system (SMS) that lays the foundation for the OLAP/BI.
- The OLAP layer is built mainly on summary materialized views or cube series.
- At the highest level, a small top layer has now totally sublimed. So brilliant like a multi-faceted gem, it is stunning in its connotation of depth combined fluidity and dynamic visual effects, the most notable by far is BI Executive Dashboard, which support strategic decision making.

By pyramidal design, we can build BI applications above all the underneath layers. Note that relationships/transformations between hierarchical layers are vital. We either take excellent care of these relationships/transitions between the superimposed layers, or suffer collapsing loss due to the lack of support and bonding with them.

Data tends to converge as it travels upwards in our DW pyramid. The lower levels are the bases of those higher levels, containing vast amounts of detailed data. Further up, the data will be computed, aggregated, tailored and condensed into a more compact and brief form. The upper layers contain information that is concentrated and is more meaningful to the upper management, and is therefore more elegant in nature; data is highly polished to show quality, often presented in summary views or cubes. As the elevation increases (to wards the top of DW), so does the degree of convergence. At the very top of the pyramid, where business intelligence (BI) represents the loftiest form of all, can be easily used for visualization and strategic decision-making. It is here that users can get a Bird's Eye View of overall business performance.

As with any pyramid, a solid foundation is essential for its structural integrity and stability. Similarly, relationships between layers must be carefully defined, created and nurtured, otherwise the whole things may fall apart. So, a wise guy will ask:

- What is the base on which my DW is built?
- Can each layer adequately support those that will sit on top of it?
- Whenever we think about adapting or adding new applications such as ERP or CRM, do we have to evaluate the supporting systems first, to make sure that they are adequate? Can we define a foundation layer in advance that will support future DW/BI applications down the road?
- How do we provide highly concentrated, intelligent information flow and pump it to the upper layers feeding top management needs?
- Given that all organizations are unique and they may not fall neatly into generic layers, how should we structure our DW to best represent our enterprise's business management practices?

While there is no one-sentence answer to those questions, it relies on clearly understanding the data model and a careful layout of layered model design and continue innovation on DW architecture, plus, selecting the right models and strategies that fit most with your business nature.

Transformational power place

The pyramid of data warehousing emanates great power as a transformational power place. And like the great pyramids, it is constructed in discrete steps from the bottom up. Like a high-rise building, or intertidal area, the DW is divided into horizontal bands, or floors.

1. Source or Operational Data source (ODS)
2. ETL and staging area
3. DW basic elements (facts and dimensions)
4. Cubes and nested materialized views groups (it made up of sub-divided layers)
5. OLAP, mining models, reporting systems (it also made up of sub-divided layers)
6. Business Intelligence (BI) and visualization user interface (UI), dashboard

DW for diverse management hierarchies

When different management hierarchies have been analyzed, they may not fall neatly into these same layers or levels, and their levels of each management hierarchies differs in appearance depending on the nature of the business management practices. Rather than a hierarchical, a business may opt for "flat" organizations such as cluster like, blueberry-pie like or network like management systems. By providing sufficient hierarchical information sharing across the entire corporation's body, the data warehousing model applies equally well, as far as it is layered modeled. The pyramid structure here, applies to the flows of data, the scopes, and perspective of data views efficiently rather than squeezing it into a particular mould box forcefuly.

In today's dynamic, fast-paced world, new techniques are emerging one after another in dazzling speed. Big data solutions and cloud computing as emerging data power houses and network sharing grid, handles both database and file systems with great volumes, fast speed and huge capacity.

No matter what technology changes occur, it is vital that you know what ground works need to be done to meet the challenges. Know how to architect and build your information system pyramid based on a solid foundation, so that Today's and Tomorrow's new technologies will lay on top of it which is the major subject of this book.

Data warehouse Architecture - Pyramid

Figure **2-2.1-2** DwPyramid

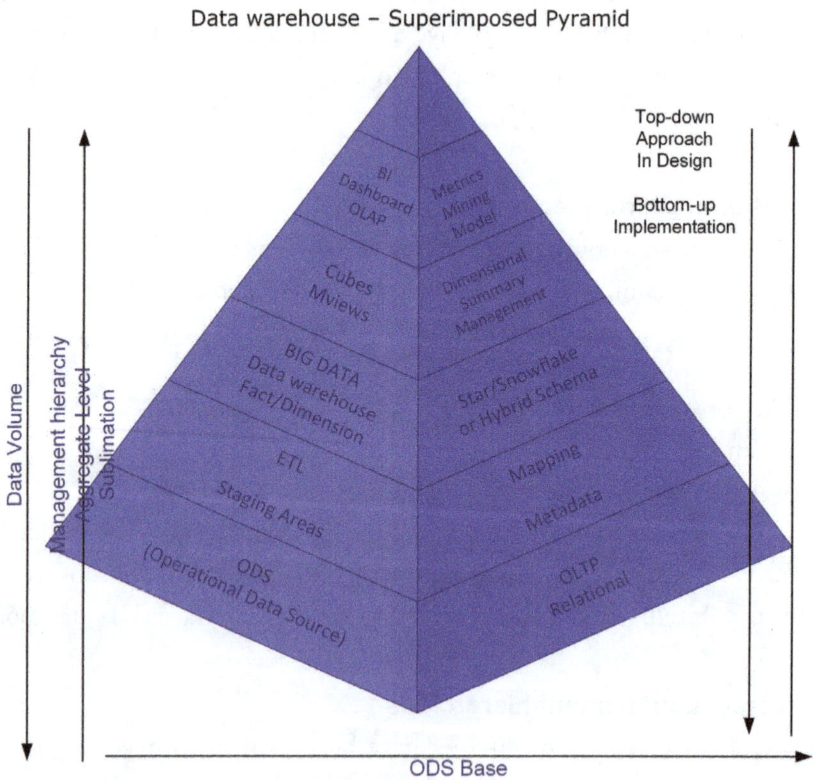

2.2 The Data Warehouse Infrastructure

The infrastructure of DW (and its surrounding environment) is hierarchical, it is comprised of four distinct layers. At the bottom is operational data source (ODS), next comes Extract-Transform-Load (ETL) and staging area which often is necessary to serve as a buffer zone between ODS and DW. Above that is the DW basic schema containing fact and dimension tables. Finaly, at the pinnacle, we find an expression layer such as summary management and cubes with Online Analytical Process (OLAP).

When you look at the following figure showing the DW and its surrounding environment, you may observe that the data flows downstream through the entire DW as data loading is performed in scheduled waves, views, and cubes refreshing after the data loading. Meanwhile invisible, *virtual information flows* upstream from top-down through the DW. It reflects decision flow from data analysis, and conrespondent follow up which then feeds back, forming a loop in business management cycles. DW support business analysis at global scale. Contrasting this with the traditional data systems, where analysis capabilities are limited due to lack of data integration.

Architecture and Environment of Online Ad Data warehouse

Figure 2-2.2-3 DwAdArch

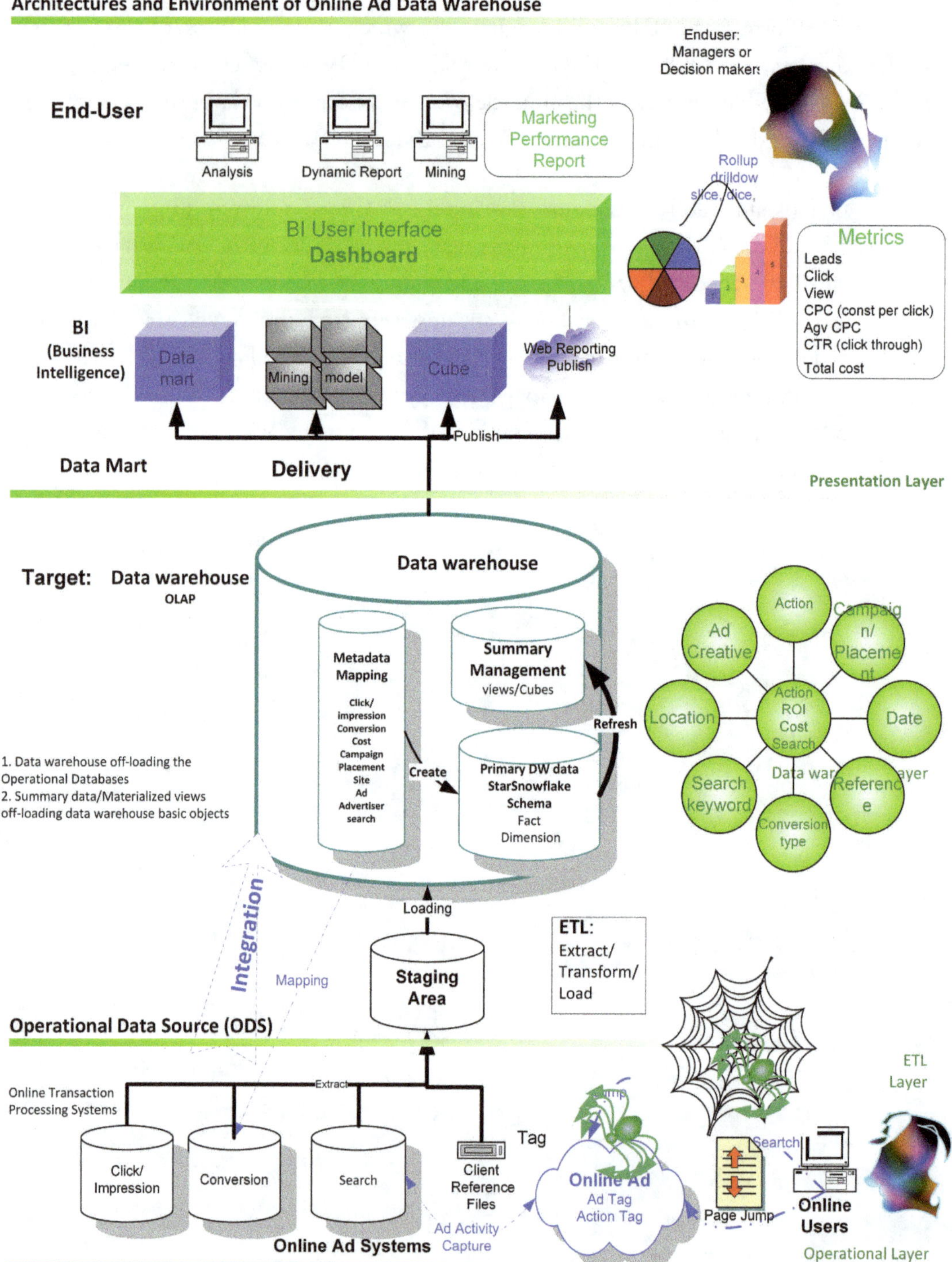

2.3 Evolving Data warehouse

2.3.1 Offloading Operational Databases

2.3.1.1 Two different models

Operational Data Source (ODS) – data of origin/operation; Data warehouse – data of analytics.

One of the most valuable assets of the enterprise is ODS; used in managing day-to-day business activities. An ODS is basically an Online Transaction Processing (OLTP) meaning that its model is organized in such a way that it is optimal for transactional process. Concurrency and atomicity issues are major concerns. Such model should therefore come up with no surprise that transaction-oriented nature of the OLTP has discouraged intensive ad-hoc queries and analysis. DW/OLAP model in other hand is basically output-oriented, and query centric – Online Analytical Processing (OLAP).

2.3.1.2 What happens when these two mix?

There are data models and technologies that may speed up query and reporting, but they tend to slow down transaction processing. For example, heavily indexing tables may help speed up query but degrade the performance in an update (insert, update and delete) process greatly. Query can be such a resource drain for an OLTP system; few ad hoc queries may bring it to its knees.

2.3.1.3 A flashback

Back in the old days, many enterprise's databases carried mixed tasks, as operational database, it's pretty much tied down to day-to-day business transaction processes and more often, it took many query loads to meet the management analysis and reporting needs. What happened in such a system? Sure, it was quite miserable and full of uncertainty.

Our story began, but not quite the end...

Days started brings many people of a corporation out of their residential retreats to begin their daily works. Few others finished their night shift. Some staff came out at dawn and so did the managers, sales representatives, customer care personnels, data entry staffs, programmers, and business analysts. They were adding, updating or deleting data, replying to and sending email messages, dealing with the inquiries and bookings, checking weekly reports, pulling the data for preparing reports for morning meetings ... All these online activities seem to be under the watchful eyes of DBAs. - Looks like another busy day in office. However, such a mixed system ran just like messy highway traffic, some users claimed the right of way for their tasks, others were asking special privilege as an emergency vehicle or VIP convoy by holding off all others. When this was the case, everybody else had to get out of the way quickly.

Results were chaotic

Pressured by the manager who needs to get reports for all regional clients, a series of ad-hoc queries were launched by business analysts against the tables which was under heavy update during online transactions while trying to avoid the watchful eyes of DBAs, resulting in serious competitions and eventually drained the systems resources.

Ad-hoc queries had sat there forever since launched because some tables had been locked. Some long transactions also had been holding off, transaction log was filled up. Some users were screaming and sending angry emails because their submitted mission-critical database jobs just got screwed up due to the table locking and resource exhaustion. Behind the scene, contention was high, database processes were struggling to grab the already limited resources, such as CPUs, tablespaces. The DBA was called to fix rollback segment errors in a haste fire-fighting mood as more and more processes jobs had been screwed up. Then there were finger-pointing and departmental blames as issues arise. Frustrated, still starving for getting information out and desperate, the users locked up for the day while waiting the storm dying down.

Impact for business was potentially not good. It was far less hospitable to end-users who desperate need quick reporting. It is perhaps a disappointing fact that the insightful information was not set to full use when they need it most. You watch fascinated as parts of this drama are played out again and again. That was our story of what happened, and is still happening in an environment lack of data warehouse.

Report server and data replication

From time to time, reporting server based on data replication have been used to resolve the issues, but by data replication alone is not enough to satisfy business user's needs due to its limited functionalities and it still ride on old model which was not quite a fit for BI/ Analysis.

Time is coming, OLTP traditional reporting's dominance has been challenged by a more powerful, innovative query-centric newcomer - OLAP.

2.3.1.4 Offloading

With coming of data warehouse, the analytical solutions blossomed in business and industry, many BI tools became available, and smart dashboards sprang up like wildflowers at such oasis. What followed was one of the most peculiar chases in BI market.

DW brings solutions for both analytical and load relief for ODS. It provides the isolation needed to protect ODS. Furthermore, it takes the challenges of the most demanding analysis requests, delivers its OLAP power. Taking this idea one step further, the DW which created with multiple layers will protect and offload internal layers – its core data. By building cubes, materialized views and summary tables as outer layer, it isolates and protects core data such as fact tables, and definitely improves system performance and security greatly (See details in Section < System Platform – Core and Shells > in Chapter Four). In summary, by providing OLAP cubes, DW takes challenges of mass access - A great load relief for the already stressed-out ODS.

The Win-win solution

DW puts information close to endusers, by providing fast and holistic views. ODS been left alone with a few internal maintenance procedures running. Unlike traditional MIS which only serve small group of people, DW is available to broader users, and even whole organization's business community. In a good DW environment, besides scheduled data loading, everyone gets a piece of toy to play without interfering with one another. End-users that have earned their rights to DW through role-based accounts/controls suddenly give way to life that has flourished, with their desire. They, now within striking distance of their reporting system, and arc able to drill down pivot tables while other managers roll them up to summaries. Senior managers probe dashboard with descriptive charts while department managers select their reports from their datamarts.

2.3.2 Staging Area

> The staging area is buffer zone between operational data sources (ODS) and the data warehouse.
>
> Like wave-whipped tidal lines along coast, staging area is periodically refreshed by ETL waved actions.

In many cases, there are needs for staging areas between sources and their targets - data warehouse. The reason is obvious. Data come from sources often need intermediate processing before reaching the data warehouse. ETL mostly likely runs in batch mode. It sometimes can't finish the job at once (extract, transform and load all together), and has to do them in the groups of split tasks. Futhermore, in some cases it is impossible and/or impractical to have direct access to the sources, or neither have direct access to both sources and targets at same time. The data must to be dumped or extracted from sources at one time, and then be loaded at later time. In certain cases, both sources and targets likely remain isolated. Data is first passed in a format of text file, which would be treated later by other processes to convert it to be the database objects.

All these demands a staging area to hold data, where it may be transformed and transported in a relatively isolated area. They may be standalone database server, file systems, or database schemas/objects.

There are many possibilities of where a staging area may sit. In some cases, it may serve as a dual host for OLAP production services, provided that one may undergo loading and refresh processes while the other stands online.

Tidal actions - ETL

ETL periodically dismantle, wash away used data objects in staging area (drop and truncate tables), then deposit (load) new data, staging area also has its high and low tides depends volumes and frequencies of moving data by ETL.

Like marine intertidal life which surviving between high and low tides, twice a day, the sea rises and falls, alternately flooding and exposing shore. In such environment, the objects built in staging area should able to survive harsh condition there, must be able to withstand not only changing conditions (expanded sources, growing volum of data) but also maintain sanitary of data.

Staging area as a buffer zone between source and DW target, has advantage of doing error checking before loading to DW. It also uses tables to track high-water mark of previous loading in order to determine next data extraction scopes. By this way, it is easier to control loading process undone earlier and more precisely, and avoid the ugly situation in which exessive/bad data have to be striped from DW.

Staging area, what does it look like? what does it resemble? the source or target?

Mimicry is a common survival strategy in nature. Octopus can change its color to mimic its surrounding, ETL does the same, it creates staging objects mostly resemble source, but sometimes resemble target/DW, or resemble neither, depending on the environment, tool used, replication technique used, performance concern, and design and/or development preferences. Their appearance also depends on how you want to distribute or split the tasks (Extract-Transform-Load) into each ETL stages. It also depends on what kind staging design principle to follow. If the focus or major concern is on extraction, you may let staging table resemble source; if focus is on transformation, in case of transfer data from low grain level to high level, staging table may more like target/DW – in that case much less data will be transported and stored as result from aggregation, filtering transform. There is another case when using staging area as a central repository – it may be further extended into the heart of DW. For an enterprise-wide data warehouse (EDW) which mostly rely on multiple ODS, staging area may become a central hub or a cluster by which many staging objects to connect ODS and DW target. For EDW, staging area can be fairly large, forming a centralized hub, most likely in a 3rd normal form database consists with your DW logical model. It normally has a data receiving area holding initial staging tables which most likely resemble ODS tables.

Soft Landing: While collected data flying on the way to its destination -DW, staging area offerings a landing buffer. Since ODS are most likely located in remote servers, and data must be moved through network traffics where there are risks of failure. Hence transport need to be done as quickly and simply as possible. To reduce the load stress, most staging tables (if they are database objects) are bare table without database constraints and been periodically truncated and loaded.

Designers may weigh each of these issues differently, considering systems, data flow waves in both high and low tide. For a distributed data marts environment, a shareable staging area has many benefits such as reducing redundancies - one data fetch from source is good for multiple data consumptions (for several datamarts).

Amazing nature - A soaring eagle, fetch the prey from remote site and bring it back to nests for whole family feeding. Let data feeding frenzy begin at your DW staging site instead of on the operational data source sites.

However, the overall goal here is to govern day-to-day ETL in a manageable manner which further requires some basic metadata tables and control tables as follows:

- Metadata which holding sources and destination/target information such as severs, databases, file locations, table definitions/properties
- Mapping tables
- Session control/log tables holding high-water mark(last maximum sequential id) for incremental refresh
- Synchronization mechanism - be able to synchronize with sources

Please refer Figure 2-1 DwEnv

Centralized Data warehouse with master staging area

Figure 2-2.3-5 MasterStaging

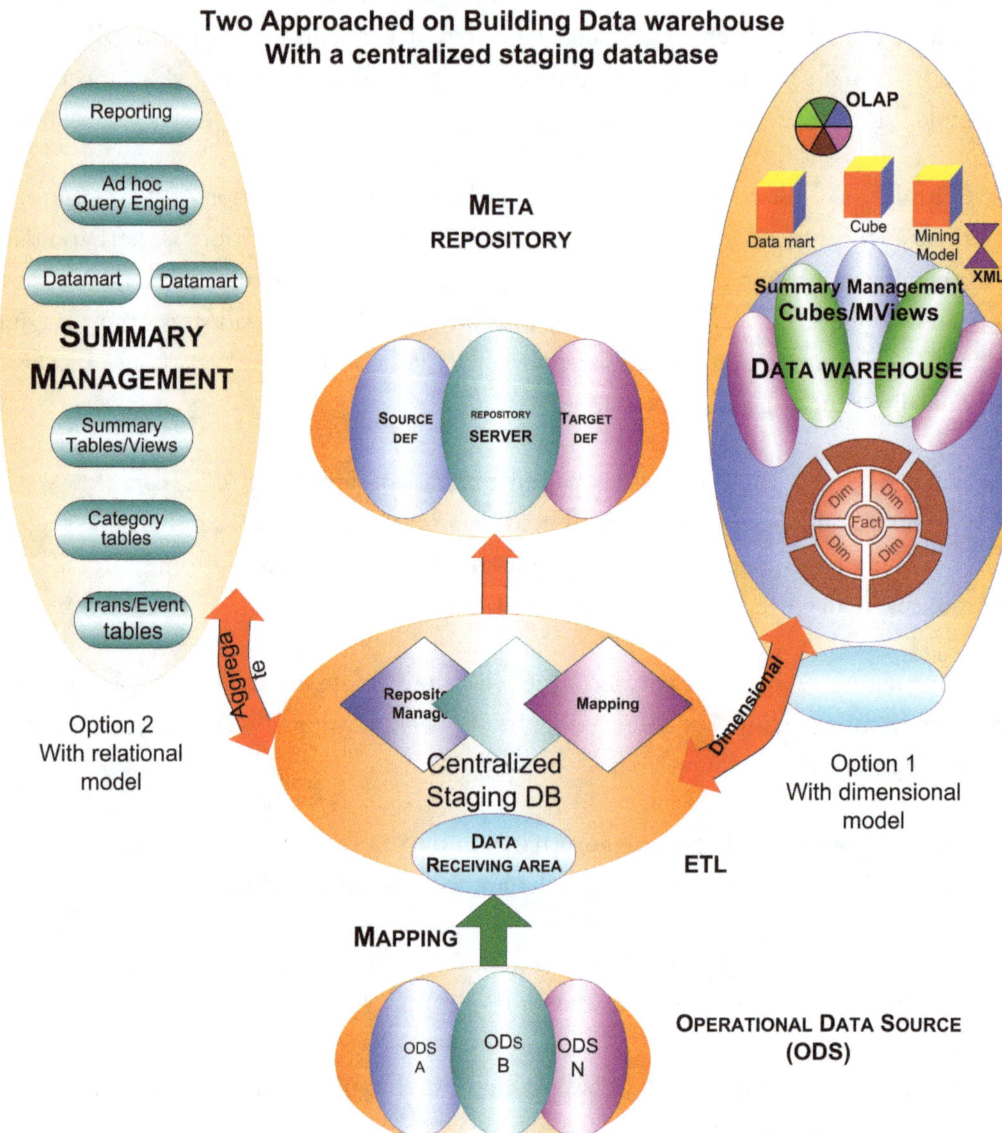

The following chart show data source-staging-target evolution

Figure 2-2.3-6 SourceStagTarget

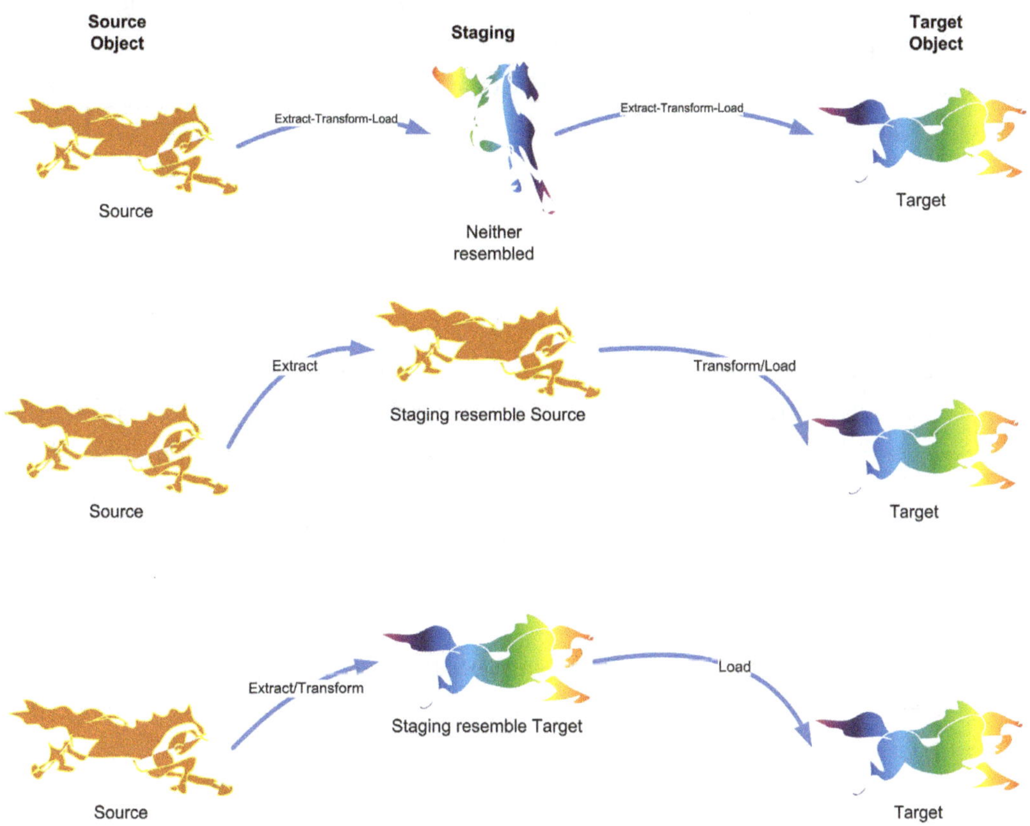

2.3.3 Cycles of birth and renewal

Dead end of data in operational databases

Traditional OLTP systems are usually constructed in an open loop fashion, data flow through the system, being consumed until transaction is done, then nothing happens after that. Data no longer flow – it reaches its dead end. Once data purge is done, a great deal of accumulated, valuable data would be washed away.

Triumph of life

> *The insect's amazing life cycle has been a fascination. Cicada's transformation from a mute nymph to a singing adult (after burying itself underground for 17 years) has been regarded as symbol of powerful rebirth.*

Like life stages of many insects in nature, data pass through from one stage to next, but still its usefulness is not over. DW gives data a new life by continue pushing it through a different kind system, kicking start a new journey. It extracts data from ODS using **ETL** and transfers data into DW. There it computes and summarizes the data into meaningful information, and direct it through the **OLAP** system to endusers. These, in turn conduct analysis and gain the valuable insights, ultimately resulting in administrative actions that changes business operations and further impact on-going data transactions. In such fashion, data presented to endusers now has its own impacts on business even after its transaction was over. You could almost say that the data is reborn into new life through an elegant cycle. We finally see a profusion of BI reporting all flourishes along its course and throughout the business management world.

Through carefully monitoring information flows from each of management stages, you may find that DW represents a central point in a loose loop, which, from ODS to OLAP; endusers use BI/OLAP to help them make decisions. These decisions will affect daily business operations, and are reflected in ongoing uploading data towards the DW and through BI/OLAP, where business performance will be measured and evaluated once again. As you can see a powerful and sustainable decision support is in place.

Cycle of life

The journey in a DW - from raw data to insightful information

A caterpillar completes the miraculous transformation into a beautiful adult butterfly.

Even though data is loaded into a DW through ETL processes, there is still a long way to go from the raw data to more informative, quality presentative data. From presentive cubes the data are aggregated, grouped, computed and well-organized for analysis and decision-making support. Summary cubes serve a dual purpose, providing quick availability to endusers and offloading core data in DW such as fact and dimension tables. In fact, management desperately need summary reports about bisiness performance and trend. For example, a manager may say: 'Give me monthly summary of sales for all the products.". A CEO may also ask for highly summarized reports about the corporation's global sales shown in BI dashboard.

Marketing example

Today, marketers are more closely looking at return on investment (ROI) which becomes more measured discipline. Campaigns are running with constantly checking of the outcomes. Management is expected to take decisive actions, with analytical results. Those actions influence business operations and change outcome which in turn will affect subsequent data and forming on-going fact table for measuring.

Let's say that a marketing department wants to study outcome of a promotion by looking at sales during the past six months and then comparing them with associated promotion costs and its effects in order to draw the conclusions to help them to make decisions and figure out better promotion strategy. After study, a new strategy then get ready for action, thus in fact influence the business operations and results in new outcome. New data from operational source about sales and costs again being extracted and loaded into the DW then become available for further analysis and business performance measures, hence provide constant flows for continue monitoring, analysis and business decision/ management adjustments.

Most of the information usually will be provided as forms of summary mviews and/or cubes:

1) sales distribution among products, channels, vendors, regions
2) product distribution among the channels, promotions, vendors, regions
3) promotion distribution among products, channels, regions
4) Compare above the past six months, against for the current month, previous month, same period of last year.

Online Advertising example

Managers create and manage online marketing campaigns using DW BI solutions:

1. In online advertising, the Ad web sites host company's brand banner, pages about products and services, conduct a high volume of transactions meanwhile using various tools tracking all user's activities (impression, view, click) through planted ad tags and action tags
2. A conversion occurs when a click on ad leads directly to user behavior marketer deem valuable, such as a purchase, signup, pageview, or lead.
3. Data collection tools capture and collect data from websites and use ETL tool transform such data to dedicate servers form DW for analysis
4. Media analysis provides the planner with an integrated view of all digital media campaigns at a customer segment level.
5. Marketer research on web content for various channels, publish site, search keywords, display format and more; monitor, measure and evaluate campaign success with conversion analytics, visitor, clicks, impressions and costs; review results, conversion rate and content usage metrics; measure return on marketing investment, ad hits and profile online users and customers
6. A BI dashboard provides insight with holistic view to support a business decision, the decision then can be made through overviewing of performance.

7. Launch improved campaign, optimized media placements, improved web content, or better-focused investments – in action. Optimize web content for better distributed media channels, publish sites, higher relevant search keywords, and attractive display format to achieve better results.
8. Gauge the success of online campaign and measure return on marketing investment, know how successful the promotions are - back to loop.

Please see Figure 2-2.2-3 DwAdArch Architecture and Environment of Online Ad Data warehouse

> *Energy may be likened to the bending of a crossbow; decision, to the releasing of a trigger.*
> *—Sun Zi*

Figure 2-2.3-7 CrossBow

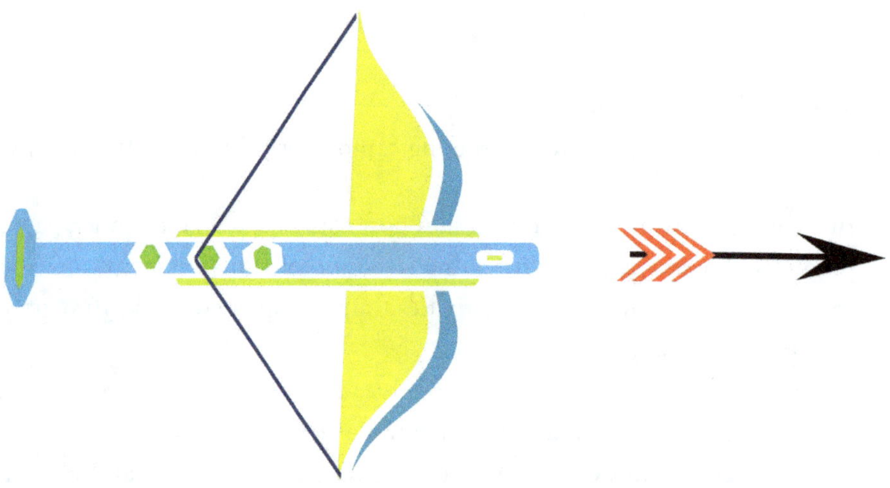

The real benefit, however, is made when the data reaches the end-users through OLAP and most importantly, management, and end-users actually use it to make conscious business decisions, and take necessary actions on business operations and strategy planing.

Data Warehouse Close the Loop and help improve business performance

Figure 2-2.3-8 DwCircularLoop

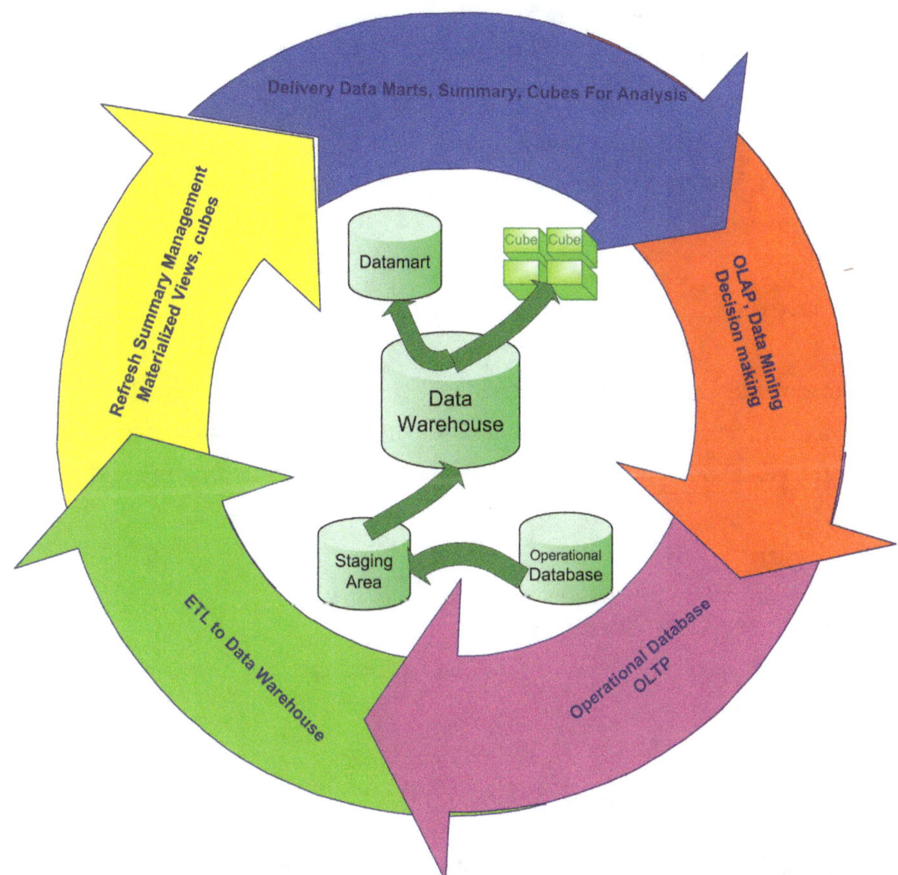

2.4 Evolving Data warehouse Architectures

Anatomy and evolution - How things shape themselves the way we see them today
The modeling, used to study almost everything - from the nature to any system creations. Let's first observe living things, their anatomies in the nature.

Living world developed through millions years of evolution, let to the highly adaptive structures which help them survive in a competitive world. There are many models which have various anatomy structures, forms, and relationships such as star shaped flowers, snowflake crystal, recursively nested hierarchical plant leaf arrangement etc. All those shapes, formations, architectures strive for one thing – survival, therefore bring many comparative advantages:

- High adaptation to environment change
- Rapid growth rate
- high productivity
- adaptive resource control
- cost-efficiency optimization
- damage tolerance
- increased stress tolerance
- high capacity loading or distribution
- high capacity transport and exchange
- performance
- stability
- connectivity

There are reasons why things shaped themselves so much to the advantages. It is therefore to be expected that architectural autonomy features of living things are related to functional aspects. For all over the years, we as human beings always try to understand nature and learn from it.

Anatomy of DW

2.4.1 DW Primary Components

There are three primary components (ETL, DW core data, and summary management/ OLAP) for us to discuss.

Each of the three falls in its own glory. Together they constitute a near-mystical data warehouse.

1) ETL (Extraction-Transformation-Loading) and staging area
Transfer data from ODS to DW

2) DW Core Data
Star, snowflake or hybrid schema (normalized or dimensional)

- Facts
- Dimensions

3) Summary Management/ OLAP

- Materialized views or indexed views
- Cubes
- OLAP on top of the star schema with supporting summary management
- Query engine, user query navigator
- User interface (UI), BI Dashboard
- Reporting system framework

Metadata is the roadmap for DW developments.
Together these three elements constitute a world of decision making support DW and business intelligence (BI) that is far greater than traditional systems.

2.4.2 Multi-dimensional Model

> *In respect of military method, we have, firstly, measurement; secondly, estimation of quantity; thirdly, calculation; fourthly, balancing of chances; fifthly, victory. Measurement owes its existence to Earth; Estimation of quantity to measurement; Calculation to estimation of quantity; Balancing of chances to calculation; and victory to balancing of chances.*
>
> *—Sunzi*

Timely assessment is essential for business success. DW objects such as fact tables are designed to measure the business operations based on the key indicators such as sales, cost, profit, quantity, and production. The dimensions which describe fact tables in many ways, for example time, customer, products, promotions, and channels. Dimensions provide various important aspects of measures. Whole schema (the star formed by fact and dimensions) is used to measure and evaluate business operations and performance in order to be successful in the competitions.

Data in a DW is often organized in multi-dimensional structure. This take the form of star or snowflake that make database queries fast and straightforward, thus enhance query performance greatly for decision support applications. The processes of building a DW involves reorganizing OLTP data stored in relational models into OLAP data stored in multidimensional schemas such as fact tables, dimension tables, summary materialized views (mviews) and cubes.

Star Schema

Star is one of the glories of the universe, so is star schema in DW. It is most notable model form which involved with multi-dimensional schema. A star schema has a fact table in the center, and has more radiating points where dimension tables at the tips tied together by referential keys to form a star like structure. It is a query-centric model.

Shining Star

Star schema can be viewed as clearly grouped data model. It is symmetrical, well-formed, balanced, standard, correspondence organized. You may have various data model of OLTP, they look like maze, but once converted into star schema, they all look similar in pattern – star (one fact table with its associated dimensions) or group of stars (several facts with its satellites - dimensions).

Star shaped things can be found everywhere in amazing nature. Living things are highly organized and structured. Star shape is one of the beautiful shapes. A star shaped flower, with several petals radiating outward from the center is so common, a star shaped DW resembles just that.

Snowflake

Snowflake is one of the most fascinating and unique formations. They have been considered as symbol of symmetry of nature. From perspective of DW, a star schema often extends to more indirect relationships between fact and dimensions thus form a snowflake. For example, a fact table F link to a dimension D by key, and dimension D link to another dimension D1 through key. In another word, dimension D1 link to fact F through dimension D – indirect relationship. The Fig SnowflakeDWtopo show a snowflake used in a global training system where fact table Course activity linked to a master dimension personnel which is a hub connecting to many personnel related dimensions such as status, geographic hierarchy, management hierarchy… etc.

The same snowflake diagram (Fig SnowflakeDWtopo), also can be used to present a totally different structure- a nested master-slave architecture.

Beautiful and unique

Is it really true that no two snowflakes are like?

> *Every crystal was a masterpiece of design and no one design was ever repeated*
> *Wilson "Snowflake" Bentley 1925*

Close up snowflake- Crystal Patterns

Beauty of their intricate shapes have made snowflake a perennial favorite when it comes to DW design, snowflake topology is star formed star, here are some currently frequently seen.

Snowflake – nature's wondrous beauty

Formed in the clouds, it all start from tiny water droplets freeze and become ice particles. Water vapor assembles on the ice particle, causes it to stretch out into a hexagonal prism and then to shoot out branches parallel in all directions, creating a more complex crystal shapes -a nature's beauty, snowflake is born.

But there are so much more than just these beautiful crystal snowflakes. Their structures are striking and highly inspiring!

Secrets of beautiful snowflake

To truly see beauty of snowflakes, especially their star dendrite form, look at them from three different viewpoints:

A crude look at whole, you will see a shining star crystal. If you look closely, you will see that each star has a center centroid as a central hub from which six crystal branches grow parallel radiating outward. If you look more closely, perhaps with a scope, you will see that each branch tip may actually be made up of small star.

Perhaps one of the most dramatic form is stellar dendrite which has the following remarkable miraculous characteristics:

- To emphasize conceptual simplicity of model, snowflake in whole is a star, each tip of star is also a star by itself, and so on forming star of star - nested star snowflake.
- Radiated branches have independent, parallel growth. – they expand beautifully!
- Symmetry balanced – that is aesthetically beauty of snowflake
- well-balanced braches with explosive tips which grow more dynamic and chaotic rise to the side branches in similar shape of main branch.
- Parallel independent growth of branches – exciting fast and dynamic
- Natural copy - It replicates itself in similar shape.
- It can be hierarchical, nested, or has certain degree of iterations

Though mechanism governing Snowflake growth are not well understood, study for her amazing beauty, has given us tremendous inspiration, and you will find that what snowflake topology intend for you goes far beyond anything you can imagine

It is not just beautiful but structurally striking, and very useful in many architectural designs.

Snowflake topology/forms, which widely exist not only in natual world but also in human civilization; from hierarchical social classes, centralizatioin of society to urban development and expansion. Man-made construction projects, road traffic/ communication network, water supply network, crowling of residential areas, most of them appear to be snowflakes shpes containing many connected stars; these are true if you look at them from far away or from the sky. Regardless what their initial intention/design was, results most likely going to form the shape of snowflakes.

To advance this concept further, let's look at DW model in snowflake topology their miracle structure layouts give best performance, flexibility and extensibility, and manageability.

- A control center which act as a communication hub with surrounding satellites - Well connected
- Cooperation – keep growth amazingly symmetrical balanced
- Cluster together - many nodes hook together form a grape-like, master-slave process structure.
- branching system which provide internal flows to maintain vital functionality
- Transition between nodes through major branches and side branches, each node with its own ability to develop different levels of structure and has its own complexity – suggested an architecture that handle many parallel independent processes which then can be merged into main process channels for succeeding downstream processes.

Snowflake topology resemble communication and data sharing in organization hierarchical levels in many ways. It also suits information flows naturally in DW. Topological snowflake we observed can be employed in much broader contexts. It sure significantly helps on modeling.

Advance this concept further, let's look at DW model in snowflake topology using zoom in and zoom out views, the following hierarchical levels are recognized:

- This is a nested structure with several levels represented from lower levels to higher levels
- Group together close-related essential elements forming a star cluster
- A master dimension linked to its sub dimensions, together, forming a star or cluster
- A fact linked to its dimensions, together, forming a star in high level
- Multiple facts, all together consist a cube, in such case, facts might be considered as "dimensions "of this cube
- Business subject area or DW with its cube group all together, forming a star in higher level where multiple cubes become "dimensions" of this business subject area
- EDW system center with multiple DW subject areas joining together forming a super star, in such case each DW might be considered as "dimension" of EDW
- Master slave cluster architecture, consists of many side branches with grape-like hanging nodes (slave nodes) forming a nested master/slave systems(processes), and they also can be merged into the main branches tie to a data system center. In such case, each node group in lower level might be considered as "dimension" of node which at higher level

Extending this concept even further, it can be implemented in modeling designs to achieve successful outcome – high adaptation to the environments:

- o Star and snowflake, like hub and spoke satellite layout that can achieve connections among all nodes with least communication routes. The smaller number of routes, more efficient use of transportation resources. It also helps data sharing.
- o It suits information flows naturally in DW ecology
- o Since all nodes in a snowflake is in a connection group, using bridge-like main branch can join another snowflake and bring in a new set of connection group, another way to say: Any group of snowflakes can link a snowflake by a single joining.
- o Centralized star joining maintain all components related in a consistent and coherent way
- o Snowflake may be considered as extended star, hierarchical star - stars in hierarchical arrangement

Snowflake is so simple, yet so complex

Hybrid and hierarchical topology can be set as centralized, centralized + distribute (nested centralized), but there is more, just think about joining snowflakes together forming the stacked distributed matrix, that would be fairly complex. However, it can possibly be synthesized to produce structure that is more powerful and more effective than either one alone.

- o Distributed cluster nodes – master/slave nodes
- o Distributed centralized - combine distributed as centralized
- o Centralized distributed - snowflake union to form another round iteration
- o Centralizing over multiple distributed systems
- o It can be hierarchical and can be embedded centralized or embedded distributed system
- o Embedded centralized into distributed – view as distributed in global view
- o Embedded distributed into centralized – view as centralized in global view
- o Snowflake topology can hide detail and complexity duo to its hierarchical feature

The aesthetically beauty of snowflake topology

Due to snowflake hub-spoke architecture, the data systems can be grouped together and organized clearly in hierarchy levels – make the complex simple and easy (please refer to figure 2-2.4-10):

- o Its hierarchical view able to hide detail and complexity, thus help us focus at the different levels – clearly see from high level to low level – every view is focused on a specific level - from global view to grain level view

- Snowflake topology can make group connections with the least joins possible
- Easy to mend and expand
- New elements can be easily created without much disturbance or reconstructions. A new group can be easily added by attaching it to main branch or side branch
- Unwanted elements can be easily dropped, a group can be isolated or dropped by detachment from the branch
- Remodel and renovate is much easier, thus costly dismantle and rebuild existing systems might be avoided
- Join and union is much faster and easier at their hierarchy level
- Replication and communication can be done in hierarchy level
- Interface control become easier, thus interface can be set at higher level such as at group level
- Cluster by integration which form the groups or grape-like master/slave bundles
- Parallelism can be nicely coordinated
- Good coordination at group level, and at hierarchy level
- Good for independent and parallel growth
- Balanced architecture in a complexity evolving system
- Configuration and operation can be done at group level
- Resolve duplication and redundancy with easy – easy to spot, easy to clear
- Provide advantage such as more economical maintenance and support
- Can improve loading
- Can reduce construction cost
- May provide advantage over other topologies
- Provide better stability
- Scale up influence maximum rate of exchange
- Improving overall performance

So much about snowflake! Let's go with it!

Growing snowflakes in clouds – future star snowflake infrastructure

Clouds as mysterious water vapor formations in sky, in our atmosphere have been always our passions and poetries. Solar energy make hot air uplift moisture water vapor into sky where it condensed into clouds. Carrying tremendous amount of load, clouds moving around, floating drift, swirling and showing the colorful displays: like white unicorn horse graceful tail which suggest weather change; rainbow, polar lights with brilliant prism of the color spectrum.

Clouds with **great transformation power** also turn water vapor into snowflakes, ice crystals, hails, rains and storms. Yes, it **has huge delivers** by discharge mass amount of snowflakes, raindrops into Earth feeding hungry and thirsty lives. When angry, it got electrified and release stunning thunders and dazzling lightning.

Based on Oriental legend, the Dragon, which has magnificent power governing haven, was born in clouds.

No matter what beauty or beast cloud is, **all living things in Earth cannot live without cloud**.

We are in the information age, and IT innovations have brought another magical creature into our live – cloud computing!

More and more organizations leverage the cloud to build and deploy data applications, thus we need clouds, as these are the places where our snowflakes are born.

the data warehouses, data technology solutions mostly like to be star snowflake- shaped, and they will live in cloud computing provide much needed data sharing and resource saving.

Can you imagine that in the near future almost everything will be done in clouds. Wherever you go, whatever you do, you will be hooked into clouds. While you conduct inquiry, connect to social channels, search the travel plans, purchase products and services, high on the sky, someone is watching, all your web activities, clickstreams have been gathered, uplifted to air, transformed and processed by cloud based data warehouses and big data solutions for predictive analysis, user behavior analysis, and to discover some insightful for their business strategies – that is real-time data discovery!

There would be million shining star snowflakes come from the clouds, flying and swirling in the air, floating in the sky, delivering effective information services that we all need in our lives. This natural phenomenon becomes inspiration, which results in conceptual model transformed into something of reality of data system infrastructure.

Let it snow! Let it snow!

Figure 2-2.4-9 Snowflakes

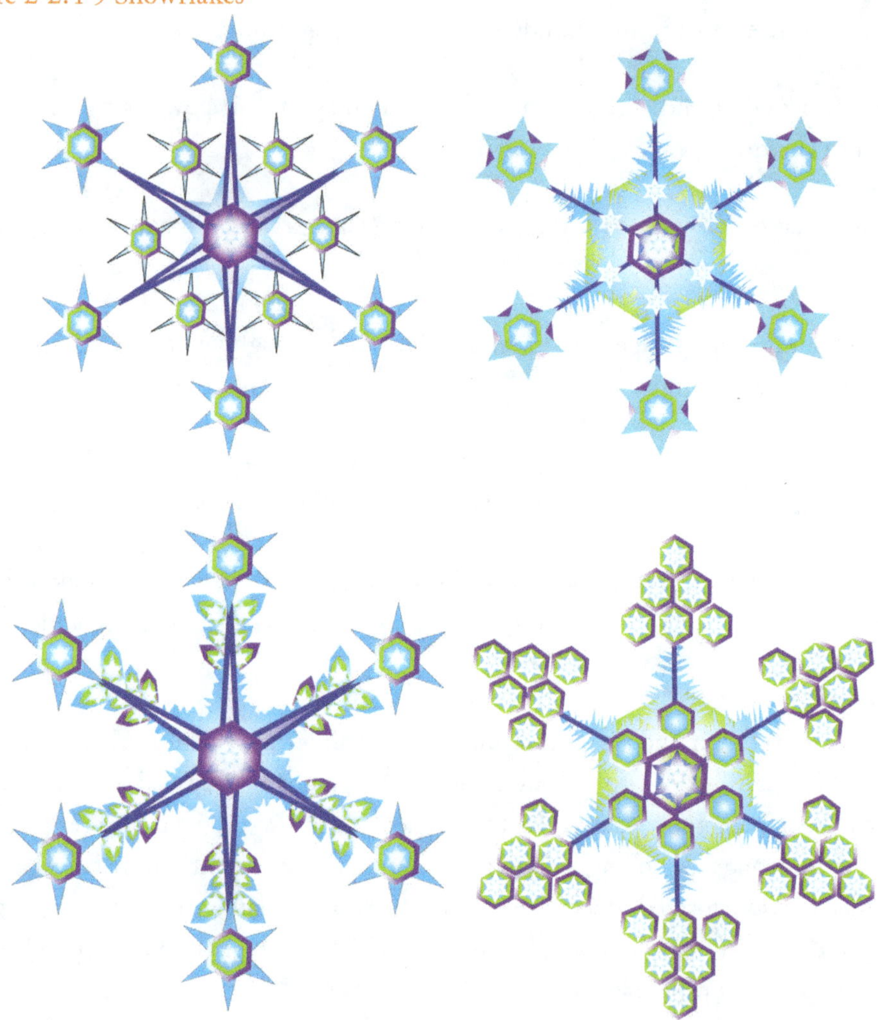

Depends on its presentation levels, a snowflake may be considered as a hierarchical, nested, iterated topology in the following:

- A master dimension with group of sub dimensions (in green) forming a cluster dimension
- A fact with multiple clustered dimensions (in blue) forming a star
- A business functional area with multiple facts forming a star in higher level
- Enterprise wide DW (EDW) a centralized star with multiple stars each represent a business functional area (in black)
- EDW – centralized DW with conformed dimensions (green) delivering multiple data marts
- Big data – snowflake topology
- A master node with group of slave nodes forming a star or cluster

- o A centralized data store linked to many stars which include master node and surrounding slave nodes from distributed data sources forming snowflake in higher level
- o Big data center (star center) also feed DW OLAP which are in fact somewhat stars/ snowflakes

Seeing Diagram (Diagram 2-2.4.10) snowflake topology in four different persipectives representing zoom in and zoom out hierarch level views.

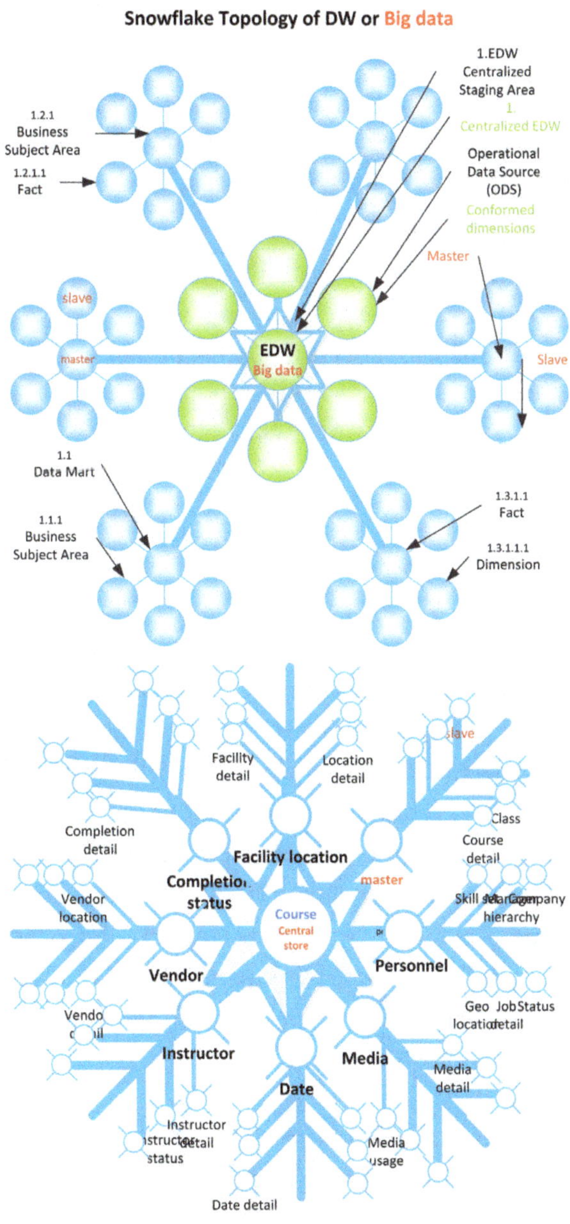

DW topology - Snowflake

Figure 2-2.4-10 SnowflakeDWtopo

Fact

Fact table include numeric fields for measures, which are of primary interest to end users. Data items in fact table are numeric and additive – can be summarized. Data might include sales quantity, sales amount, costs and the number of certain activities such as clicks on web applications. Fact table may also contain semi-additive data which can't be uniformly aggregated across all dimensions such as daily snapshot of number of employees or stock prices but it can be set in a certain way for aggregation such as average, first day of month, last day of quarter etc.

Fact table includes keys which link (via a foreign key – primary key) to dimension tables. The relationship between the fact table and dimension table is of a child-parent. The fact tables are the more dynamic part of DW. When business interests shift to the different areas, the fact tables and their measures must be modified or rebuilt based on upcoming business changes/requirements accordingly.

Measures

Numeric fields in fact table such as sale, cost, number of clicks, and other metrics are called measures.

See details in the Chapter Five <**Data warehouse Development**>, the Section 5.1 <Logical Design>.

Dimension

Dimensions are used to describe facts in specifying categories. They are usually formed in hierarchies which can be used in summary, aggregation and various prospecting. Dimensions also provide a way to prospect facts and cubes with drill-down analysis. Dimension table can be referenced by fact tables or other dimension tables. The relationship between dimension and fact is typically that of parent-child. Contrasts to fact tables which are fairly dynamic in nature, dimension are relatively static part of DW. If business interests shift to new areas, fact tables such as products and services may have to be dropped or reconstructed but some dimensions such as personnel, organizations, customers, and geographic locations may still remain useful provided that they were built in an integrated and generic fashion. Building reusable dimensions is the key to a successful journey of DW modeling if they are well-defined with broad vision.

Some dimensions called slowly changed dimension (SCD) that are major two types ; type 1 which overwrite change data and type 2 which keep historic data by adding new entries and mark effective begin and end date of events.

In a grand scale, term dimension can be interchangeable at specific hierarchy levels:

A master dimension with associated group of subdimensions, thus each subdimension is "dimension" of this master dimension.

A fact is tied with its associated dimensioins, thus each dimension here is dimension of that fact table – this is original and basic definition of dimension.

A cube with a group of associated fact tables, thus, each fact here is "dimension" of that cube.

A business focus area together with a group of associated cubes, thus, each cube here is "dimension" of that business focus area.

A DW together with a group of business focus areas, thus, each business focus area here is "dimension" of that DW.

A EDW together with a group of DWs, thus, each DW here is "dimension" of that EDW.

Depends on how deep you want to go down, how high you want to go up, just follow the same logic, and so on go to next iteration level.

Using snowflake topology, you can describe the DW hierarchical architecture above.

(Please refer the fig 2-2.4-10 SnowflakeDWtope)

Slowly changed dimension (SCD)

Figure 2-2.4-11SLD_type

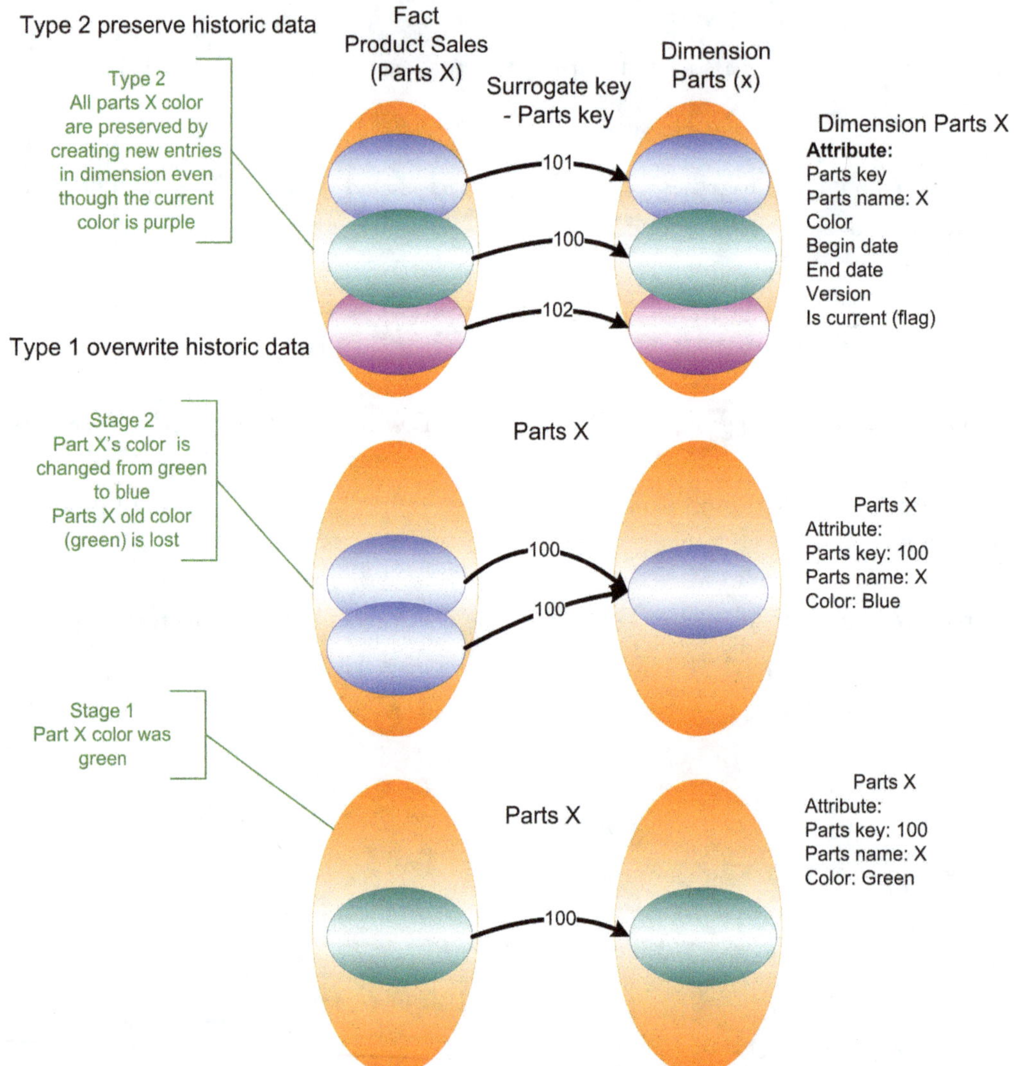

Dimension cluster – one of the patterns of snowflake

In real world of DW modeling, there is a case when one or more dimension has a dominate role and serves a central point of a group dimension then forming a cluster, former presents as Master dimension or Dimension hub and later as sub dimensions.

In example in a personal training program DW application, (called *CourseStart*), there is a dimension *personnel* which can hook multiple related data objects such as Organization, location, position, department, status thus form a dimension cluster, then it links to fact table such as *Cource.* Normally, such dimension cluster is reflection of the business nature – business focus area. Other good examples are customer dimension in a CRM or campaign dimension in an online Ad BI solution.

Please refer to Figure 2.2.4-10 SnowflakeDWtopo

Expansion of Star

- Add new business instance/subject area – form new star
- Add measures - Add it into fact table
- Add new dimension – add it into star, make fact table link to new dimension
- Add new sub dimension – add into dimension cluster – make it link to fact table through master dimension (snow flake approach)
- Add attributes - Add attributes into correspond dimension
- Likely, single star may expand like snowflake growth as dimension added to tip of star, split in radiating forms. Snowflake in a fairly complex form, look like stellar dendrites with many arm-like branches.

Prospecting path

Dimension is hierarchical in nature thus lay the summarization paths.

An example is the time dimension, whose hierarchy is organized by time, day, week, month, quarter and year. Analytical aggregations can be based on similar hierarchy: daily, weekly, monthly, quarterly and annual reports. Another example would be associating customer dimension with a geographic hierarchy such as zip code or postal code, city, county, state, country and region. A typical request from manager might be "Give me a summary sales report for all the customers in California and Florida fall in the particular zip code ranges.

In an online advertising BI application, based on likely analytic path, dimension called *campaign* will has hierarchies such as Media plan contain level of Media plan, site, placement; hierarchy search key words may contain level of publisher, category, keywords.

An example of Online Advertising BI application is formed by fact tables (Click/impression, conversion, search, cost) link to dimension Ad, Act, Date and Campaign, Campaign dimension can be used as a hub connected to multiple other dimensions.

2-2.4-12 DwAdFactDimension

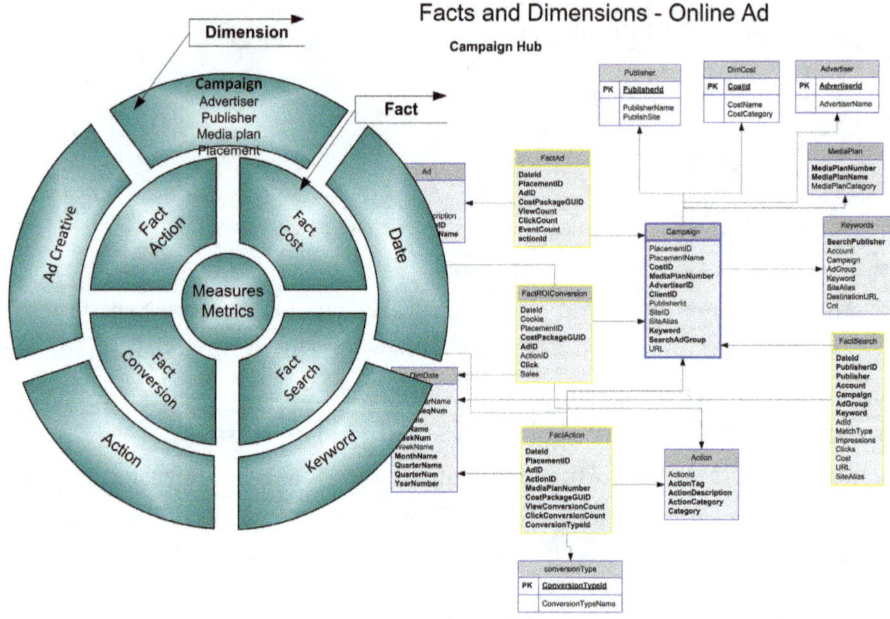

From Star Schema (Fact & Dimension) To Multi-Dimensional Cubes

Figure 2-2.4-13 DwStarCube

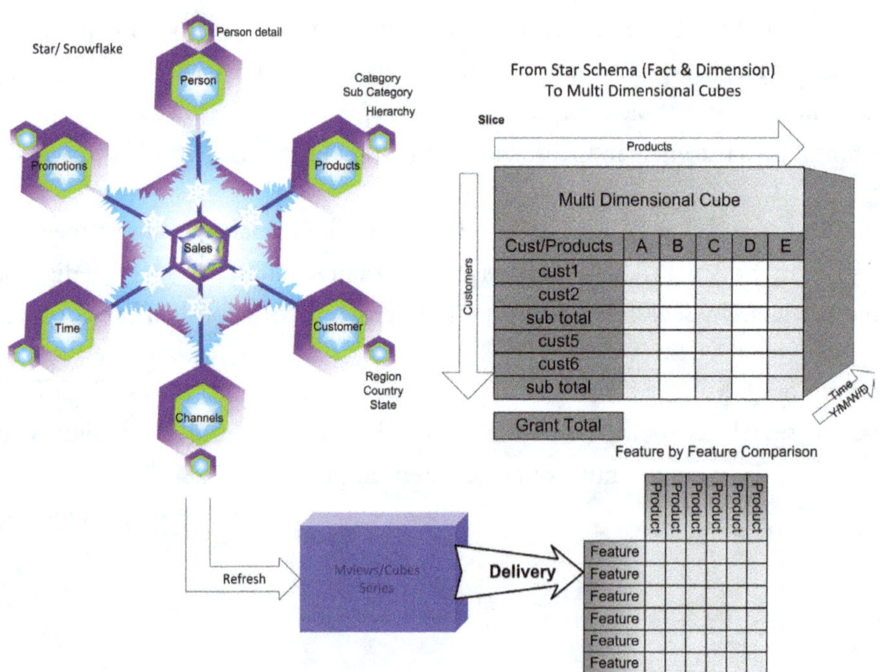

Snowflake (course activity as an example)

Please refer to Figure 2-2.4-10 SnowflakeDWtopp

2.4.3 OLAP/BI

> *Now the general who wins a battle makes many calculations in his temple even before the battle is fought. The general who loses a battle makes but few calculations beforehand. Thus do many calculations lead to victory, and few calculations to defeat: how much more no calculation at all! It is by attention to this point that I can foresee who is likely to win or lose.*
>
> *—Sun Zi*

Figure Owl

2.4.3.1 OLAP, a natural extension and continuation of data warehousing

Laid on top of our DW pyramid, Online Analytical Processing (OLAP)/Business Intelligence (BI) is a natural extension and continuation of DW. Summary management and OLAP are certainly the most demanding and the most rewarding areas in decision support system. While no expert is infallible, no novice is hopeless. The real benefit, however, is realized when data reaches endusers as insightful information through OLAP.

Data undergoes a renaissance in OLAP where transformations make it become meaningful and intelligent information for endusers. Through computing, conversion, formatting and association primitive data is miraculously made recognizable, interpretable, understandable, and visualize to human eyes. Data that has been highly aggregated/summarized offered as a well-organized multidimensional cube series. This enables summarized viewing, drill down to details, graphic analysis and slice and dice for particular portion of the interests. Upper management receives quick answers and can analyze current data as well as historical data for summarizing trends and patterns.

Cube

The concept and practice of multi-dimensional analysis appeared in the form of cubes, which are key elements in OLAP. Along the main course of the data warehousing, data has been transformed into the formation of cube, which plays a very important role. It serves as an intermediate central hub between the DW base layer (fact and dimension tables) and final presentation layer (reporting, dashboard and other delivery).

Species of cube

Cube here, refers to any presentation in form of multiple dimension structure, in some cases, it may present a materialized view (mview) with summarization/aggregation. This is a deliberately broad definition, so as not to be restricted by rigid concepts based on specific database products.

The design of cube series for summary management is a paramount issue in OLAP, and is particularly important for BI and decision support. Almost whole works of OLAP/BI rely on cube design. In a cube series, data most likely will be organized into predefined multidimensional structures to facilitate exploration of information. Such a structure should be built based on the following guidelines:

- **Prepare** well organized sources for cubes, this include fact tables, dimension tables, views, mviews, and summary tables. And in doing so will lay solid ground for all ongoing cube building.
- **Grouping major business activities**/segments as measure groups in form of star or group of stars so that it would reflect overall business aspects clearly.
- **Build customized dimensions** with primary key defined, specify all hierarchical levels ready for rolling up or dill down data, rename dimension name, attribute names as descriptive as possible that are understandable by ensures and can serve as formal business report titles, headers.
- **Design well-formulated performance indicators** calculated based on measures for business performance analysis.
- **Perspective** is sub-cube. Specify perspectives on top of cubes so that each user group has their own views of cubes. Create the restricted scopes and filtered views by cutting it vertically or slice it horizontally according to the organization hierarchical levels – then form your OLAP/BI pyramid.
- **Evaluate** the relationships between business segments such as production, sales, supply and finance by using conformed dimensions cross DW for potential drilling-across.
- **Define security** in role-based security control in order to handle access scope according to endusers group privileges and their organizational hierarchies.
- **Optimizing Cube refreshing mechanism** in order to keep it in sync by partition and other strategies.

An example of online advertising BI application may contain cubes with various measures, such as click/impression, conversion, search and cost. – Please refer to figure 2-2.4-12 DwAdFactDimension

2.4.3.2 Cube lays the foundation of OLAP

A fact table itself virtually is a big cube with measures and all associated dimensions (through dimension keys), meanwhile dimensions always been used to prospect cube to handle hierarchies and descriptions and rollup to summaries and drill down to detail during analysis.

Generating cubes is a way to bring information closer to the users. A DW reaches out to endusers by preparing computed values through extensive and expensive computing and joining operations on vast of data thus form a series of well-defined cubes in advance, rather than at execution time. Materialized views or cubes, once created, will persist in systems thus greatly reduce complexities, costs, and accessing time. Ideally, endusers are just a click away from getting their desired reports such as those highly aggregated, summary information from BI dashboard.

Cubes shields underlying tables

Like living things that depend on each other, a cube series as a top layer in DW depend on underlying fact/dimension tables while provides isolation and offloading underlying tables in a multi-shell multi-sector DW system. For details, see Section <Platform – Core & Shell> in Chapter Four <Development Highlights>.

Pattern of cubes

There are also relationships between cubes, let's look at one of the very important cube that other cubes may depend on.

Foundation stone of cubes - the cornerstones

Like building masonry foundation, laying a cornerstone is an important first thing to do. The same goes for building your DW OLAP. A kind of cube serves as the foundation/base for a whole cube series, so let's call it ***cornerstone cube*** (or in some cases, a cornerstone materialized view). It is perhaps one of the powerful and influential summarized forms, along with the cubes. This primary/master cube directly derived from fact and dimensions, and serves as a base or ladder so that other cubes will be built on top of it. It is therefore the core object for your cube series.

Serving as a central hub in OLAP, cornerstone cube stands the position as an alternate usage of fact table. Unlike the final presentation-oriented cubes tend to be, it mightily branched most of the way up forming the tree structure. This is a very useful and productive structure for supporting OLAP.

Because cornerstone or primary cubes can be readily generated to provide bases for various nested mviews/cubes, instead of scanning entire monstrous fact table, thus they have received the most attention from OLAP developers.

Tree, trunk, braches and tips

Any normal tree with a trunk and branches that are attached to trunk, tips here may refer to terminal points (of braches) where end-users' touch point of OLAP is located. Tree structure with its trunk and branches will grow more naturally. In such tree-like view, terminal points (tip) come from middle or intermediate nodes which was supposed to have been processed and readily available, alternately will shortening preparation and processes paths. It is a much easier route to final presentation from cornerstone mview/cubes than going through a much large and detailed fact tables. Compare with radiating shape (everything come from the center), developing branch pattern that can reduce length of travel and congestion of lines at the center so developing cube or summary view series is the way to go.

Tangled bushes – a real mess in structure of cube groups

A plant, like suckering bush, every sucker (branch) is attached to the root, suggesting excessive repeated/redundant processes and paths in OLAP world.

We have seen a lot of this type of messy bushy structures, it is disoriented, distorted and overly complex, and certainly has poor performance. Therefore, layout a cornerstone cube with smart cube refreshing paths is a good way to start your design; otherwise, it is easy to get lost in maze of cubes with tangled, jungle-like relationships and refreshing paths. Through the pruning or trimming might still necessary to maintain your cube tree, getting good layout in your design phase would be a better choice. You are far better off working on good layout than playing trailblazer in a messy jungle – invasive and costly changes down the road.

Review your tree – your cube tree design

Step back and take time review your overall design, do not adding things in haste without looking the whole tree, check existing and reusable objects, take all possible advantages or short cut if you can, and figure out smart way to generate new reporting views from nearest points instead of from beginning of root.

Nested Cubes (cube here more likely refer to mviews) - **propagation**

Perhaps the most interesting creations, however, are nested cubes (mviews), which can be dependent of other cubes (mviews). One may rests on top of others, thus forming a pyramid. This is also called a nested mview, depends on the types of database objects involved. Great care must be taken when constructing a group of nested cubes. We want to form a solid structure in a skillful way, not a wobbly hair-rising circus pyramid of acrobats that is prone to collapse.

The cubes or mviews with further summarization and calculation are based on other cubes/ mviews; specially cornerstone or primary cubes, and are propagated through OLAP system and eventually form a magnificent tree canopy.

Prospective of cubes:

A perspective is a subset of the features of a cube. By creating associations between users and groups of data objects, such as product sales, salesperson activity, or region distribution you build customized views from cubes with associations among several business aspects or subject areas, thus help users to focus on the area of their interests. It also provides security and privacy by filtering sensitive or unrelated information.

An ill-constructed cube - sparse matrix/cube

This is a more troublesome cube contains many empty cells, primarily caused by too many dimensions and poorly-set hierarchical levels. Dividing the cubes in question may be a solution. However, an ill-structured dimension also can contribute to this sparse cube, the lack of standization in data modeling may be a culprit, more often as the result of duplicated or inconsistent data introduced into DW. One of the major defects of a sparse cube is that it lacks ability to convergence or aggregate during the cube rollup operations. See example in Section <2.5.2 The transition and transformation> and Section <4.3.8 <Dealing with Dirty Data in Chapter Four.

2.4.3.3 OLAP/BI Reporting tools

Once we have cubes, you may develop reporting solutions, reporting frameworks and query engine against data. The more intelligent the query, the more business insight will be revealed.

By incorporating intelligent queries, powerful/centralized database stored procedures, well-defined reporting systems, user-friendly interfaces, expandable system architecture (such as n-tier hierarchical web-enable structure), well-prepared cube series (and take full advantage of it), and suitable delivery methods, we are able to skillfully forming an integral OLAP which is not only a combination of multiple information pool but also a comprehensive tool on which end-users can do business analysis, evaluate market position, critical business factors, measure potential for success, discover insight, identify problems, and test alternatives. Generally, OLAP provides a platform on which data can be transformed into information and knowledge visualized for management.

A well-designed report framework provides many benefits. These include:

- Centralizing the control and administration of report generating processes
- Allowing each user group to see and control processes at an appropriate level
- Centralizing and consolidating exception handling
- Reducing network traffic
- Simplifying deployment and maintenance

With the advent of new database products, more analytical tools and functions become available, and we now have more options to choose from. But whatever OLAP tools or applications you may have at your shopping list, you still need work hard to bring out its best features advantageously, and to minimize less positive features. Furthermore, tool only release their power in the presence of a well-defined model. BI tools bring end-users close in striking distance on analysis. These tools empower endusers with analytical tasks, such as delivering summary information in linked cubes to Excel spreadsheets, Crosstab, and PivotTables for further viewing - clice, dice, drilldown or roll up.

2.4.3.4 Refresh – find optimal path

Cubes are so good and powerful for end users on analysis. However, there is a price to pay for getting cubes. The mviews and cubes must be refreshed to stay synchronized with the underlying objects such as fact/dimension tables. Like ETL loading, mviews and cubes will be refreshed in fashion of waves. Great attention must be always paid to ensuring that all cubes and mviews have been refreshed successfully, and that optimal refresh paths with carefully defined dependencies and sequences must be built to get jobs done quickly.

DW model and architecture, layout, table/view partition, index strategies, ETL, and stacked (nested) materialized views all contribute to performance of cube refresh.

See details in the Chapter Five <**Data warehouse Development**>, the Section 5.4.4 <Refreshing the Materialized Views>.

2.4.3.5 Design a clean cube

Skeletonize mviews and cubes to boost performance and to reduce data volumes

If fact table contains many descriptive columns, it becomes very wide (fat). A fat cube take tremendous space thus slows down the processes. It may become even worse when OLAP tie everything together (facts and all dimensions) for overall cube analytical interface for endusers. If you are not careful about data design, you may end up creating your own monster that you can't control. An alternate would be skeletonizing cubes which contain only keys (surrogate key) and measures (numbers), especially in those intermediate cubes, so that all aggregate operations will be against a skeleton cube instead of a fat one during pre-calculations. It will gain fat (in a final stage, join dimensions to get descriptive information) only when pre-delivery or delivered to endusers. Although a skeletonize cube may need more joining for getting descriptive data, it can be a viable option when performance become a real issue, and furthermore provides more flexibility and efficiency when update descriptive data (it quite often in reality) down the road – it can be done in relatively small dimension tables instead of huge fact table.

Walking a fine line

Bear in mind, though, that exactly the reverse can also happen, excessive cube generation may grow prolific, and become difficult to manage, overly complex and error-prone. As a result, users are often overwhelmed by the number of analysis objects they have to deal with, thus weakening the overall simplicity and directness. There is always a trade-off between the cost of batch refreshing (processing) time and reduced system online response time. A fraction-of-a-second online response time is bought by the time and cost of cube refreshing which usually done during off-peak hours. For a DW that will handle mass user accesses or public accesses, more pre-calculated summary mviews or cubes should be built in order to gain instant online responses.

Tips for good refreshing (path) design:

- Generating mview is a resource-intensive process, which is better scheduled during off-peak times.
- Take great care planning overall construction of cubes series.
- Make full use of any mviews/cubes that are already built in place, use it.as a shortcut for generating final presentation, going through mview/cube series instead of doing full scan against fact tables. Remember, you don't need to start everything from scratch, or you don't need to start everything from bottom root which is very expensive and time-consuming. A great deal may be accomplished by defining just a few core mviews/cubes.
- Investing in mview/cube creation and refreshing will pay off when instant system responses coming to play for endusers.

From Star schema (fact & dimension) to multi-dimensional cubes
Please refer to Figure 2-2.4-13 DwStarCube

Building shortcut objects in DW to gain fast access data

Figure 2-2.4-17 DwMvShortCut

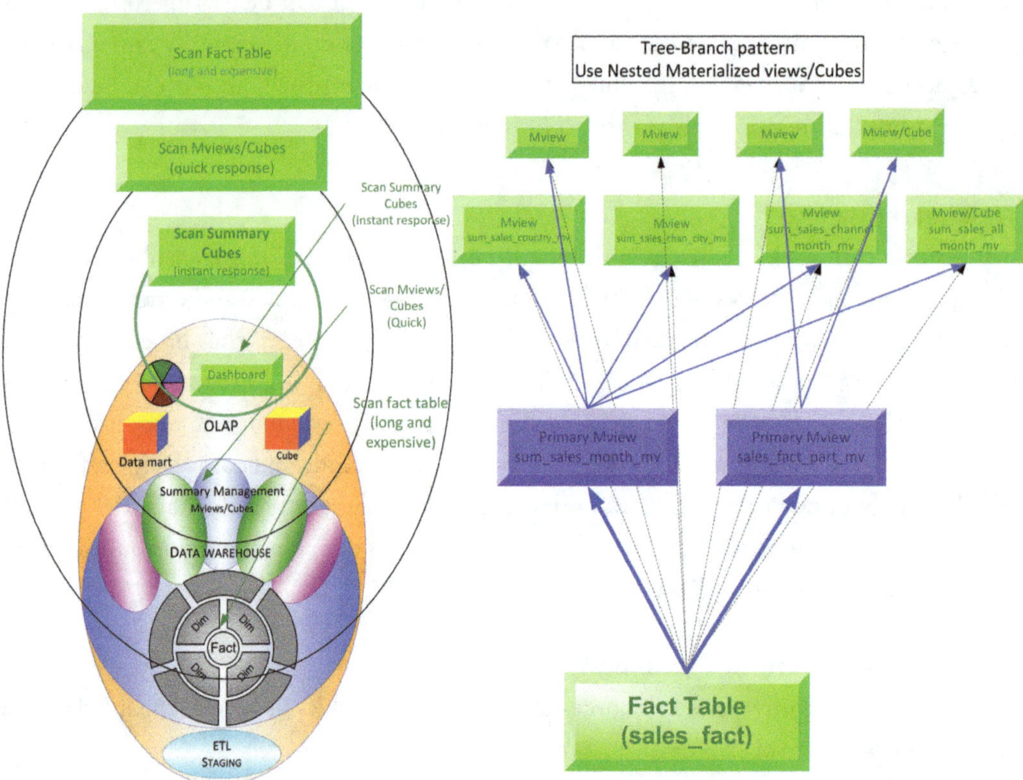

2.5 Mapping

> *Amid the turmoil and tumult of battle, there may be seeming disorder and yet no real disorder at all; simulated disorder postulates perfect discipline, simulated fear postulates courage; simulated weakness postulates strength.*
>
> *—Sun Zi*

Note:

Manage chaos and mess into orderly. Even if the world seems very complex and maze-like, there is often an order which can be perceived.

2.5.1 What is mapping?

Essentially, mapping is a structured process that directs data flow from one or more sources to a destined target. It also involves changes that convert data into meaningful insights. The whole of ETL relies on elements of mapping in its design.

Mapping ties sources and targets together by building the followings:

- o Links between the elements that may reside in the different systems.
- o Cross-references from each source schema to the target schema.

You may begin the mapping process once you have a rough sketch of DW model in place.

Mapping processes include:

Business Subject/Functional Areas

Defining business subject/functional areas is first step on mapping, everything else are based on, restricted, and focused by this. If subject/functional area include financial/ Billing, customer management, market, services, products have been defined in BI report areas so do the corresponding source mappings. It includes source and target definitions {Locations, names of servers, databases, network addresses, links, schema, objects (tables, columns), file folder, files, structures and access methods}, references {lookups, standard references, dictionaries, name and value checking and validations}, and transformations {conversions, filtering, renaming during processes}, etc.

2.5.2 The transition and transformation from ODS to DW

From ODS world to DW world, a new stage of life is born through a miracle change - mappings:

- ➢ From process oriented to subject oriented
- ➢ From disparate to integrated
- ➢ From distributed to centralized
- ➢ From non-standard to standardized
- ➢ From inconsistent to enterprise-wide consistent
- ➢ From transactional to analytical
- ➢ From relational to multi-dimensional or other hybrid
- ➢ From detailed to aggregated (summarized)
- ➢ From raw data to informative and knowledge

From process oriented to subject oriented

Mapping the data from each function to each subject area shows that there is a fundamental restructuring and realignment of data, which must be read in a transactional format and written in a subject-oriented format. For example, in an online purchasing system, there are multiple intermediate stages have to be go through, and there are many data objects to hold transaction processes. An online user is viewing, moving from page to page, click for actions, shopping cart, etc. then bang! – Purchase/Sales. Only final action triggers the sale is counted for sales analysis.

From transaction-oriented relational model to multi-dimensional analytical model

From disparate to integrated

Knowing that data usually comes from multiple sources, Mapping cross-references the same item across multiple systems. The different forms of applications must be intertwined into a single form. In other words, data is weaved from multiple ODS into a single OLAP system.

From distributed to centralized

Data from various sources most likely will be put into a centralized repository include metadata. If it is not going to be a physically centralized DW, due to restriction of budget, resource or user preference, a set of distributed data marts may be a feasible option, but those must be under a conceptually or logically centralized model design and layout. We will talk more about this at other chapters.

From non-standard to standard

Non-standard data must be reconciled and become standard across the entire enterprise. Data is stored using different data types in each ODS, then converted to a standard data type used in the OLAP system. At the same time differences in encoding between the different ODS are resolved. For example, the measurements have to be in one uniform format, not mixed (kilogram, pound, inch, yard and meter). Similarly, naming have to be uniform across the entire system, for example, car, carmaker naming should be uniform, (VW, volkswagen, vw, etc.) = Volkswagen; (Ford, FORD, ford, ford company, Ford Company, etc.) = Ford Motor Company.

From inconsistent to enterprise-wide consistent

The title speaks for itself.
For example, customer and product dimension no longer for a particular department, it will be the all department-facing dimensions instead.

From transactional to analytical

Data come from ODS where it is organized in the normalized form. In the journey to the DW, data most likely will be modelled as star or snowflake schema with a multi-dimensional structure to be suited for rapid analysis and query. Even in hybrid approach, some data may still remain normalized in a DW staging area, but soon or later data is likely to be delivering as analytical form – multi-dimensional cubes or summarized mviews when presented to endusers.

From detailed to aggregated (summarized)

Mostly, detailed data will eventually undergo aggregations and calculations forming many hierarchical mviews or cubes for analysis. A type of mapping also directs data from the data warehouse data storage layer to its destined target, such as an OLAP representing layer in the form of multi-dimensional cubes.

From data to information and knowledge

During this incredible journey, data in raw state has gone through such amazing transformations, become more meaningful, visualized, and is ready for endusers.

Translate data to something more understandable

Translating data to vocabulary used in the final presentation layer make sense to endusers

See details in the Chapter Five <**Data warehouse Development**>, the Section 5.3 <ETL>.

Figure 2-2.5-20 DwMapTransition

Top down approach – from user's perspective

Very often, DW mappings must be start from user's requirements, business goal, then look for where and how to get ODS and how to create workable paths from source data to user desired reports.

Data Warehousing Mapping:

The questions being asked about mapping:

How to resolve differences, inconsistencies and discrepancies in data?

How to live with the ODS which have problems such as inconsistencies or discrepancies?

How to deal with the ODS that most likely are external data sources, some of which are beyond your control?

What is mapping table? What it used for?

What is the dynamic data-driven approach (DDDA) in mapping?

There are many questions/answers about mapping, however, there are number of strategies and tricks may come to play.

2.5.3 Mapping levels with degree of abstraction

Why do we address the mapping level issue? Because we want to build a hierarchical mapping model framework to steer clear of the complex mapping pitfalls. In the mapping levels, upper levels which steer away from numerous data objects and details thus have higher abstraction, while lower level is more detailed- oriented, specific. Using snowflake approach will be very helpful in mapping. For snowflake topology, please see later chapter.

- Business scope, Global, enterprise, branch\departmental
- application level – server/database
- Subject areas
- schema level – object group
- module level - group
- entity level - table
- element level - column

Mapping path/methodologies

Since most ODS are transaction type, there are many data objects been employed during transaction stages, from OLAP perspective, those may look redundant and need to be mapped into a single, well grouped DW object through the following methodologies.

- grouping
- divide-and-merge
- split
- branch
- cross
- filter

Figure 2-2.5-21 DwMappingPattern

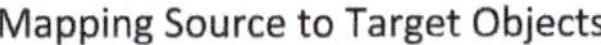

Data mapping involving many mapping patterns: Split, Merge, Cross

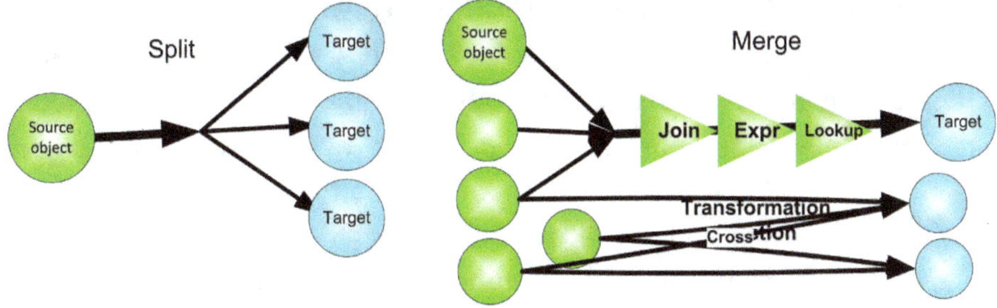

Create mapping tables to map various source values to the standard values

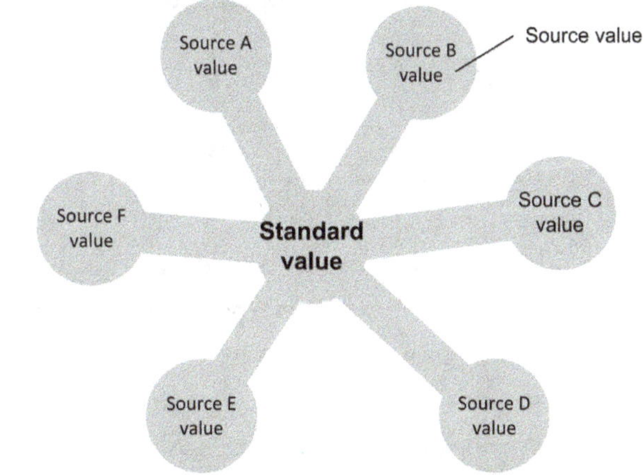

DW Item name	DW Std value	Source	Item name	Source value
	100	A	Table/column	abc
	100	B		f88
	100	C		ww
	100	D		456

Mapping Source to Target Objects

Enterprise level of data warehouse EDW model might be based on at least a virtual relational conceptual model which may physically become a staging database or core database, based on staging and core database, further define and create multi-dimensional model for OLAP, cube, and solutions.

In such large scale EDW solution, immense mapping have to be done to cover multiple existing reporting systems (data marts). Existing data marts have considerable redundancies, overlapped reporting, repeated ETL extractions against ODSs, extensive and duplicate data feedings, different groups grab same data from same ODS and feed to multiple data marts. Problems in existing systems are consequences of lack of integrated design in the past.

For integrate design approach, Consult Chapter Four – Data warehouse Development Highlights.

2.5.4 Mapping strategies in an ever-changing world

The business is a fast-paced, ever-changing world. Frequently, ODS, especially those of external sources are quite unpredictable, it is subject to change without notice. As a result, developers are often overwhelmed by the number of changes they have to deal with down the road.

To cope with such volatility and to avoid too much code changes in our mappings, numbers of tactics may come to play. The basic guideline is to use a dynamic data-driven approach (DDDA), avoiding making code changes as much as possible by changing data in special designed mapping tables instead of changing program code.

Dynamic data-driven approach (DDDA): it includes building mapping tables, creating business rule tables, and developing the read-parse-interpret-compose (action code) then execute abled software mechanism. Unlike 'flying blind', this kind mechanism should be able to learn a) what it is instructed to do; b) where to start; c) when to stop; d) how to log the record or notify other related processes regarding critical events; and e) perform read-interpret then execute procedures with encapsulation engines handling. Specify a trained program to read mapping tables and then execute whatever it is instructed to do. The big advantage here is that this part of the software may be reprogrammed to change functionality "on the fly". The idea is simple and very useful in practice, especially if you try to keep current mappings updated in a volatile business environment.

Avoid hard-coded conversion rules in the programs. Design dynamic packages or procedures that can read instructions from designated repositories (for example, tables) about conversion rules, formulas, source origin and accessing methods, then compose correspondent queries/codes and execute those accordingly.

Mapping tables are major ETL metadata objects which include the followings:

- conversion rules and formulas,
- reference values, which may involve multi-step referencing
- mapping level and hierarchies – mapping path
- function library and calling parameters
- target system locations, server/box, access methods and parameters
- source database locations, names, server/database access methods and parameters
- table list, column list, primary key list, etc. Such system information also can be fetched through metadata-driven dynamic procedures or functions.
- conversion dictionaries

Good mapping tables are visible for all parties involved, developers are able to see it, so do users, managers, engineers, staff; and they are maintainable by non-computer personnel thus makes the mapping changes simple –it simple as data update by anyone has appropriate permission instead of code changes by only computer professional. Good mapping tables along with a set of dynamic data-driven procedure (DDDP) make ETL work so efficient that stand for hundred programs and hundred thousand lines of code.

2.5.5 Create a logging mechanism shared by multiple processes

Use well-defined logging mechanisms, dedicated tables or files to provide a snapshot for each process stage, thereby coordinating multiple processes in a controlled manner. In addition, define the sequential execution logic, this is much like an execution-tree structure, providing all possible execution paths and dependencies that associated procedures and/or processes are enable to follow. It is extremely useful during the ETL and DW refreshing processes, as well as management of end-user sessions in OLAP processes.

2.6 ETL – Life support for DW

In the natural world, plants cannot survive without supply of water and nutrient, plants will eventually wilt and die. The same goes for a DW without ETL.

ETL (Extract-Transform-Load) is one of the most important processes/tools in DW. It create/maintain DW by extracting data from ODS and transform it into required formats (standardized, consistent, cleaned up). It also loads data into DW core elements – fact and dimension tables. Furthermore, ETL is involved in a series of processes such as data capture, cleansing, incremental loading and error handling in a log-based job control. Initial ETL run for a new DW is most important step, like transplant life data from ODS to DW - It give DW a life.

Journey of data flow – Controlled by ETL
Keywords for features

- *Communication*
- *Connection*
- *Couple*
- *Correspondence*
- *Construction*
- *Convergence*
- *Combine*
- *Conversion*
- *Correlation*
- *Cleansing*

Driven by ETL, a profusion of data all flourishes along its course and throughout the DW all process phases.

ETL serve as communication hub, which link to all ODS through well-established connections, each connection involve couple – target and source setting in one-on-one session. Data travel from disparate ODS been combined through convergence processes into integrated data which also undergoes many amazing transformations until it reaches the OLAP/BI system, where it becomes meaningful, insightful information for endusers. But before data come that far, it must pass through many process stages, involving more cleansings, conversions and computing. Refreshing materialized views/cubes is followed soon after data loading is completed. DW is now been constructed by ETL.

Preparation for cleansing data – build supporting utilities

Laying the groundwork for your ETL is first thing to be considered. Always keep a firm grip on building useful utilities as foundation of ETL development, since integrity of your ETL processes and extendable developments will rely on it.

The data world is full of unexpectedness. To resolve inconsistencies, discrepancies and spelling errors originating from various ODS, a series of standard name dictionaries and lookup procedures must to be built before adding data to the DW. Building lookup tables not only saves coding efforts. but also make processes transparent. Some transformations or translations can be done by just looking up the tables as following:

- Person names
- Forbidden names (offending or dirty words may appear in name) you may not want to send email and call someone bad name such as "Dear #@$%^&*..." even someone named himself/herself as such (the funny scenarios in some internet online user registrations).
- Location names (county, region, state/province, city, town...)
- Zip or postal code lists
- Other common standard names
- Cross-references
- Function and subroutine libraries for conversion/transformation processes

A gigantic octopus in riding boundary of data warehouse and sources

Like an immense *octopus*, sprouting multiple tentacles the ETL reaching out to external data in remote ODS, capture and load it into the DW.
Please refer to Figure BookBackCover - Octopus

Dynamic data driven ETL (DDDETL or 3DETL)

A DW with many ODS that may reside in many different locations, spread over numerous servers, databases, involve thousands of tables, and hundreds of thousands of columns. ETL as a central communication hub with all necessary connections must recognize each connection name and able to act on it in a sophisticated way.

How to design an ETL to handle this? 3DETL is a way to go. Instead of coding million lines of code in programs against data objects, build a dynamic ETL using a data-driven approach (DDDA). The architectural model of a data-driven design provides generic flexibility for varying ETL coverage. Customization is done with easy maintenance on metadata. Additional scopes, requirements and the corresponding functionalities can be dynamically expanded as new requirements are identified through metadata. The approach involves in creating proper metadata to point to sources, staging and targets; dynamic SQL is the backbone here.

3DETL like a giant octopus, which changing into almost any color of the rainbow, blending into surrounding environment, even matching the texture of other creatures. Staging area as a landing base for incoming ODS data, most likely resemble the sources, 3DETL clone data objects in staging area through accessing and interpret metadata – systables from remote data sources. ETL - octopus finally changed its color by reading its surroundings – from metadata. The dynamic ETL makes itself independent of the specific data objects. It is configurable, data-driven and parameter-driven tools that suitable for ever-changing environment.

See example in Chapter Five <DW Development> 5.3.7 <Design your own DDDETL Tools>

Bad example with hard coded…This was what's happening in a database server migration. There were several database servers were going to migrate to a new environment that require server name changes, database name changes, but almost all existing programs, stored procedures were hard-coded mean that all server names, database names were buried in lines of codes…So server migration task became all out war on mass code-change – almost all existing programs had to be edited with miserable headaches to make them function in a new environment. After migration finally done, once up runing, anxious, keep fingers crossed! Whoops! Odd thing happened! Several omitted programs went against the wrong targets - old servers. It point and shoot wrong target. What a hazard!

ETL - From Sources to Target

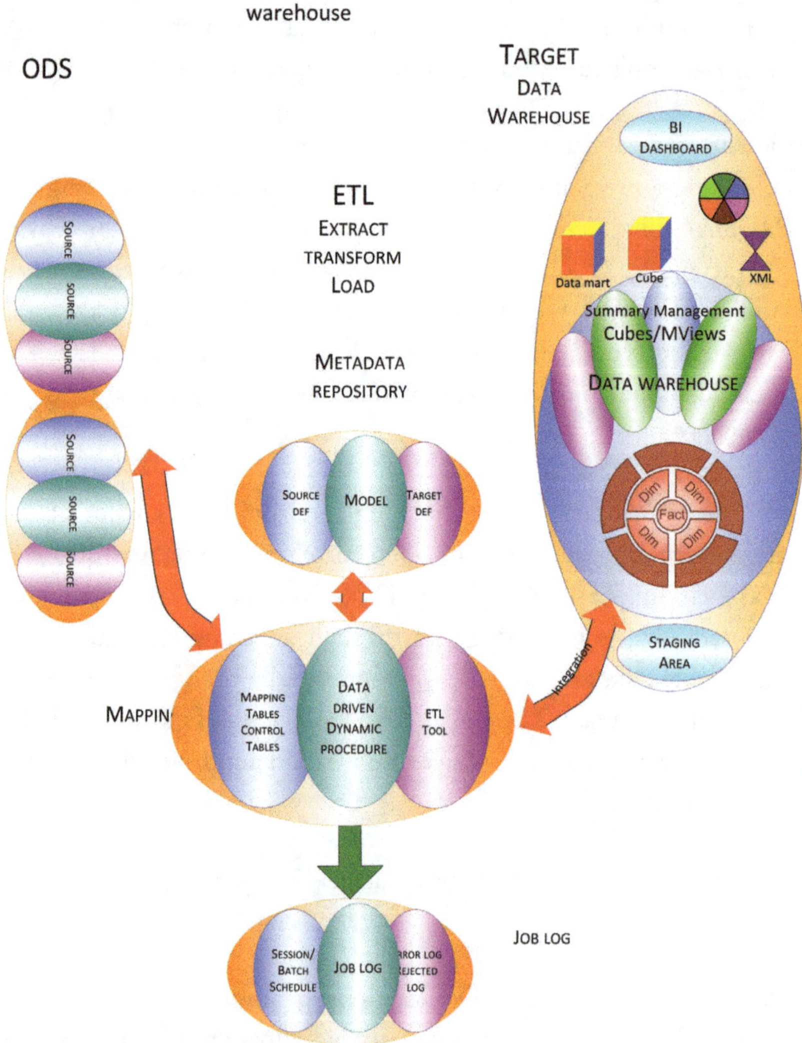

Figure 2-2.6-23 DwEtl

ETL Processes – handle sequence dependencies

To handle complexity of the real world of data transformation, ETL may need multiple steps to complete (extract, transform and load). Each process may depend on other processes, and vice versa thus form sequential order and dependencies among processes. Load a fact table normally using dimension table to lookup (for keys). For example, a sales-based fact table, product key in fact table actually depends on the product dimension table (as its primary key). – The product dimension has to be loaded prior to fact table loading. The ETL batches and jobs must be defined to including sequence and dependency handling, job handling, and signal to the corresponding party/task involved when there is dependence among them.

A well-defined logging system can provide **communications** between all processes involved, and coordinate the sequence of executions and logic in ETL jobs.

Creating and maintaining a dependency tree is the best way to increase visibility of workflows, sequence dependencies, it can be done by using tables to store sequential orders and dependency linkages between jobs, procedures and other data objects such as tables and views. It would help along the way of design, development and eventually detect errors; however dynamic update mechanism is desired when you want it handle propagation effects in your sequence dependencies and cascade update it accordingly.

See details in the Chapter Five <**Data warehouse Development**>, the Section 5.3 <ETL>.

2.7 Rotating and Rolling Data

Divide and conquer strategies have been tirelessly used throughout the power struggles in human history.

Key point to gain your superiority over your opponents is to divide them in pieces. Now let's look how to control data volumes by rolling up data and rotating data on partition-based approaches.

2.7.1 Size

In the initial stage of building a data warehouse, size poses few problems. But as the DW grows, it quickly becomes very difficult to manage. Fact tables become very large and drag down ETL processes, materialized view/cube refreshing, and queries. Eventually it reaches the point where a monstrous data volume could bear database performance down quickly unless you can find adequate solution.

2.7.2 Partition and rolling the summary

This data monster must be tamed by way of partition and rolling up of data:

- Split tables into more manageable sizes
- Rolling up summary data in a timely manner

2.7.3 Influential factors of size

If you are creating a new DW, you must first decide what level of granularity is and you need to be aware what impact it will be. General speaking, lowest grain level (same as ODS's) have more potential – you never know all in advance about user's requirements that may pop out at any time down the road. Obviously, a more detailed base can support more numerous types of reports - As your screenplay unfold you have more to show. However, there is a price to pay.

Granularity – The number of dimensions or type of dimensions greatly affect granularity. Adding new dimension into star schema usually changes the granularity and size of the fact table dramatically. For instance, in a sales fact table with customer and product dimension, if we add a sales person dimension or delivery location dimension, the granularity of fact table will increase.

The data model and schema design has most influences on size. My recommendations would be: Creating slim (short column length, short row length) fact table instead of creating wide and fat (long column length, long row length) one . The former hold equivalent information while keep relatively small volume and it can grow like a ***magic pea***. The later like a messy, stocky ***pumpkin***, it is very time consuming to process. This is well illustrated in Figure Narrow your fact table.

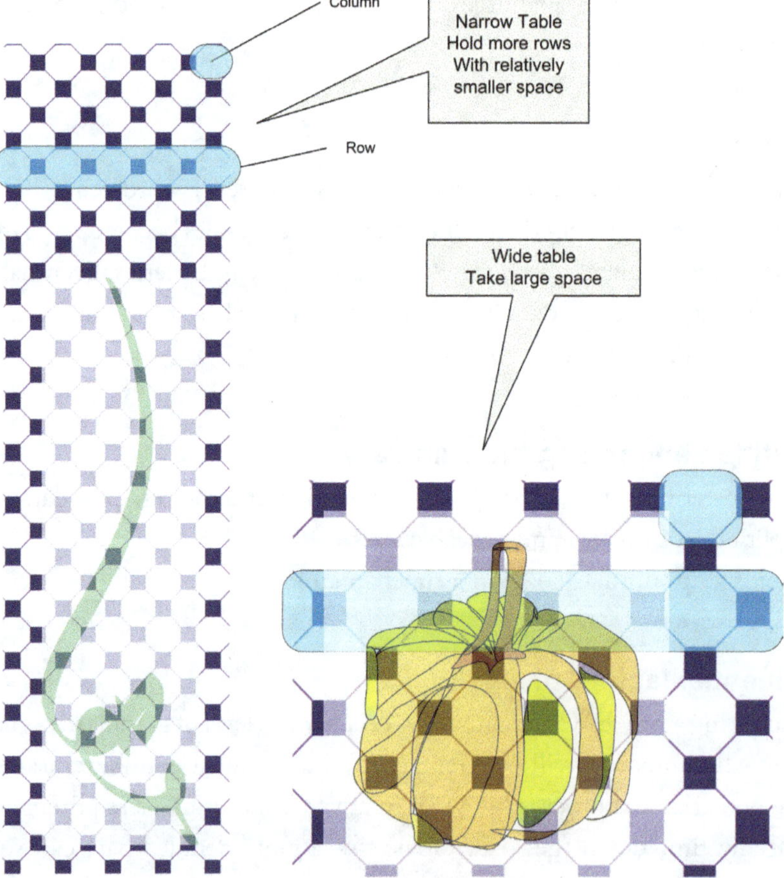

2.7.4 Data aging and retention

An aging process is necessary so that data does not accumulate indefinitely. Also, minimizing the amount of data online improves database performance.

But how old is old when it comes to data? – This is the question you will ask yourself and ask your end-users, and unfortunately, there is no easy answer. Some data, though not active currently but still has potential value for trend analysis or historic comparisons, etc. But how long it will be kept? It depends on the end-user's preferences, business nature and management needs.

For example, an e-commerce company may keep detailed sales data for the past 24 month. But an insurance company or health care organization/hospital may keep clients or patient information for life time. A real estate company may keep historic data such as flood histories forever.

From a planning perspective, the projection of future size and usage will shape your data model and data arrangement (partition, rollup summary) based on balancing of data volume and processing costs.

2.7.5 Rolling up summary data

Summary management is one of the most important parts of any data warehouse, particularly for decision-making analysis. For example, an executive dashboard shows all important key business indicators for organization such as sales, products and resources in highly summarized form – demanded by management.

As time go by, data volume increases, the usefulness of detail diminishes. The rolling summary data is the best way to convert data to an aggregated dataset for much reduced volumes. During the summary rollup processes, data granularity is in the evolution from lower to higher as data being further aggregated or summarized. The detailed daily data become totals by week, month and year. From business requirements, you may find that many reports (trend reports for example) may only require historic data in the summary level. If this is the case, consider retaining historic data only in the summary.

A detailed discussion is provided in Section 2.4.2 Multi-dimensional Cubes and 2.4.3 OLAP in this chapter.

2.7.6 Rolling windows - an intricate question

Probing the data obsolescence. When data is no longer worth keeping? This brings out to the rolling window and partition strategies. Address this earlier is better, resolve it during the logical modeling and design phase. Otherwise sooner or later you have to swallow bitter medicine and your system will suffer performance deficits.

Generally, we need to determine the rolling window for data aging and implementing the partition technique. If rolling window is 24 months, so as 25th month data entering database, the oldest data such as data before 24th month will be roll out of online system, or will be aggregated in format of summarized or compressed as read only and put in the less expensive offline or secondary storage thus save space for incoming data.

2.7.7 Divide and conquer – approach as a universal Truth

Common sense tells us that a very large object like a watermelon or a birthday cake must be cut into pieces in order to be consumed. Similarly, using partition technique can make an enormous data system manageable and scalable. Partitioning large tables improves performance and simplifies maintenance. By splitting a large table into multiple smaller tables, queries can access only a fraction of the data instead scanning the whole. Maintenance tasks, such as rebuilding indexes or doing backup, can execute more quickly and easily. Tables can be partitioned by the following categories:

- time
- geography/region
- categories (product or service categories, etc.)
- business unit, and other categories

Also, parallel process offered by database system to increase process speed can be utilized once partition is done. For a large fact table or dimension table, refresh is always extremely time and resource consuming. If it has been partitioned by time such as by day, so daily refresh will be very fast since only newest day need to be processed, whole fact or cube would be refreshed incrementally which is very desirable for performance improvement.

Usage frequency

Categorize data based on usage frequencies, and divide it accordingly. So that dataset has lower usage frequency won't drag dataset that has high usage frequency. One example here is employee dimension in a sales data mart. Employee is a big master dimension including many attributes, beside most frequently used dataset such as names, dates, title, and phone number; there are also a lot personal details that are in low usage such as family related, technical background, etc. which is a very big chunk of data. If we can separate them, dataset with high usage frequency would move faster, would get far less time to be processed. When using snowflake topology modeling a big dimension also consider such factor as usage frequency. A big dimension table can be modeled as snowflake structure – multiple linked sub dimension tables.

See details in the Chapter Five <**Data warehouse Design and Development**>, the Section 5.2.3 <Partition and Parallelism> and 5.2.3.6 Figure DwPartition_Quarter

An example of rolling up summary approach

A large system infrastructure consisting hundred servers and support a world class web browser which handle millions requests in a glimpse of an eye. There was a need of reporting and analyze all online requests and handling activities, domain pages calling, directions, server service status etc.

But there was a problem. Mountainous data collection that far exceeded those of the existing database spaces to hold it.

Users/engineers need extreme detailed data in order to trouble shoot over the large system for **live situations – data in lowest grain level with short period time**.

There were also needs for the after fact analysis reports based on historic data – **data in high grain level with long period time.**

Users also like to browse report to see "Is everything OK today?" what happen and where it occurred in the hundred server groups at a very high and broad level and then able to drill down into details, moving attention to the area of interest.

By keeping recent detail data (one week) and rolling up summary the reporting system provides detail of reports which trouble shooting services, machines, domain and pages in near real-time fashion. And summary reports based on rolled up data (by day, week, and month) for server, services, domain pages, and service usages. Summary and high level views also provide a broad view for users to browse in a global scope, quickly spot the unusual high rate of failures and able to dive deeper to current detail through the hierarchy/path provided. It helped engineers to listen to heartbeat or feel pulse of large online infrastructure live system.

Together, rolling up summary, data sampling solution and partition strategy help to hold system on the line, otherwise mountainous data from online request logging pour in just like a snow avalanche flooding all over the spaces.

2.8 Metadata and Model

The control of a large force is the same principle as the control of a few men: it is merely a question of dividing up their numbers.

Fighting with a large army under your command is nowise different from fighting with a small one: it is merely a question of instituting signs and signals.

—Sun Zi

There are not more than five musical notes, yet the combinations of these five give rise to more melodies than can ever be heard.

There are not more than five primary colors (blue, yellow, red, white, and black), yet in combination they produce more hues than can ever been seen.

There are not more than five cardinal tastes (sour, acrid, salt, sweet, bitter), yet combinations of them yield more flavors than can ever be tasted.

—Sun Zi

My note:

- ✓ Turn chaos and mess into orderly; the method is to count the components and sort them out – thereby controlling complex and massive database systems by maintaining the few metadata – a structural way to manage data.
- ✓ Grasp the few key factors in order to control the whole. Although metadata is very small in terms of volume, it describes virtually everything about data processing world. Grasp the metadata; you will get a grip on all concerned.
- ✓ The system design principle is standardization and simplification.
- ✓ All things in the universe can be sorted into fewer categories. Data standardizations allow you to deal with a few instead of a massive mess -nonstandard, inconsistent data.

2.8.1 What is metadata?

Metadata is the data about data. One example is a data dictionary in the database. It defines and describes data structures, processes, relationships, data management and its environment. It also describes where data come from and where data is going. - It is "the road map to navigate the data maze".

2.8.2 Data warehouse lays on the metadata

Good metadata is essential to a DW. It is of course indispensable for ETL, especially for dynamic ETL for data capture, extraction and transformation. Metadata describes mappings from ODS to DW or from OLTP systems to OLAP systems, source, updating/refreshing, algorithms. Lack of metadata maintenance in DW development is like trying to rebuild/remodel a house without a blueprint.

The data model describes how data is organized, and relationships among them. As we all known that the major goal of data warehousing is to provide analytical abilities and decision support, so that DSS output requirements are the major driving factors in data modeling and design. The Top down approach is primary path during define phase meanwhile bottom up is a primary approach to build up model and fill up void. Such modeling process is in reverse direction against data flow. Start from output requirements (analytical results, summary reports) towards data elements layout. On other hand, because DW is built upon top of operational data source systems, so data modeling and analysis also against sources that involved. Such as how to transfer data from sources into the target (data warehouse) following the natural data flows. Sound data modeling must therefore in combined, bidirectional analysis path.

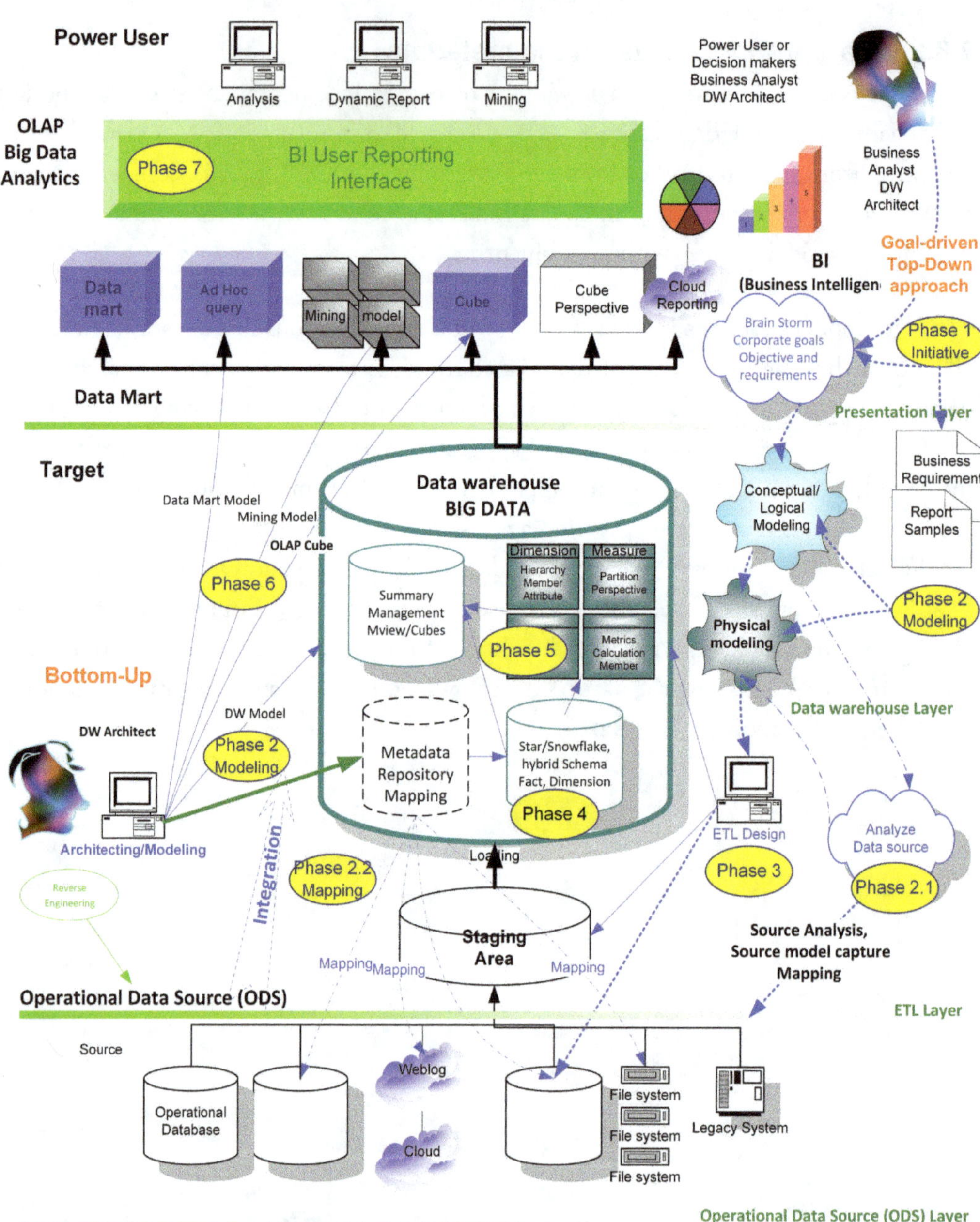

Top down Architecture modeling, Bottom up Implementation
Architecture of Data Warehouse -Design
Please refer to Figure 2-2.8-24 DwArchiPhase

2.8.4 Common nomenclature

The real world of business data is full of inconsistencies in naming. People just can't stop naming things even though things they try to name are essentially the same. Different names are often used for the same thing, or vice versa. However, to get the maximum benefit from the DW, we must insist a common nomenclature as one of the prerequisites of building simplified, integrated DW. A very name should suggest the same thing, same definition, same property. Different names should not refer to the same thing in same DW. Two names referring to the same thing that make confusions in the system. Once the uniform data definitions are built, we can go ahead and integrate data that comes from disparate systems through the adequate mapping processes. Building uniform documentations, specifications, data dictionaries and shared metadata repositories certainly is the route to success.

2.8.5 Build a centralized metadata repository

As a powerful integration of multiple data systems through shared metadata, a central metadata repository provides a holistic view of enterprise-wide source data definitions, data models, target databases, and transformation rules that convert source data into target data objects. Such **proactive** centralized metadata provides a general guidance for overall design and development. But there are gaps between theory and practice. Very often, exactly the opposite is true! A problem we commonly see in the data modeling is a passive metadata repository system which falling behind the runaway developments. Like a poor guy chasing his runaway bulls down the road, there is no guidance for developments but only after fact checking – backward system documentation.

Recommended best practices

- Proactively use and maintain a centralized metadata repository to store metadata and data definitions on a global scale.
- Before designing or modifying a database, review the metadata repository and check existing standards and proposed data elements. Do so before implementing new database changes to ensure that data elements are defined according to standards. Also, reuse as much existing data objects/elements and types as possible. Avoid introducing redundancy into the data model.
- While databases are going the direction of distributed systems, metadata management would be better off by going toward centralization.
- Use metadata as driving force and develop your dynamic ETL which is generic, extensible and configurable for your specific requirements.

2.8.6 Metadata maintenance

Documentation: retain knowledge and intellectual properties

The data model should be visible to all parties involved, including architects, developers, programmers, user groups, and management. Metadata, which relates to source and target systems, should be maintained and remain update and refreshable with the latest changes so that the metadata repositories and documentation can be used by team as the blueprints of project developments.

Reverse engineering and design capture

Reverse engineering must be used to capture models from source and target systems, and thereby create your metadata repositories.

Separate business rules from application programing codes

Using Data driven approach: will-defined stored procedures or packages with generic features should be able to take instructions or hints from metadata provided and able to execute tasks accordingly. This is good way to implement business rules. See details in Section <Platform - Core & Shell> in Chapter Four <Development Highlights>.

2.8.7 Metadata definitions and managements

Metadata definitions and specifications Includes the following:

Source

- Using Snowflake topology layout overall data sources and connections
- Locations, network connections, access methods
- Computer platform definitions, operating system definitions
- Servers, databases, nodes, file systems, access methods, schema, tables, data elements
- Source database links
- Reverse engineering and source design capture specifications
- Metadata exchange definitions

Staging area definitions (captured source metadata may sit in this area)

- Using Snowflake topology layout overall data sources and staging maps
- Source-staging mapping (servers, databases, tables, columns)
- Staging-target mapping
- Source-target mapping
- The file transport specifications
- The file specifications and usages
- The file pre-or-post event processing specifications (empty, cleanup, compress, backup, etc.,)
- Staging database usages and pre/post process specifications

Target definitions

- Using Snowflake topology layout overall data and system architectures
- Star/snowflake schema, hybrid schema
- Fact table definitions
    - Measures (metrics)
    - Foreign keys (link to dimensions)
    - Primacy key (suggest using surrogate key)
    - Index definitions
    - Validation constraints
    - Data range validations
    - Partition specifications
    - Storage specifications

- Dimension table definitions
    - Primary key (link to fact)
    - Slowly changing dimension (SCD)
    - Hierarchies
    - Levels
    - Members
    - Relationships
    - Dimension sharing
    - Dimension versioning
    - Database integrity constraints
    - Type (type 1, type 2 for SCD)

Mapping definitions

- Source-target mapping
- Primary data-summary mapping
- Methods
- Standardization dictionary
- Conversion dictionary
- Lookup tables
- Mapping tables

ETL definitions

- Conversion rules and methods
- Data cleaning specifications
- Batch job specifications
- Loading frequency
- Incremental slice control specifications (the last loading date or batch number)

- Filters
- Rollback specification and policy
- Stripping and modification against loaded data (undone or apply patch)
- Conversion function library
- Transportation
- Loading
- Replications
- Session management
    - Scheduling
    - Pre-batch and post-batch job events
    - Logging (Batch log, Session log, Rejected log, Bad data log)
    - Error handling (Log, rollback, Email notification)

In DDDETL approach, metadata may serve as driving factors for dynamic ETL. It is normally done by lookup database sys tables/category tables to fetch source and target item names such as servers, databases, table names and guide ETL to create generic, configurable action codes instead of specific, hardcoded rigid one.

Summary management definitions

- Fact and dimension-summary materialized view(mview) and cube mapping
- Summary object -summary object mapping
- Summary mview/cube layout
- Aggregation definitions
- Materialized view definitions
- Cube definitions
    - Sources of Cube
    - Shared dimensions, dimension used
    - Relationships between cubes
    - Dimension usage (dimension- measure usage relationships)
    - Dependencies of nested materialized views and cubes
    - Grouping of cubes
    - Measure group partition
    - Calculations (metrics)
    - Key Performance Indicator (KPI)
    - Cube perspective (customized view of cube)

- Refreshing definitions
    - pre-refreshing and post refreshing events
    - methods (complete, fast)
    - groups

  - dependency sequence
  - frequency
  - monitoring

OLAP and reporting definitions

- Query engine
- Intelligent query extraction
- Cube/view definitions
- Mining modeling methodologies and algorithms
- Mining models
- Reports
- User interface definitions
- Access methods
- Delivery methods
- Result set transportation and rendering
- User log in and activity tracking,
- User logging and error handling
- OLPA user manual

Application software specification

- Version control
  - Database application version
  - Software and program version
- Function-data object references (dependencies between programs and data objects)
- Packages/stored procedures/functions
- Function library
- Components
- Hierarchical level model
- Architecture – N-tier structure
- Library
- Rule-base control policy
  - Business rule tables
  - Associations between business rules and business policies

Quality control and security definitions

- Security policy
- Audit log
- Error trapping
- Error-tracing methods and specifications
- Database access and network traffic logging

2.8.8 Avoid duplications

Lack of knowledge about organizations' data can lead to wasteful duplication of efforts. Fortunately, this can be avoided by having sufficient and unified metadata. The initial expense of properly documenting data with complete metadata clearly outweighs the potential costs of having to recreate the redundant data, which is expensive and time consuming. Before you start a new development, should look at this road map first, looking for any useful data system and determine how you going to use it – look before you leap.

Data in its raw state and then transform into the work of art through Meta model
Please refer to Figure 2-1 DwEnv

CHAPTER THREE

ANATOMY OF DATA WAREHOUSE

3.1 Stackable layered architecture

The DW is a multilayer structure reflecting multiple process stages throughout the entire data stream. Each layer in this stacked structure depends on its base layer (layer underneath) and it also provides data stream to support to its upper layer. This is the major characteristics of DW architecture, and tremendous efforts will be made to implement and optimize such structure.

DW is made of many different and distinct layers which can be clearly defined and well-structured in the followings.

Core and shell

Looking at DW system platform and its internal structure from different angles, it stands like a pyramid as described in Chapter Two <the Great Pyramid>. You may also think of it as a solid sphere with multiple layers, sectors and the shell (the outermost layer) – it also resembles a coconut, stone fruit or walnut.

Multiple layers

Like natural fruits described above, the DW has three body segments, the outermost layer - *shell*, the middle layer – *mesocarp*, and the inner layer – *endorcarp/core* respectively. Each layer may be further divided as sub layers vertically, sectors horizontally. Now let's look at it layer by layer in a perspective view.

Start with the bottom (innermost) of this multi-layered object, looking upward or from very central section – *seed* core data, looking inside out.

The core: this is the primary data layer, which is made up of facts and dimensions (F&D) with underlying ETL and staging area. ETL techniques and processes are implemented to build and maintain F&D layer.

The middle layer: This layer is inherited from the core layer. Here we find the information layer. The transition zones exist between the core and shell, such as a summary management system (SMS), or multi-dimensional cubes. OLAP refresh processes keep cubes sync with underlying tables. This layer may also have its own (multiple) sub layers such as preparation layers for final presentation and delivery layer.

The shell - The outermost layer
This would be just the tips of the frontal lobes. It is there that BI presentation objects reside. BI presentation is the layer in highest level and is the effective interface of OLAP system to its endusers. It senses the user request and responds to it. It consists of several sub layers or sectors such as report delivery layer, user interface, reporting and cube perspectives, BI dashboard and data visualization.

3.2 How do layers of the DW form?

3.2.1 The pathway – from the core to the shell

Each layer is nourished by the layer underneath it, and it in turn supports its upper (or outer) layer; And so on so forth forming the layer step by step until natural and stable layering evolves.

Communication between adjacent layers - Layer binding
ETL layer is a sub-layer of the core layer. As a central communication hub, it maintains both network/database connections and provides point-to-point communication sessions; offers major establishment and transport services to staging area and DW core data sector (fact/dimension). It is also responsible for the propagation across DW of changes in servers within it. It works as a bridge between ODS and staging area/other core data sector, also as a bridge between staging area and core data sector – facts/dimensions (F&D) respectively.

The masses of data that flow from the bottom to top – all contributed to the patchwork layering that gives todays DW's their distinctive banded appearance. Pushed up from ODS or staging area, transformed, and cleansed, data is ready to be passed to the next higher level/layer, then ETL strip away the unwanted noise and build linkages, not only from the fact tables but also from the dimensions around and between them, and created the rich sanctuary for DW that is the base of OLAP/BI. It is within this sheltered bowl that cubes are to make their homes and it is from this level that we build up our BI dashboard and reporting.

The mission of building any new layer is to provide quick services while creating much needed isolation and protection for the inner objects. This is what recommended core-shell system architecture consisting of multilayers and multisegments.

Data here is organized in many layers staring from the core to the outer layer and in many segments based on user group/applications. Most objects in the outer layer are derived from inner layer; inner layers are derived from the core – data layer. In an ideal DW environment, information would be pushed as close as possible toward endusers; meanwhile, users should be prevented from accessing the inner core, as strict as possible. With prebuilt materialized views, summary data and shell, fast access can be achieved. Each outer layer provides offloading of its inner layer, meanwhile shields its inner layer.

Data and its expression sets may be logically or physically partitioned or tailored into multiple sectors based on the scope of applications or user groups.

As the layers built up over duration of ETL/Aggregating processes, they are compressed and cemented together, solidifying into summary layers with many levels of hierarchies. By the time the last/highest level created, the raw data has turned into insightful information, the details have turned into the summaries, the historic data become available to make the trend comparison charts, and so on creating something like the layer-cake looking we see. Tiered with staging areas, facts/dimensions, summary cubes, OLAP, and BI dashboard, data warehouse rise in splendor – the highest comprehensive platform on business management world.

3.2.2 Zones of transition

In order to achieve data visualizion for end users, it is better to allocate more ready-made objects in higher layers than doing it in lower layers, instead, lower layers should be kept "slim and mute" while higher layers can expand to cover broad spectrum of objects in high-visibility show fashion.

Data becomes better-organized as more layers are built. Taking this idea one step further, we can build materialized views/cubes to isolate/protect our core data such as fact and dimension tables.

As described in the Chapter Two <OLAP and BI>, summary mviews and cubes served a dual purpose of quick availability to end-users and offloading the core data elements such as fact tables. Furthermore, due to the presence of summary mviews/cubes, the core data element - fact table will be shield, and can be largely unaffected by many user access.

DW Multi-layer structure - Core & Shell. Build solid core and use inside out data push
Figure 3-3.2-1 DwShell

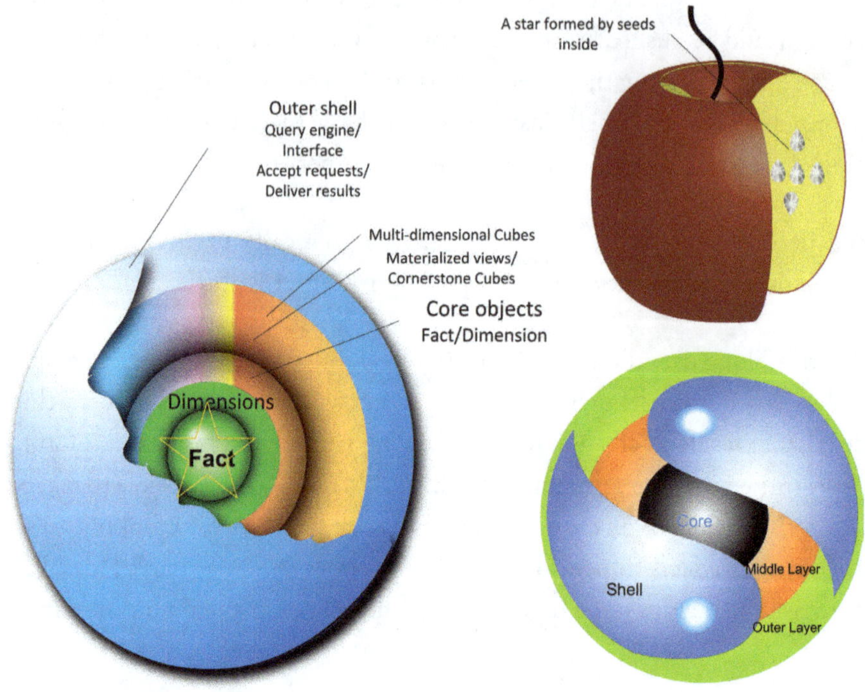

3.3 Deployment of presentation layer

Presentation layer

BI presentation layer is a high-level layer and is effective interface of OLAP system to endusers. It connects to the ready-made objects which are located near high level of layer for delivery. This layer offers key reporting establishment and transport report services to both endusers and report applications. It is responsible for propagation across reporting publishing nodes. It also routes requests from endusers to OLAP, fetch and return result sets. The requests travel top-down and corresponding results return in the reverse direction.

It serves as communication or delivery/access layer. Here formatted data is transferred from the presentation layer to clients who initiated requests. Visual presentations, reports, charts, and graphics are typical categories in this layer. OLAP or reporting delivery tools handle requests and deliver the result sets to users via user interface, web interface, and user access control.

Preparation for this layer has been done in the layer beneath it – the middle layer. Cubes and summary views have been created; business analysis required metric such as calculations have been defined; performance indicators (KPI) been created. Cube perspectives which suitable for intended user groups have been clearly defined and set, all ready to answer the calls from the higher-level layer.

From this point on, BI Dashboard – already a powerful force upon DW – becomes one of the greatest user interface tools of OLAP. Standing on Grand view point, from high level above confluence of data streams, you survey one of the stark of these landscapes in business world. The view is grand indeed- especially at global level. So much of visualization is done here to make it like a brilliant multi-faceted gem.

As discussed before, the summarized views and cube series are our firepower, and should be created then deployed close to the front. This design technique using prepared summary mviews/cubes in the front, and therefor use much lighter demand on computer time and database load. This is because expensive computing and table joining have been done during scheduled (off-peak hour) times, thus support many users with fast response for online services. The core components such as fact and dimension tables being the important source of OLAP, should be put to the rear in a protected fashion.

DW push information streams from its core data layer (facts and dimensions) into the presentation layer – cubes and data marts

Figure 3-3.3 DwPushCube

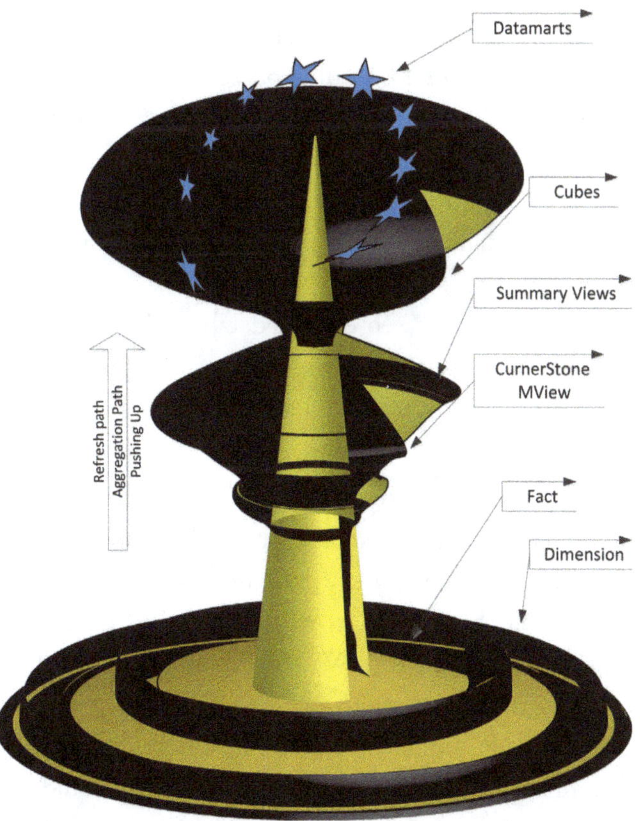

3.4 Multi-layer, multi-sector (MLMS)

First, let's consider a military deployment strategy that has been proven successful in real battles:

> *The battle line is drawn with such deployment:*
> *For effective strength (manpower): heavier in rear, light in front (in much protected fashion);*
> *For firepower: heavier in front (in much firepower delivery fashion), light in rear.*
>
> *—Anonymous*

Note: Deploy manpower LFHR (light in front, heavy in rear) basis, firepower on HFLR (heavy in front, light in rear) basis. – The same goes for DW; put core data in rear with protected mode ; and put presentation data in front for quick delivery.

Such system architecture/layout provides the following advantages:

- Performance gain
- More balanced system load
- Offloading the core data set such as fact/dimension tables. In certain cases, OLAP can still produce analytical reports meanwhile DW core components such as a fact table may be undergoing ETL loading processes.
- Security gain. Each layer can provide isolation to its underlying layer, making it hard to hack something like a multilayer system. Each segment can be isolated from others, thus avoid spoiling or disturbing rest of system in case things go wrong.
- Provides adequate management and accessing scopes and controllable depths for users.
- Ideal for the systems such as web-enabled databases (E-commerce or E-government) that face the public or feature mass-user access.

Security gain

As one of its defining features, stacked layered DW provides facilities for carrying out security functions, protecting established core data and transport of data, and controlling processes. It builds on the basic security framework by isolated layered structure. The layered data sectors which shielded by its outer layers and outermost shell that is the cornerstone of security architecture of DW. The toughness of a multilayer/multisegment object (think of a walnuts fruit) is related to its internal structure (multilayer, multisegment/ multiple compartments). This is inherently different than a single-layer object that is fragile and easy to break (think of glassware or a balloon; how fragile and weak they are). The internal structure here refers to the architecture on which data and application software is organized. Armed with its multilayers and its hard shell which serve as access controls, make it a hard nut to crack for any intruders. It is similarly immune to another security threat - human stupidity. Furthmore, it can survive the roughest hits that online nature can devise, and is very well adapted to harsh conditions of the internet environment.

Please refer to Figure 3-3.2-1 DwShell

3.5 Software infrastructure

Deployment strategy

In this section, we will focus on deployment strategies for web-enabled data warehouse, especially where and how to outlay the architecture of business logic and business rules in a centralized system approach.

Client-server platform

As client-server platforms replace mainframes, two- and three-tire architectures have been popular in the database world. Benefits of the platforms are obvious, especially for three-tier architecture as it

1. provides scalability, reliability, manageability, security, interoperability and flexibility
2. increases system throughput
3. increases security
4. deliveries cost/effective solution

Centralize data control

A DW as an integrated solution for enterprise-wide management against regular database systems bears the following characteristics:

- o Central repository over distributed source systems
- o Central metadata repository over various disparate (inconsistent) ODS
- o If web-enabled, it provides broader services to end-users, offer open for public access.
- o Readiness for quick query/analysis availability
- o Using backend database objects, stored procedures to centralize data control. It will serve as the core of application's backend to accelerate the deployment of new services and reduce the total cost. By doing so you can centralize the controls and administration of report generating processes. It also allows each user group to see and control processes at a level of detail appropriate to the group's needs and privileges.

Stored procedures – the core of database software applications

The stored procedures as the executable forms, offer many advantages in performance, productivity, and scalability. It is a heavy weight champion of data processes in database arena.

A central repository is achieved through centralized metadata and stored procedures. These are database objects, and can be called and executed quickly and efficiently, thus minimizing network traffic, and speeding up response. Furthermore, using stored procedures and packages serves to centralize controls and administration of report-generating processes as well as centralizing error-trapping abilities. Using stored procedures as core of applications in the backend also accelerates the deployments of new services, and definitely reduce the total costs.

Centralized software management

Move business logic/rules into stored procedures on the server side

Putting business logic into a stored procedure also provides a single point of control for ensuring that business rules and logics are enforced globally across the enterprise. By making use of stored procedures that perform most application, and handling data, you can minimize network round trips, thus reduce excessive network traffic.

Developing sufficient stored procedures to handle application also has security advantages. Beside the major benefits such as performance gain, it provides better security control. Users can be granted permission to execute a stored procedure to process data instead of granting direct access underlying tables in database. In other words, users can only access data through stored procedures, which restrict them to do only what they are supposed to do.

However, in reality, it is not uncommon to see some deployments going the opposite way. With application software mostly deployed in frontend (client side) instead of backend (database server side), such systems typically have very poor performance. If an organization is not able to maintain central repositories to manage changes, their changes may become costly and chaotic.

A hollow bodied jellyfish without central backbone

Database web applications with the hollow backend would be very weak in central power, and has degraded performance. Like a spineless *jellyfish*, application is complex, yet weak in central power. An awkward creature like this is very likely to create software maintenance nightmares, and is prone to break.

Bring results close to endusers

Rules of thumb here are to let client application tasks get in and out of the database server quickly. There are several strategies come into play.

Bridge the gap or shorten path between raw data and most frequently requested information, make information ready and available to users by creating objects in the layer which can deliver direct responses. As has been mentioned in the section on "Multi-dimensional Cubes", the DW meet web users with a well-defined analytical type, well-prepared summary cube series tend to minimize response time and reduce web traffic. In fact, if you can push data so close that just a click away from user's desired results, it definitely reduce response time greatly. The system built with such approach is very well adapted to the harsh environment of web-enabled online analytical process services. It is obvious that DW cannot survivor in a web application environment without a well thought-out OLAP design and/or well prepared summary cube series in place.

Separate business rules from program codes

As has been discussed in Section 2.4 < Data Warehouse Models>, it is a good idea to build business rule tables to hold your most frequently changed rules and drive so-called smart applications, which is able to take the hint from given data (conditions, logic, hypothesis, and instructions), and execute accordingly, thus making applications more flexible and intelligent. Furthmore, use a centralized business rule repository to get the most of benefits from centralized power, bring global changes from single point, and then implement broad-scale deployments.

Facing the dynamic business environment

Facing the ever-changing business environment, the development of database application is subject to frequent and lengthy changes or revisions. Application software often requires acute and global changes as a results of business acquisitions, business interest shift, direction twist, and technologies advance.

Bad practice - Rules buried in source code

Initially, business rules were simply buried in **source** code, which were scattered throughout the applications. It is still common to see those nested if-then-else clauses embedded in code bodies. That make it hard to change rules or logics without testing all other case - otherwise such changes may introduce odd side-effects and unpredictable consequences. It is a nightmare to make global rule changes across multiple applications with such coding practices because code changes can be costly. This sort of approach leads to a situation in which lack of business governance and visibility, lack of traceability; so, it is not far awy from maintenance nightmare and inconsistent implementation.

Separate business rules from application procedures

The idea is to build application that is flexible and generic, so that user can change business rules without touching code every single time, and be able to avoid code changes in some degree. Is this possible to do? The answer is yes, only if rules are separated from application program codes.

Give applications ability to read and parse rules

Give stored procedures of read-then-execute ability; besides passing parameters, such supercharged procedures are able to read instructions from rule tables and execute assigned tasks accordingly; therefore that parts of the software may be reprogrammed to change their functionality "on the fly".

Maintain the rule tables instead of modifying the stored procedures

Extract carefully choossing rules from process logic and store them in the rule tables as visualized, traceable and maintainable data sets. Hence separates rules from procedures or program routines. Together, a rule base and a shared rule-parsing function able to avoid hard-coded mechanisms (which were created inside of program source codes); this, also avoid propagation effects in procedure groups when a rule is enforced only by passing parameters. The key here is using dynamic programming (for example, dynamic SQL) to compose application based on the guiding information provided by the rule tables.

Customizable business rule properties

The business rule repository stores the rules including the access, permissions, job/task frequency, quotas, actions, action chains, chain events, and exception rules, plus their properties, including descriptive names, rule key values, creation date, last modification date and associated rule documentation. In term of specific rule properties, the Repository may include:

- Business rule descriptions which are understandable by code-blind users
- Rule code/value parse-abled by programs
- Rule ownership tracking using a rule author or rule owner property
- Effective and expiration date, as well as add/edit dates
- Status (including invalid status) which assignment permits rule-skipping
- On/off toggle
- Default rules
- A pointer to rule hierarchies or dominate/overwrite relationships
- Business unit/department dependencies – author groups
- Customer segment dependent

- Rule permission management which is preferable associated to management hierarchies
- Logging mechanism to track usage history
- Logging mechanism to track rule changing history
- Rule scale-back mechanism
- Link between business rules and related business policy source documents using rule source properties

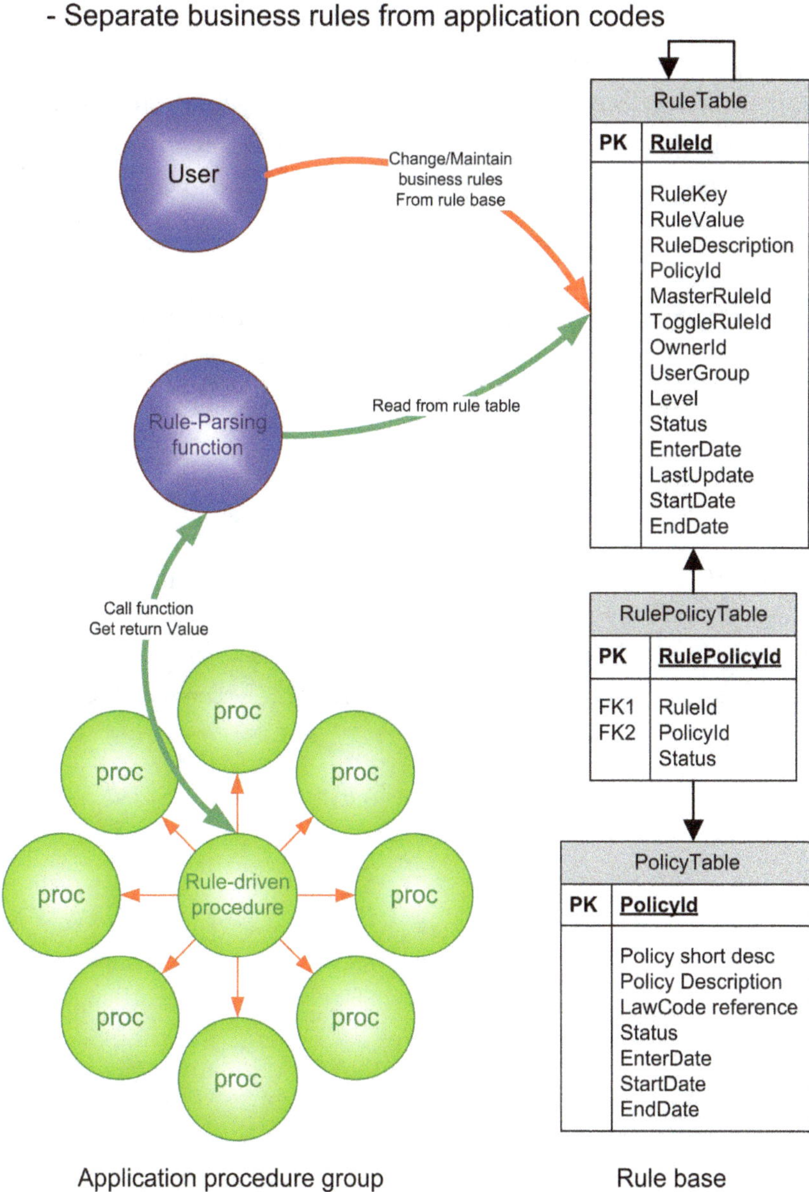

Figure 3-3.5-4 RuleBaseTable

Benefits of separating rules from source **codes:**

- o Global changes can be realized by making single point change in data
- o Rule change can be done through changing the rule related data in the tables instead of changing procedures or source codes
- o Users can change the rules to a certain degree (by editing rule tables) without asking a developer to revise source codes.
- o A central repository provides a rule-base that is maintained globally across entire enterprise.
- o Application logic and rules will be tied to the related business policies.
- o Developers can rapidly respond to the frequently changing requirements.
- o Greatly simplify program logic testing.
- o Propagations effects in program and procedure groups are reduced.
- o Additional gains are achieved with less complex design work, reduced overall testing, lower maintenance, smaller design team, and lower overall risk.

Function library

Building function libraries is a fundamental job for quality database applications. It involves breaking down processes into simplified and abstract processes and function groups. Such function libraries will be shared across many applications thus provides power to apply global changes across application software systems.

Reporting

Always strive to centralize the control and administration of reporting processes. Allow each user group to see and control the processes at a level of detail appropriate to their group. To reach that goal, create the architectures such as a schema to track users' access, activities, errors and exceptions; and to maintain user access scopes and parameter settings.

CHAPTER FOUR

DATA WAREHOUSE DEVELOPMENT HIGHLIGHT

Figure Tiger3d

4.1 Development Strategies

> *All men can see the tactics whereby I conquer, but what none can see is the strategy out of which victory is evolved.*
>
> *—Sun Zi*

> *In the practical art of war, the best thing of all is to take the enemy's country whole and intact; to shatter and destroy it is not so good. So, too, it is better to recapture an army entire than to destroy it, to capture a regiment, a detachment or a company entire than to destroy them. Hence to fight and conquer in all your battles is not supreme excellence; supreme excellence consists in breaking the enemy's resistance without fighting.*
>
> *—Sun Zi*

> *...Thus the highest form of generalship is to balk the enemy's plans; the next best is to prevent the junction of the enemy's forces; the next in order is to attack the enemy's army in the field; and the worst policy of all is to besiege walled castle.*
>
> *—Sun Zi*

> *There are roads which must not be followed, armies which must be not attacked, towns which must not be besieged, positions which must not be contested, commands of the sovereign which must not be obeyed.*
>
> *The general who thoroughly understands the advantages that accompany variation of tactics knows how to handle his troops.*
>
> *The general who does not understand these, may be well acquainted with the configuration of the country, yet he will not be able to turn his knowledge to practical account.*
>
> *So, the student of war who is unversed in the art of war of varying his plans, even though he be acquainted with the Five Advantages, will fail to make the best use of his men.*
>
> *Hence in the wise leader's plans, considerations of advantage and of disadvantage will be blended together.*
>
> *If our expectation of advantage be tempered in this way, we may succeed in accomplishing the essential part of our schemes.*
>
> *—Sun Zi*

My note:
Sunzi always advised to avoid costly war. Why shouldn't we apply the same principle in planning and starting a DW project?

Sun Zi wisely advises us not to compete in all fields, only in the one where we have advantages, using the existing systems and external sources to patch your own disadvantages and shortcoming, and thereby form sound and broad systems. Doing so, you can avoid wasteful duplicate efforts.

In certain cases, you have to make your own decision, take reality into account, and come out with a practical solution instead of obeying top leader's command blindly.

Strategic overview – Goal and path

Have a clear goal in mind and an overall plan before starting your data warehouse project. Once goal is set, path will follow accordingly. If goal is building EDW, path you are taking is different than that of building datamart, so does complexity, degree of difficulties, resources, time, and costs which must be carefully calculated and estimated.

The following diagram shows the major DW design phases or stages:

1 Initiative – plan and start project
2 Data modeling
    Logical modeling
    Physical modeling
    2.1 Analyze sources
    2.2 Mapping
3 ETL design
4 DW primary designs
5 Dimension and measure design, summary design
6 Cube, datamart design
7 User interface, BI dashboard design

There are dependence sequence, priorities and relationships between these design phases or stages.

The following diagram clearly show a **critical path** – DW modeling in design phases, it is a central hub on which almost all later developments depends and will ever affect them such as ETL, staging area, DW primary design, cube, datamart design, etc. It must be done, and done it right based on grasp business goal, objectives, user requirements, environment and available resources.

Govern overall development

It will primarily be a centralized repository. Even if it is a physically distributed system, it must have a centralized, integrated logical design in place. This will feature a centralized ETL functionality and have a logical centralized metadata repository to hold data definitions in order to ensure a high level of data integrity.

Planning big

Also consider it is multi-layer system. For example, ETL, staging, DW core data layer, summary management layer, mviews, cubes, and result delivery and representation layer. In addition, it may hold historic data. So, it is better to lay a broad base for a stackable layered DW architecture.

Finally, design and develop summarization or aggregation on broad scope in an organization or among them will form a powerful OLAP, which turns data into relevant information for overall business decisions and delivers results to broad range of users.

Cooperation and reuse existing resources – Achieving more with less

The goal here is to share IT sources as much as possible during system integration through broad-scale cooperation with the organizations both internal and external which have common interests. Doing so would enable a rapid exploration of the DW project scope. You should own nothing, but control everything; what you need is everything available for you with or without ownership. Share as much resources and ready-made information infrastructures and BI data reporting as possible. Don't start same thing parallel with your neighbors or other organization that you can (or possible) share with them. Negotiate with them and make your offer and contributions for common/mutual benefits. This principle should apply for both private and public sectors especially for later since there are more common interests than differences (conflicts) by nature.

Key words: *Share, Exchange, Connection, Contribution, Consortium, Cloud* (SE4C).
The point here is not simply suggest cutting back your budget and cost, but direct your effort and resource to something that you can't get from anywhere and focus on **integration** of existing DWs (regardless internal or external) and make them available to you.

Standardization

Look for way to share, build and implement data standardization during development, using unified data dictionaries and data exchange protocols lay a broad, solid ground for enterprise-wide, region- wide, nation-wide or even global data warehouses.

Wise choice on modeling

There is no concrete rule for data modeling, all depends on the circumstance such as user's requirements, short-term and long term goals and trade-off, so you may come up with dimensional (star or snowflake), relational (3rd normal) and hybrid model and so on.

Working group

True collaboration for business decision-making requires a high level of knowledge sharing. For large-scale information integration projects which involved cross-enterprises or cross-departmental levels, effective work groups should be formed to improve communication among the various parties. All of those will demand top management's sponsorship for a global DW solution.

Please refer to Figure 2-2.8-24 DwArchiPhase

4.2 Planning for Success

> *We cannot enter into alliance with neighboring princes until we are acquainted with their designs. We are not fit to lead an army on the march unless we are familiar with the face of the country--its mountains and forests, its pitfalls and precipices, its marshes and swamps. We shall be unable to turn natural advantages to account unless we make use of local guides. If we don't know those key points, we can't be a force with great dominance.*
>
> *—Sunzi*

We are now ready to move on to DW development with more proactive approaches.

4.2.1 Design work steps

Evaluating the business needs - Study business objectives and organization's mission and goals

Before choosing an approach for building DW, you should think carefully about your business needs. Only when you have determined and selected approaches that will best accomplish your goal.

As we already know, DW is integrated solution for enterprise management. The development team must therefore have a good grasp of its subject over numerous and complex business areas. Still, those who look and watch carefully will discover much in this BI wonderland.

The diversity of interests among users is certainly a factor to be recognized by the development team. When start a project, it is essential to get a global view of organization, both horizontally across departments and vertically across management hierarchies – an overall enterprise view.

In this chapter, we use one of Online advertising BI solution examples – OnlineAd.

Business area: Online Advertising

Goal: Ensure market success and ROI that maximize money making opportunities; as a result of analysis, the solution built should help corporation to develop better customer relationships, increase sales and generate greater brand awareness.

Please refer to Chapter Two 2.3.3 Closing Loop – online advertising

Topology in forming DW – the world of snowflake

Grouping subject areas

The following steps describe how to group subject areas in a way of hierarchical **embedded star** – snowflake. As such decompose progressed, a star radiating multiple star – detailed model form in recursive manner. If we do this recursively, we get a series of successive stars, from which form our snowflake – overall architecture.

- DW is roughly a superstar form – BI major subject area as a center, connect to multiple data marts derivate radiantly from main DW base. Its radiating shape can be presented in diagram in first layer as set (1) > {1.1, 1.2, 1.3, 1.4}.
- Data mart itself is also a sub-superstar form – connect to multiple subject areas (sales, services, marketing, and resource). There may be overlap on data marts and subject areas. Its radiating shape can be presented in diagram in next layer (second layer) as set (1.1) > {1.1.1, 1.1.2, 1.1.3, 1.1.4}.
- Each subject area can be further decomposed as a star form that made of a subject and connected multiple business activities (transaction or event). Its radiating shape can be presented in third layer as set (1.2.1) > {(1.2.1).1, (1.2.1).2, (1.2.1).3, (1.2.1).4}.
- Each business activity also can be decomposed as a star (fact) and multiple dimensions surround it. Presented in diagram fourth layer as set (1.3.1.1) > {(1.3.1.1).1, (1.3.1.1).2, (1.3.1.1).3, (1.3.1.1).4}.
- Dimensions themselves can also be a star form - a master dimension as its center, link to other sub dimensions. Presented in diagram fifth layer as set (1.4.1.1.1) > {(1.4.1.1.1).1, (1.4.1.1.1).2, (1.4.1.1.1).3, (1.4.1.1.1).4}.
- And so on for next lower level split.

Note:
This is a hierarchical nested snowflake topology with certain degree of iteraton.
Nodes and paths from layer 1.1 to layer 1.x.x.x.x are omitted on this hierarchical decomposed radiating shaped, layered diagram to help simplify matter.

From now on, if you unfold/expand all above in detail, it looks like a super, complex snowflake form made of multiple stars and less complex snowflakes.

Please refer to Chapter Two Figure 2-2.4-10 SnowflakeDWtopo

The snowflaking stages in general

Growing like snowflake crystal – ideal development model approach

- Start from the core(nucleation), from which everything grow in diffusion and coalescence manner
- Hierarchical level control -the way to handle complex control problems
- Two basic types of mechanisms contribute to formation of balanced developments of DW project: diffusion control and interface control

- Let radiated branch projects have independent, parallel growth
- Design a symmetry balanced architecture and approach in an environment with explosive tips (fighting edge) which grow more dynamic and chaotic that may give more chances to rise to new height of innovations
- Symmetrical beauty must be maintained by well-balanced strong coordination over a dynamic, chaotic development ecology. Communications within or cross team/organization is essential for overall success, that discipline team and impose the development constraints whereby it retains much of its form and function
- Natural copy, share their orientation with their neighbors - selective breeding and clone to save time, cut cost, and avoid duplicate efforts. It can pave the way for similar applications.
- Based on such ideal model, shoot for rapid growth rate, high productivity, cost-efficiency, and adaptive resource control

Snowflaking during the DW design phase is **Top down design**, like nature, generally growing like snowflake. Start from center core then grow a star then further radiating out to form snowflake. Depends on business nature and degree of complexity, this approach may continue go to next level and layer – **imbedded star** suggesting such architecture. Here are the stages of snowflake growth:

1. Major business subject area – form the core of business object
2. Consider overall subject areas – include multiple subject areas
3. Form a star
4. Business activity areas in each subject – from a central star radiating to form snowflake
5. Completing snowflake (include data marts, facts and dimensions)
6. Recursive progression – may go further down to lower levels or layers (multiple stars and snowflakes)
7. In a big data ecology, snowflake topology come into play when a central data store supported by multiple master nodes which in turn control multiple slave nodes. Snowflake topology clearly show how big data evolve in a distributed environment, how it expands, and how easy to mend.

This diagram demonstrates stages of snowflake growth.

Figure 4-4.2-0 Snowflaking

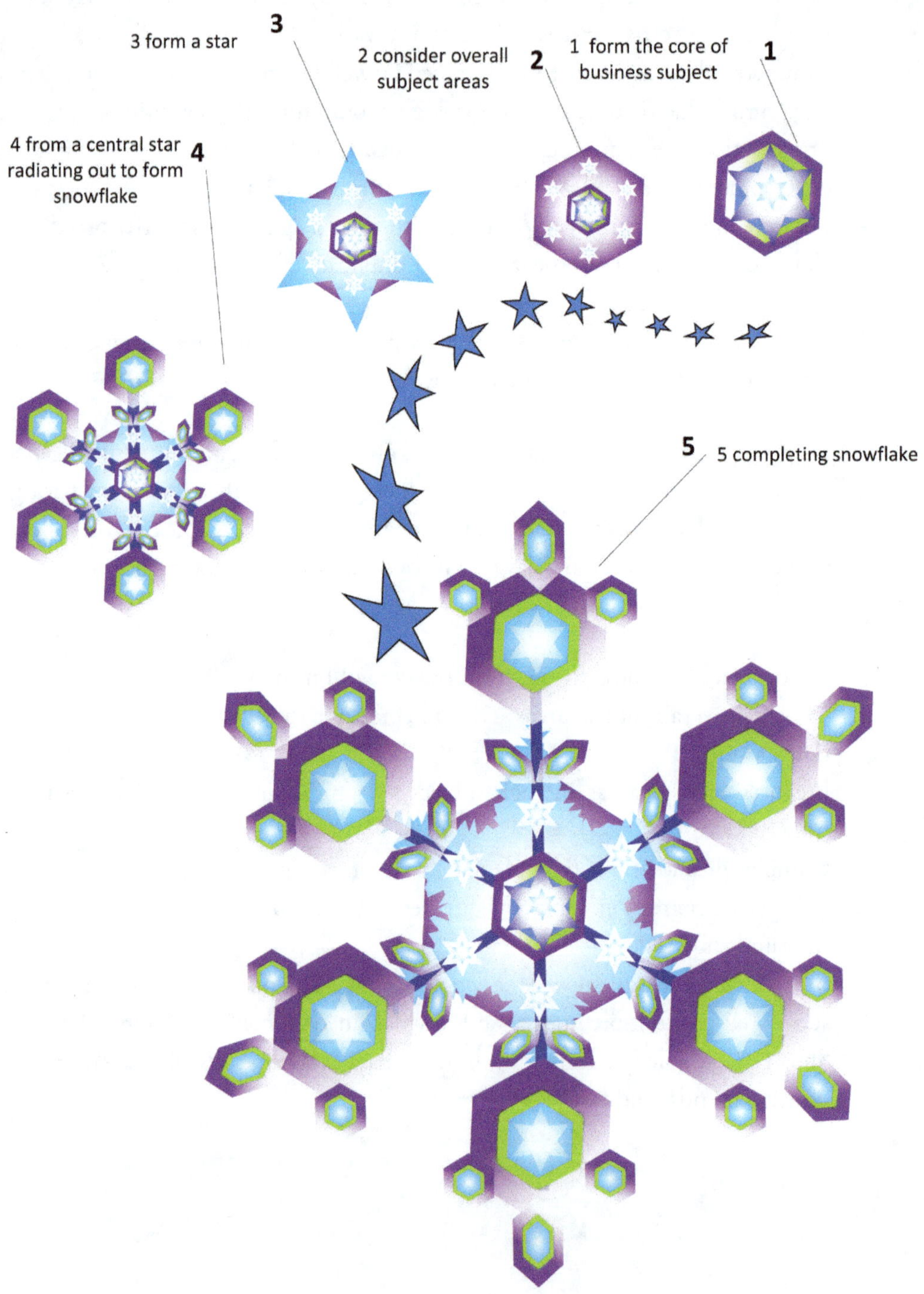

Another example of Snowflake approach which applied to a global Talent BI system was based on the same DW topology: Major business subject > several subject areas > Business Activities > fact > dimension.

Figure 4-4.2-1 SnowflakeTalent

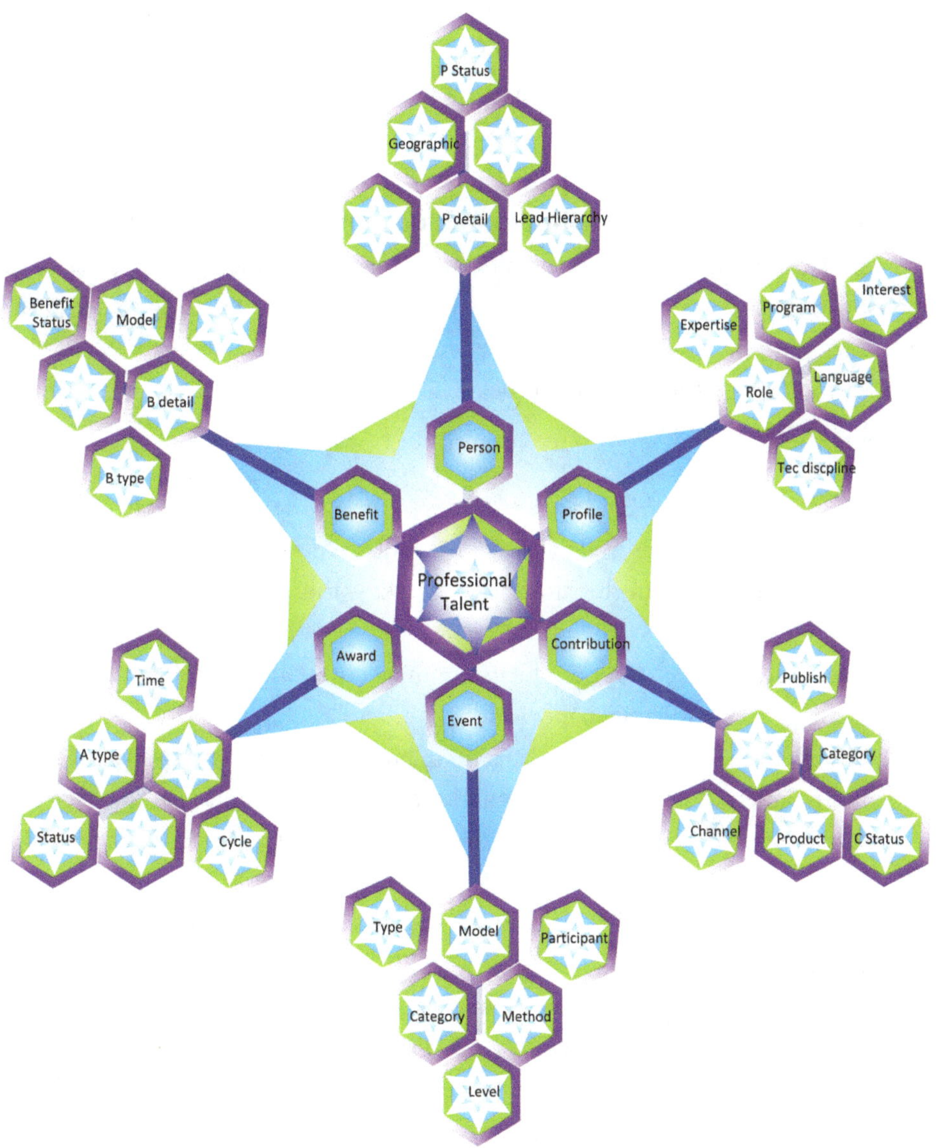

Professional Talent BI

Next step – compose/combine dimensions

Once it is done in decomposition in each subject areas, fact and dimensions, you may work on DW conceptual model integration – shared or conformed dimensions. Combine/integrate similar dimensions into fewer shared, conformed dimensions for overall enterprise wide DW. This is delicate approach because too many snowflakes suggest many joins that could slow down queries, but solo star schema cannot resolve complex data relationships and some monstrous dimensions with too many fields that also problematic and have to be split into a group of sub dimensions in order to be efficiently updated. Finding a right degree of star/snowflake combination in the middle ground is always an interesting challenge.

Verify the concept through well-prepared documentation

Document your findings and show them to the management, then get their responses and opinions, correct and enrich the all you got and so on – you are getting closer to the real picture. This is the way to close the gaps between what you think it is (or it would be) and what they think it is (or it supposed to be). The same does for what you think they want and what they think **they** want.

General guidelines of subject search

- Confronted by time and client constraints, we must put our already limited resources and time in the most needed tasks – those are most interesting subjects we are search for.
- Start digging wide, and then focus on important points and digging deeper. Start small then extend your scope later.
- Choose topics which are fundamental to business success and future developments and represent those urgent needs and great interest to users. Do the deep dive is a must, a superficial research like a dragonfly skimming surface of water – will not get you into the real business matter.
- Strive for simplicity of both concept and execution with an elegant and focused design.
- Develop searches simultaneously in other areas of interest.
- Read the minds of the power users and business decision makers through effective communications.

Topics

- The characteristic of this Ad BI solution is campaign-centric which drive everything these people do.
- Find a master dimension which position itself as a central hub - Campaign and placement

- Define major subject area: action (impression/click), conversion, Return on Investment (ROI), search, and cost.
- Monitor or measure campaign performance regarding banner, products or services
- Tracking user activities – impressions and clicks which trigger purchases or sales
- Gage Ad Campaign performance and campaign impact on conversion
- Measure website performance and efficiency
- Get holistic view of ROI conversion on digital media
- Optimize search keyword
- Evaluate ad costs, investment effeteness and distribution

To build online Ad BI solution, the followings are needed:

- Data capture and collection tools
- ETL to extract, transform and load data into DW host staging area
- Customize business requirement – marketer's reference data loading and process
- Define DW schema such as star/snowflake or hybrid (mix of dimensional and normalized) model
- Well defined dimension hierarchy
- Layout aggregation or summary management design and implementation
- Create cubes to include comprehensive view of marketing data
- Present data to executive management in the best, dynamic, high-level view – design BI dashboard

Major Development Steps

Analyzing sources - Mapping

Analyze source systems, and pay attention to their objects. You may find that some of them can be used for prototyping your DW tables. Also, the report systems from the operational sources may be of a great value for starting your OLAP design. When you analyze sources, evaluate them carefully, because most sources are origins and birthplaces of the DW. Some obvious or inherent flaws in the new born DW most likely originated from here. This could happen when you did not study/evaluate source system carefully and just took whatever is available.

Online Ad example

Please refer to example OnlineAd in Chapter Two 2.3.3

- *Ad action data*: Come from online advertising host sites, which host Ad brand banner, pages about products and services, conduct transactions and track user's activities through planted ad tags and action tags.
- *Conversion data:* From user actions against ad campaign and convert to meaningful action such as sales, registration or signups

- *Cost data*: pay by impression (view) or by click
- *Customer related data*: visited ads by sites, and state
- *Ad Search data*: Come from Google, Yahoo, MSN and other publishing sites where customers search for products and services were captured.

Fact table layout

First, we need look for the primary measures of fact tables. They may be sales, costs, profits, or customer activities such as number of clicks on the web.

In onlineAd example:

To provide an integrated view for marketer, there are several fact tables needed:

- Ad Action
- Conversion
- ROI
- Costs
- Search

A diagram shows how to split transaction table into fact and dimension tables. Please refer to Chapter Two Mapping 2.5.2 Transaction and Transformation and figure 2-2.5-1 SplitFactDimension

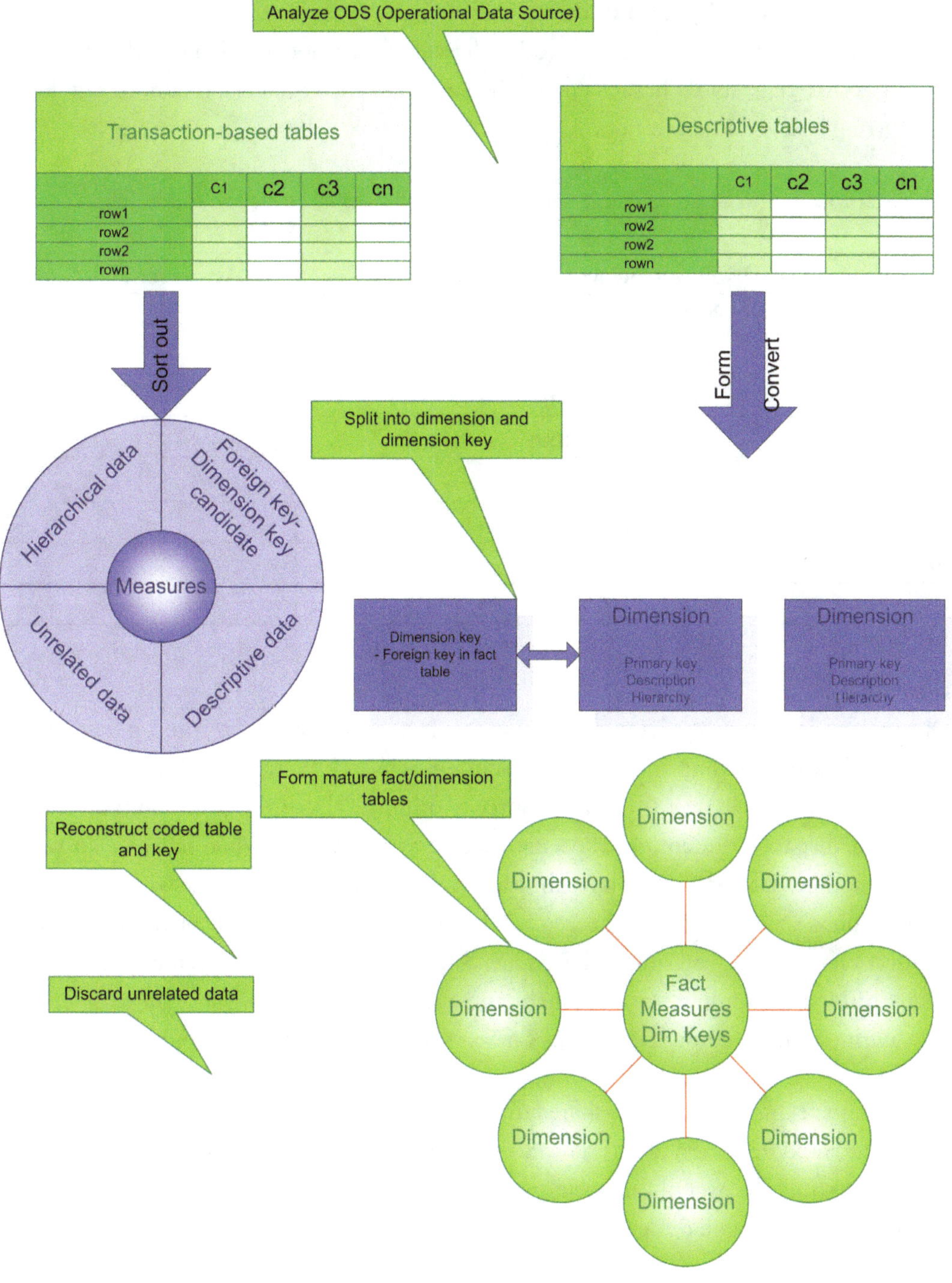
Analyze ODS (Operational Data Source)
Transaction-based tables
c1 c2 c3 cn
row1
row2
row2
rown
Descriptive tables
c1 c2 c3 cn
row1
row2
row2
rown
Sort out
Form
Convert
Hierarchical data
Foreign key-Dimension key candidate
Measures
Unrelated data
Descriptive data
Split into dimension and dimension key
Dimension key - Foreign key in fact table
Dimension
Primary key
Description
Hierarchy
Dimension
Primary key
Description
Hierarchy
Form mature fact/dimension tables
Reconstruct coded table and key
Discard unrelated data
Dimension
Fact
Measures
Dim Keys

Skeletonize fact tables and cubes

Reduce size of fact table by creating code reference dimension - code table that take care of descriptive, flag, status in fact table. The code reference dimension contains code key (1,0), (true, false) and description.

One example would be status table serve as code table containing the following:

Status	**Description**	**GroupId**	**IsCurrent** (as filter)
0	NA		
1	Descriptive name1		
2	Descriptive name2		
3	Descriptive name3		

FlagName	**Descripton**	
0	No	
1	Yes	

Dimensions

Dimensions provide categorized descriptions for fact tabled, on which you can further drill down and extended your analyses. As discussed before, DW with obvious and inherent flaws might be carried over from their source of origin - ODS. One common type of flaws lies in the disparate dimensions. Because each department or division has its own way of looking at data, same data may have multiple names or formats associate with it across the organization. Once these have been loaded into data warehouse, all of the troublesome duplications will give you quite a headache. Similarly, you will have tremendous troubles and confusion in summary management and OLAP, since you will end up with a sparse cube with too many empty cells. That can get you into some serious trouble!

How to resolve this problem? Use shared dimensions as a tightening gate. Shared dimensions enable the standardization of business metrics among different departments and divisions. When you study the overall dimension at layout, use shared dimension whenever possible. In another word, merge dimensions and make them shareable across the enterprise for all areas concerned.

For a simplified example, consider geography location dimension which should work at global level instead of domestic level, also consider how postal code is used. Five-digit US zip code which only work for US but not fit to other regions across world. The postal code in particular, should be set for global (data type, format) level if there is the case that business organizations abroad are involved. The same goes for other dimensions such as account, product dimension. Those should be set not only for specific departments but also for overall enterprise. It is also a good idea to leave some breathing room for both specific user group and overall enterprise – each may have their own code and naming conventions which can be linked/bridged together through references.

A typical dimension includes the following types of fields

Column Type	Description	Usage	Type
Dimension key	Surrogate key	Primary key	Sequential number
Business key	Meaningful key name	May be update/ duplicate	
Dimension Name	Descriptive generic name	Global level	
Customized Name	Alias name	For specific user group	
Source Name	ODS name	Map to source/ origin	
Attribute	categories, hierarchies		
Attribute	link	Foreign key link to other dims	
Last updated	date created/ updated	DW load/update	Date

Additional fields for slowly changed dimension (SCD) type 2 (historic usage)

Column Type	Description	Usage	Type
Begin date	Effect date	For type 2 historic	Date
End date	Expiry date	For type 2 historic	Date
Is current	Mark as current	For type 2 historic filter	Flag
Is active	Mark as active	For turning off/filtering	Flag
Version	Version number	Track change history	Sequential

In example OnlineAd
To get perspective of analysis in cube form, there are several dimensions may be used:

- Ad creative
- Ad action
- Campaign/placement
- Conversion type
- Search keyword
- Date
- Other marketer's reference

Uniqueness

We strive for uniqueness; however, very often, the same item goes under a variety of different names in databases. For example, same car maker may have multiple different names and spellings, such as "Ford Motor Company", "ford co.", ford, Ford Motor, FORD (those names may come from different ODS). In worst case one model or product item even has more than a dozen different names. And when such thing happen, these nonstandard values present huge problems in analysis reports such as generating swollen or sparse cubes with duplicated presentations. In order to prevent such problem, every object in dimension must be **uniquely defined**.

Company	Car Sold	Sales
Ford Motor Company	100	2,000,000
ford co.	12	260,000
Ford Motor		
FORD	5	150,000

It should be summarized like following:

Company	Car Sold	Sales
Ford Motor Company	117	2,410,000

Properly designed ETL or mappings can resolve the problems mentioned above.

- Dimensions describe the fact tables. In order to reflect the historic data scopes, timestamps should be added into the dimensions.
- Handle the slowly changing dimensions
- Versioning of dimension is necessary in case of tracking the dimension change history.
- If possible, build primary key in dimension with logical or business sense . Build alias name lists (perhaps in separate table), and link to the primary name so that both primary name and alias name able to serve the needs of enterprise and local departments.

Dimension hierarchy (OnlineAd example)

Campaign hierarchy

- Advertiser
- Mediaplan
- Publish site
- Placement

Date hierarchy

- Year
- Quarter
- Month
- Week
- Day

Search keyword hierarchy

- Publisher
- Category
- Keyword group
- Keyword
- site

Dimension hub

There is a dimension which has dominate roles among the group of dimensions - master dimension. For example dimension ***campaign*** here can associate to multiple dimension-type tables such as *advertiser, publisher, placement, cost, search keyword* and so on thus form a hub or cluster. Such model structure reflects the nature of online ad – Campaign centric.

Overall data model is a form of star/snowflake; several stars that consist of five fact tables with shared dimensions form a cube – a snowflake; several cubes (snowflakes) form a Online AD BI solution – a complex snowflake - stellar dendrites.

Summary management and OLAP

Summary management and cube should be built based on user requirements. Include a refreshing mechanism, and defined refresh cycle and latency, an intelligent query engine and finally - the reports delivery methods.

Following diagram show Online Ad data Flow and BI solution
Please refer to Figure 2-2.2-3 DwAdArch

Please refer to Figure 2-2.4-12 DwAdFactDimension

4.2.2 Iterative development

Now the general who wins a battle makes many calculations in his temple even before the battle is fought. The general who loses a battle makes but few calculations beforehand. Thus do many calculations lead to victory, and few calculations to defeat: how much more no calculation at all! It is by attention to this point that I can foresee who is likely to win or lose.

—Sun Zi

4.2.2.1 Two distinctive styles

It has been widely discussed about two distinctive styles for building a DW - "Waterfall" and Interactive approaches.

Classical "Waterfall" style is characterized by that development cascades down from top to bottom where system will be handed over to users. It includes the following clearly defined stages:

- requirements gathering
- analysis
- design
- programming
- testing
- implementation
- delivery

Iterative

Another style - the iterative (or the "**heuristic**") approach, under this, the prototyping of the warehouse is quickly constructed, direction of development going in the cycle or loop. It is frequently changed or adjusted. This looks like "direction-less" at the beginning (reflection of real nature of this kind project) with multiple probing directions, and then gradually becomes more focused on the essential points. There are many interactive communications between developers and endusers as a means to steer us in the right direction.

4.2.2.2 Iterative Development in the DW Environment

And so appraise them and know the plans for gain and loss. Prick them and know the pattern of their movement, action and inaction. Form them and know the ground of survival and vulnerable Force him to reveal himself, so as to find out vulnerable (vital) spots. . Probe (using small force) them and know the strength and weakness.

—Sunzi

Grasp initiative

Data warehouse project poses many unknowns for both developers and endusers. Contrary to traditional OLTP development, the picture of the OLAP is not so clear at the beginning so that developer need acquire as much hands-on experiences and knowledge of business as possible as means to picture what the would-be OLAP, and use it to approach endusers and start dialogs in interactive manner. In such environment, only cooperation and collaboration between the user community and development team can enable a rapid exploration of the projects.

> *Toss out a brick to attract jade*
> *—Chinese proverb*

- A way to elicit other's idea about the topic.

The initial iteration is essential work as means to explore what DW can possible do and demonstrates it to endusers thus excites a variety of responses. Whereas some shy away from it, find it cold, unresponsive and perhaps even forbidding, others are fascinated by its revealing power, and, once fascinated, are liable to become obsessed with management decision support. This initiative must illustrate the promise of DW, thus to trigger the responses from endusers for new ideas that may lead to success.

Feedback and redesign

Feedback from end-users forms the basis for the redesign of the next iteration, and so on in the development loop cycle. Step by step, this iteration will be continued and perfected.

Spearhead unit and reconnaissance

What is the first step in a military campaign? It is reconnaissance. Have a small group to act as a reconnaissance unit, which conduct touch trigger and probe the responses as a means for pinpointing the right direction before launching any major attacks, otherwise the coming campaign will be too costly and may unfortunately miss the target.

Data probe areas

- **Source:** locations, access methods, models, data extraction modes.
- **Data:** where do we get data and how do we get it? What is the scope of data? Which set of data is most interesting to us?
- **Mapping:** target-source mapping, reporting-base data mapping
- **ETL:** methods, approaches and procedures
- **Staging area:** may consider using centralized staging database or small scattered staging areas hooking to their source

- **Summary management**: hierarchical levels, aggregation and grouping
- **OLAP:** Start looking for key indicators of the enterprise, summary cubes, reports and report samples that reflect key indicators; those should be quickly constructed. Have those studied and evaluated by end-users.
- The core of these aspects is your prototyping report presentations such as Business Requirement (BRD), Functional Requirement (FRD), business process model, data model which include Logical data model and physical data model, dimensional model with hierarchies on which all aggregation will be done, quick ETL and simple staging area, primitive fact/dimension and cube which can be shown to endusers to get their feedback.

Search and discover (S&D)

Probing the unknown depth must have been an awesome experience for these adventuring explorers – DW architects/analyst. As another old saying goes: "*Throw a rock to probe the deception path*"

The designer must be in a discovery mode, like a treasure hunter wading streams searching for jade boulder or gold nugget. He or she will fan out as the search advanced, frequently refocusing on the key points and concentrating efforts on major directions. Strive for success and success always belongs to those who leave few places unexplored and unexploited.

Figure 4-4.2-4 DwInteractiveExplore

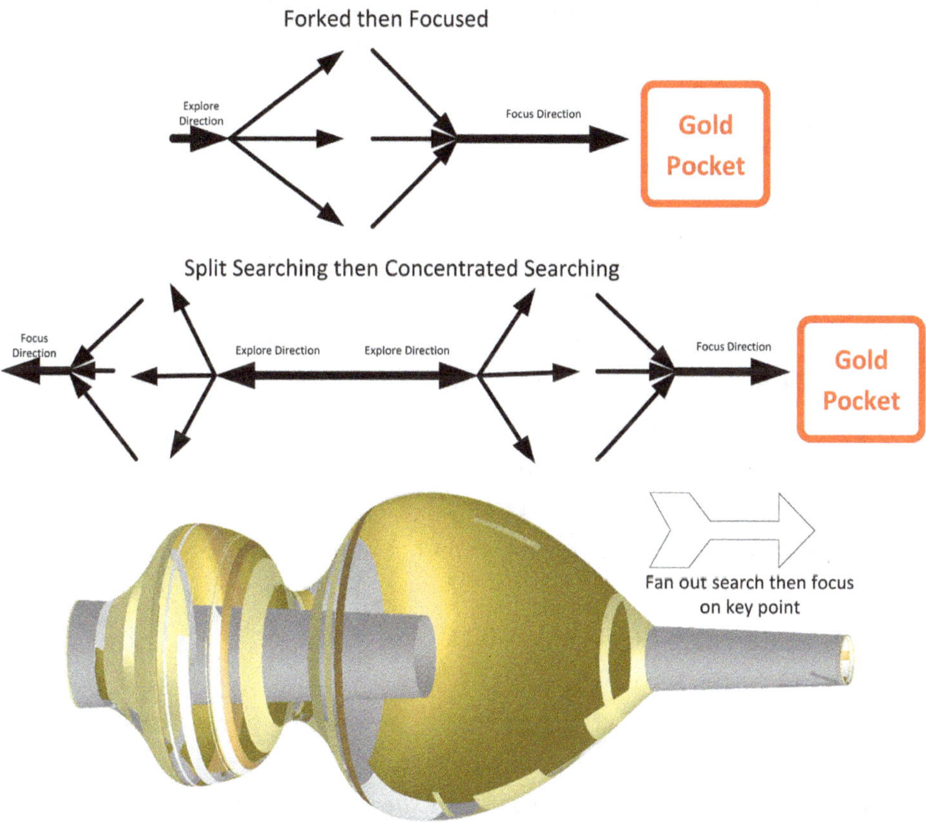

> *Thus it is that in war the victorious strategist only seeks battle after the victory has been won, whereas he who is destined to defeat first fights and afterwards looks for victory.*
>
> *—Sun Zi*

Prototyping will help you knowing what to expect.

Use the following spearhead prototyping tactics:

- In a small, fast iterative manner
- Respond quickly to feedback
- Mock up report
- Reduce work load. Simplify processes and design by focusing on something critical.

- Build an experimental DW serving as a backend and the stepping stone to your final product. It may resemble the source, the would-be DW target, or something in between. This is where you remodel everything in the backend based on results from front-end prototyping, cubes, and reports. You really want to know in advance, what happens in the front (cubes, reports), And how to remodel backend data architecture in order to get your desired results.
- Use prototyping to generate analysis results or reports that expose the major functions and problems/issues in order to help to speed up development. For example, a quickly populated OLAP cube series, like a show window that expose any major function and underlying data schema issues or problems.
- Skip the details and move forward quickly before moving into finer design, you can always add details at a later time.
- Overall simplicity and directness of approach is essential. This is accompanied by a proficient of execution on everything.
- If prototyping is not appealing to end-users, the whole thing needs to start over again. This is complete normal during the prototyping period. Don't afraid of failure at the beginning, the methods employed in prototyping are not totally wasted, and will be fashioned into another form down the road.

4.2.2.4 What happens when there is lack of prototyping?

It may result in a costly defeat.

- Lack of much-needed early exploration. The major problems/issues perhaps remain hidden or undiscovered, the project already gone in the wrong direction for a very long time. And by the time you learn the disappointing truth, it is too late for redesign the whole thing. Lack of user active involvement has been a major concern because there is no prototyping for user review that may give a chance to invoke their reactions and feedback, especially for those entitled "power users".
- Fail to reveal the critical, potential problems.
- Never actually going through the whole process flows, even in a simple experimental manner. The critical problems have not exposed, some important solutions are barely based on wishful assumptions.

Chart description: Because management and user group's feedback is so important, the feedback loop between end-users and the DW developers is one of the most important factors for success. The following figure clearly shows:

- Iterative vs. Traditional
- Iterative Development in Data Warehouse BSDLC

Figure 4-4.2-5 DwIterativeDevFlow

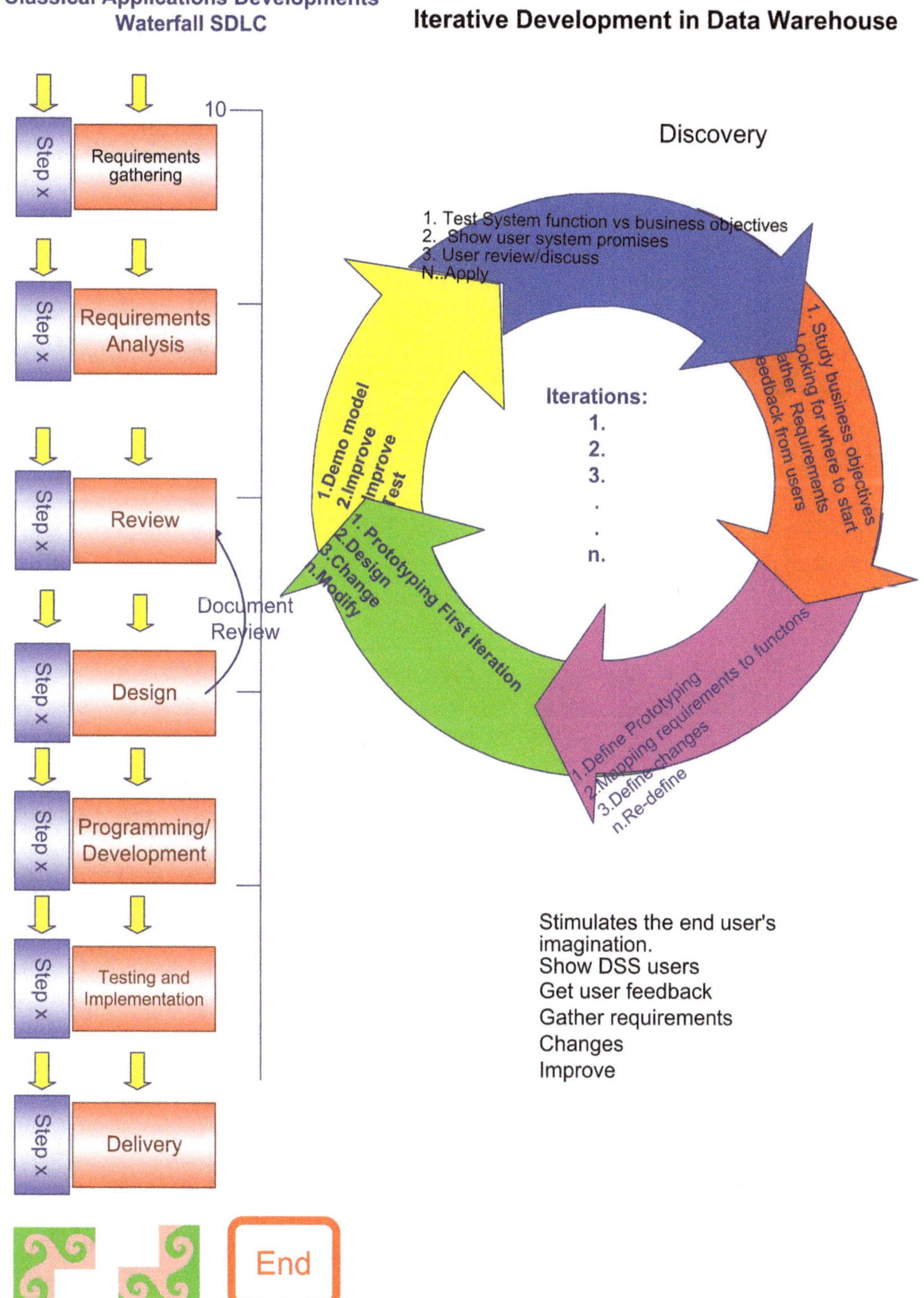

4.2.3 Stages in ecological succession

> *When you engage in actual fighting, if victory is long in coming, then men's weapons will grow dull and their ardor will be damped. If you lay siege to a town, you will exhaust your strength.*
>
> *Again, if the campaign is protracted, the resources of the State will not be equal to the strain.*
>
> *Now, when your weapons are dulled, your ardor damped, your strength exhausted and your treasure spent, other chieftains will spring up to take advantage of your extremity. Then no man, however wise, will be able to avert the consequences that must ensue.*
>
> *Thus, though we have heard of stupid haste in war, cleverness has never been seen associated with long delays.*
>
> *There is no instance of a country having benefited from prolonged warfare.*
>
> *—Sunzi*

> As W. H. Inmon has pointed out, "*In a dependent data mart architecture there is a central corporate data warehouse that feeds the dependent data marts. This architecture is sometimes called the "hub and spoke" architecture, where the data marts are the spokes and the data warehouse is the hub. The hub and spoke architecture has much to commend itself*"

One of the greatest virtues of DW is that it is an integrated solution for an organization. But how to strive that goal is actively debated. It is great debate that led to different paths of integration.

Relationship between data warehouse and data mart

Based on "hub and spoke" concept, data marts should be derived from DW as a part of DW products, this is an integrated solution for entire enterprise. Another word, building DW first, and then generate data mart naturally. **It drives overall design/development from conceptual modle towards logical model!**

However, sometimes there are limitations on money, resources and technic maturity; So we have to start on a small scale. It is not a bad idea to build the data mart first, gain the necessary experiences, and then start another one when conditions are mature. But bear in mind that what we want to achieve is an integrated solution for the enterprise through data warehousing technology. A data mart, ideally, no matter how small it is, must be built based on the overall logical design of whole DW frame. In other words, wisest approach is to build small, physical data mart based on the grand logical DW model frame (design).

Centralized design for inclusive development

In either approach, the **design** must be centralized. Any data mart development must be under the guidance of the overall DW logical architecture - that include, implementing standardization and building shared objects for the future design of the overall DW. It also includes the all domains, entity-relationship, attributes (data fields) defined across whole organization/enterprise. When you build your dimensions, for example, consider customer dimension in a particular departmental level (there may be only include limited fields in one department), but for the enterprise level (all divisions, departments), the field set that fit in a department may not enough to fit rest of all departments, somehow a bigger data field list (attributes) have to be created in order to satisfy all in a global level, the same goes for hierarchies and naming conventions in dimension design. **It should be inclusive.** Do the same for all other dimensions. Bring the frame to a more generic, global level even if only for one or two departments currently – you will save big and avoid much more headaches down the road. Moreover, any useful data mart design/development experiences/techniques need to be integrated into the on-going overall DW design. Without a global-scoped logical DW model in mind, is definitely a route heading to a pitfall of its own digging.

Data mart silos - The disadvantages - reintroducing drawbacks of old OLTP

What happens when you build several data marts first without considering the overall DW architecture at global level?

- Redundant data starts to appear. Here we go again, are we backing to old disparate systems?
- Lack of integration – Sounds familiar. Are we talking about operational data sources?
- Many redundancies exist in DW, duplicate dimensions, repeated extractions, transformations, and loadings that make ETL exhausted. Everybody is trying to grab data from everybody else; launching so many ETL processes just like shooting swarm of arrows from all the directions and fall all over the places.
- Numerous interfaces between the data mart and its sources. - Is this a centralized repository or it is just another hollow-bodied jellyfish? A creature like that would most likely create nightmare.
- This kind of datamart most likely will be short-lived due to its design flaws in the integration. It is however a throwback into the conventional disparate data systems

Issue here is really a test of organization management and the developer's prowess for how well they can grasp the data warehouse/data mart project as a whole.

In war, then, let your great object be victory, not lengthy campaigns.
—Sunzi

Dilemma between centralized DW and distribute data marts

Most developers are caught up in a variety of conflicted situations and expectations when building DW:

- not enough budget
- uncertain support and commitments from the top management
- short delivery cycle
- short of resource, lack of DW experience and maturity
- rigid deadline
- frequently changed user requirements

All those factors make the distributed datamart solution appealing to them - It happens very often and for a good reason. But if the developers just doing one piece of work single-mindedly without considering overall DW model and framework, the outcome likely will be the inconsistent, short-lived datamarts. To avoid this, the key to success is "**Integrate using conformed dimension**" as **Ralph Kimball** suggested.

And for DW especially for enterprise-wide DW (EDW), there are several critical requirements must be met:

- Integrated solution
- Historic tracking
- Holistic or global view
- High level summary views
- Enterprise-wide solution – cross departmental level
- Stable, consistent reporting and presentation
- Accurate and detail drill-down
- This demand totally integrated EDW
- Single source of truth

All those requirements push the design towards a centralized DW solution.

Stages of ecological succession
The plants first established in a barren land as pioneer plants which pave the way for later, more complex, taller trees. When these pioneer plants die, they begin to form foundation in which other, more complex plants begin to grow and eventually replaced by them, and so forth, forming climax community.

These challenges sometimes force the developers make tough choices necessary to keep project going. One way is surviving on the middle ground – Hybrid approach and centralized staging database.

Start with a simple plan, you may get quick result that you can enjoy immediately and elaborate later upon when time and money allow. Start small and grow piece by piece. Usually start to gain footholds such as data marts, soon followed by BI reporting, ETL processes, and Staging areas –all ODS data whose small section of tables are easily rooted. As soon as one application becomes established, it creates a kind of welcome mat for others by extract data and staging are providing landing base. Life attracts life. Before too long, a miniature of DW colony is thriving on the site bare expanse, easing the way for the growth of such larger, solid DW applications composed as the EDW.

The first datamart for an enterprise should not be an enclosed silo. It should serve as a stepping stone for the next development instead, and leading to complete integration of enterprise wide DW. A **miniature of DW on a grand scale/frame** (could be based on large scale logical model design) may be the one that you should strive for.

The nature has shown us evidence of ecological succession, like pioneer plants, datamart usually are established first and gain the ground for further grow; it has short life span and eventually will be taken over by more powerful, complex, stable, integrated data warehouse. Eventually it goes to highest stage of ecological succession – ***Climax Community*** – Enterprise wide data warehouse (EDW).

A centralized staging database - stepping stone to successful EDW

- All these centralized staging area as stepping stone for EDW
- Centralized data repository
- Data receiving area holding initial data objects mostly resemble ODS
- Well-defined relational or hybrid model, and are able to transform to dimensional model
- Interface to both ODS and DW
- Overall metadata repository and management
- Comprehensive ETL driven by metadata

Centralized Staging (db) lays a solid ground on which DW will be built with appropriate choice of architecture. It holding a data receiving area (tables and/or files here mostly resemble source tables) for incoming data from ODS. The core data here is relational in an integrate scope of EDW.

Well, once we have our centralized staging database and DDD ETL built, we are still standing at cross road to decide which direction to go in further developments.

Ideally "Hub and Spoke" approach will be pursued if conditions favor us and resources are sufficient. Typical dimensional model with many OLAP and analytical tools certainly has tremendous firepower in processing and presenting reports but its structure is hardly to change, too often, any structure changes on fact and/or dimensions will demand reprocess whole cube, this is costly and time consuming.

Fortunately, **there's more than one way to do it**
For more than a decade, there has been growing interest in exploring and discussing about DW modeling architectures, new approaches in building DW. The typical data models created by various master architects addressed hybrid approach in improving developments of DW… thus definitely enrich our DW modeling technologies and methods.

A chart bellows shows EDW approach: from the master staging source to 3rd normal form model, or multi-dimensional model

Please refer to Figure 2-2.2-3 MasterStaging

4.2.4 Dynamic data driven ETL (DDDETL or 3DETL)

First at all, can you remember how many times schema changes brought your system down? How cumbersome when you work on source codes which include tiresome table names and long list of column names which always give you headache whenever you modify such programs. Besides, when database server migration occurs, with tight timelines, you have to to revise those hard-coded server names, database names which were buried inside program source codes. To deal with such headache, 3DETL is a solutioin! Either stoods by itself or combined with other utilities, 3DETL can be a rewarding part of your DW development. To make your life easier in continuous DW developments, building 3DETL is a way to go.

Build flow – create ideas or concepts - thought process

- ➢ Analyze processes required and study the cases – the more you know about them, the more simpler and clear they become.
- ➢ Abstraction: filter out physical referents, distance yourself from particular objects, draw essential process logics, and the business rules
- • Simplification: mapping multiple different piece of objects/processes generic into a single piece of abstract object/process logic based on similarities in these objects/processes
- ➢ Build metadata to capture physical references such as ODS (sources), server, database, schemas and tables. Get physical referents – from general to specific
- ➢ Build generic procedures with pre-built process logics, able to read feeding metadata, replace objects with physical referents and dynamically create and execute sql based on physical referents.

3DETL normally include the following:

Centralized metadata repository

Build or capture schema information about ODS source, staging, DW target Server, database, table, column select list, filters, conversion rule, data type conversion, mapping table. Build a database to handle such kind of metadata and let's call it "ETLMaster" for its broad scope and functionalities.

Metadata-gathering module

Most of metadata as system category objects stored in the database servers, what ETLMaster need to do is just fetch it through local and remote database connections. It certainly will do the following:

- Metadata-fetch (server, database, tables, columns, keys)
- Probe sources and targets
- Source schema fetch
- Clone tables in staging area based on the metadata (ddl) fetched
- Fetch max key value for tracking incremental loading
- Based on reading of metadata, generate extraction codes dynamically

Mapping

Create mapping tables to tie soured tables to staging or target table – table/column mapping; create views which glue all related metadata objects together to form useful ETL task lists

Dynamic data driven procedures (DDDP) – a code generator

This is where you put your general ideas and generic process logics in. Generic means take object name from given parameters or get object names from metadata. In the way of encapsulation, from the 3DDETL source codes, there are no hard-coded server name, database name, schema name or even no table name should be imbedded in source codes, instead, only using variables to hold these read-in names.

Procedure may have self metadata-fetch ability based on given locations. Design stereotypes Function library and templates (for low level tasks) that can be called and used repeatedly by main procedures. Dynamic creation and execution of sql is major feature of 3DETL.

Generic update mechanism

Pre-defined and configurable process flow
Determine Delta Trace max key datetime, ID
Change control flag
Generic routine to fetch max key or max datetime (or max last loading date)
Incremental update
Off-set measure for primary key (primary key value offset between source and target table)

Logging mechanism

Tracking loading processes, job, status, table completed, number of row loaded, deleted, rejected, log errors, issue warnings.

Standalone database may be needed, which independent from ODS or DW.

Benefits:

- o Flexible
- o Extensible
- o Configurable
- o Customizable
- o Easy maintenance
- o Proactive in developments and testing
- o Fast and short cycle in migration and deployments

A hig level solution of this ETL platform with concepts and key components is shown in Fig Figure 4-4.2-8 EtlMasterComponent

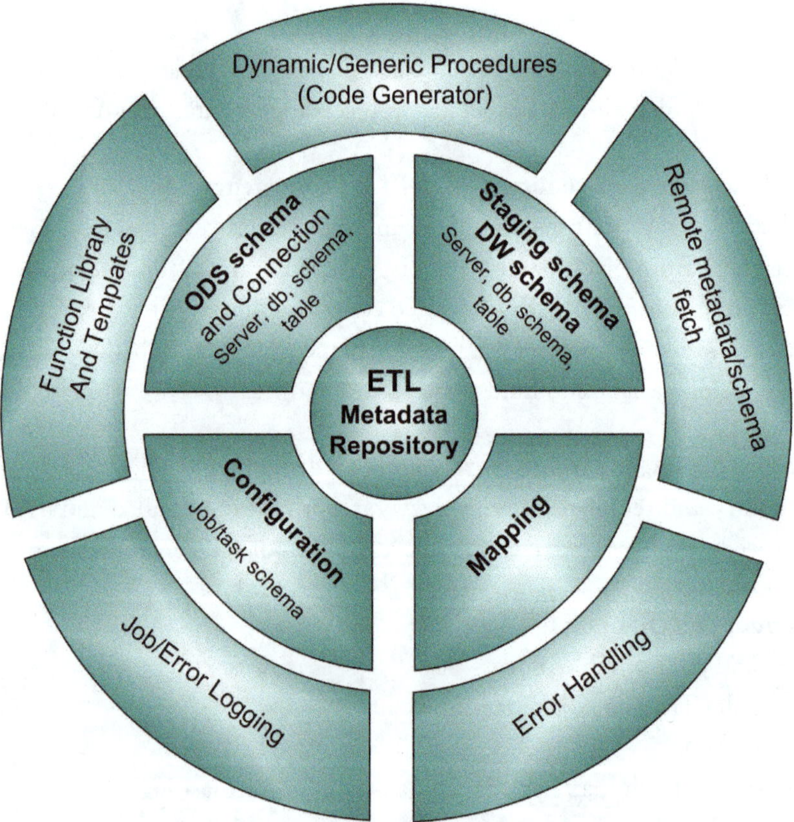

For a more detailed architecture and solution see detail implementation in Chapter Five.

4.2.5 Design your own 3DETL Tools

ETLMaster schema

Please refer to figure 2-2.3-5 MasterStaging

Figure 4-4.2-10 MetaDataDrivenETL

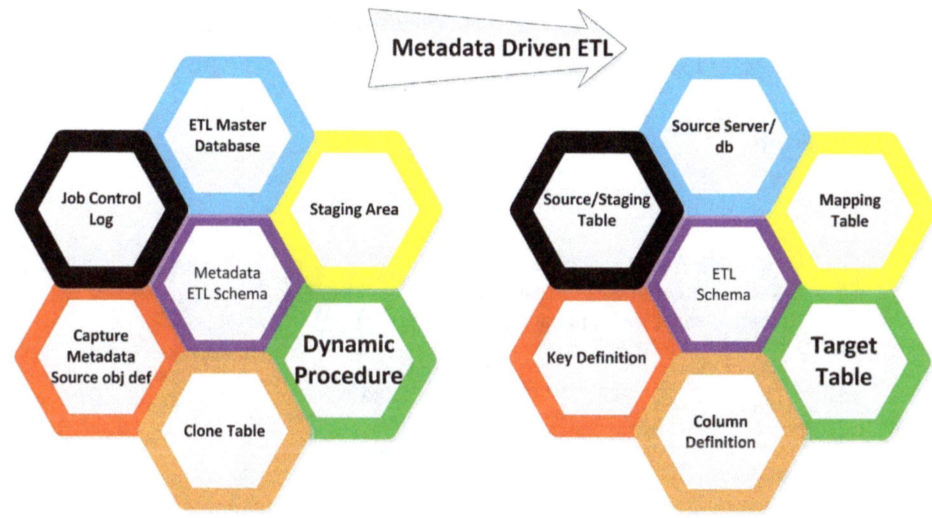

4.3 Design Quality

4.3.1 Quality is vital to data warehouse

Data in a warehouse needs to be accurate and of high quality since many management decisions will be made using its support. Poor data generate inconsistent results that makes end-users feel not trustworthy and will appeal to very limited audiences. It helps to be cognizant of quality assurance (QA) when developing of DW.

The DW environment includes many components across multiple disparate database systems, especially external sources, which as something that beyond your control; therefore QA is a big job. Be prepared to recognize this unwritten but very real variety of experience in QA. Our experience and lessons learned are presented in the following.

4.3.2 Quality assurance

Quality assurance is always a focal point in DW development and production services so a series dedicated systems and policies are needed just for that purpose.

Let's start with metadata management. From architecture point of view, good modeling and metadata management have enormous impacts on QA. It is the very first place we start. Metadata is the road map in the maze of data world. A good metadata model and documentation make the systems appear transparent to everyone involved, thus helping us understand and maintain data as well as overall quality control. Standardization also helps QA deal with only a few instead of fighting massive inconsistent and vague objects.

The testing environment should mimic environment in real production services. If condition permit (sufficient money and equipment's), deploy multiple DW instances with same capacity. One of them will be used as QA environment and in case it also can serve as dual hosts for sustainable services.

Back tracking errors

Figure 4-4.3-11 DwQaTraceBack

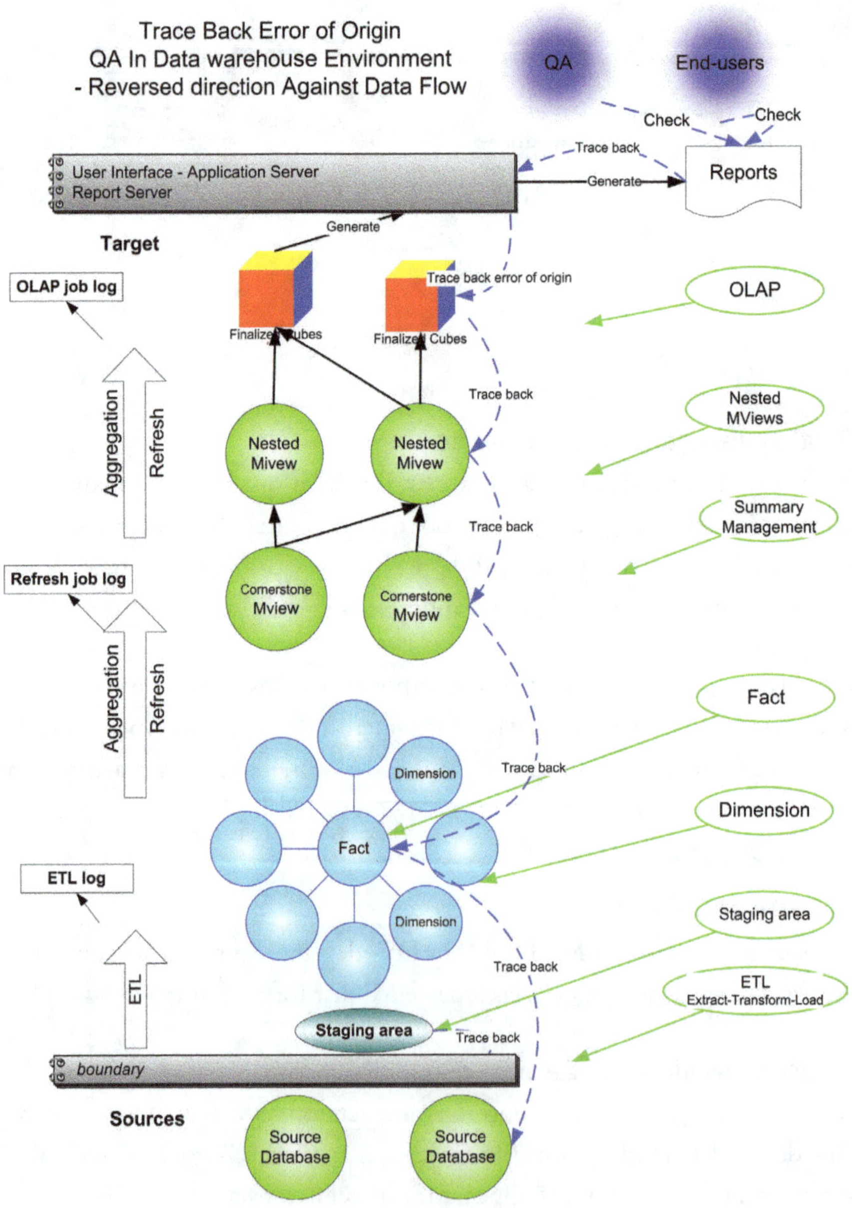

4.3.3 Error detection in a broad boundary zone

Data errors may occur at any place in the system. It could be very difficult issue for the untrained eye to detect. When we trace data flows in the data warehouse, the major areas where errors usually occur should be examined closely:

- ETL (Extract-Transform-Load)
- Staging area
- File systems
- Fact tables
- Dimension tables
- Summary data, materialized views/cubes, views and queries
- Measures, calculations, KPI

Look over system and its surrounding to define the boundary

It is not uncommon to find that some errors may actually come from ODS (operational data source). Even ODS already have been put into production service for some times, hidden errors may not be uncovered until after data loading into the data warehouse, where data goes through a series of transformations and aggregations then form the summarized cubes. Data has a better chance to be exposed in DW since aggregation help easily to spot and reveal the nature of data, including its errors; with DW report, some of them (data errors) exist in ODS would otherwise have remained hidden were exposed. Something odd may be easily exposed when browsed in cube view. It happens sometimes as a surprising discovery.

4.3.4 QA will use

- Fast error detection mechanisms
- Data audits
- Batch job statistics and verification
- User point of view (Does everything make business sense?)
- Sampling and comparison with sources
- Fast error tracking and root cause analysis
- Use the tracking/audit logging mechanism to enable developer and QA to pinpoint where the error occurred.
- Use view (or remote view) to provide a comparison between the source and target, in order to identify missing data.

4.3.5 Detect errors quickly

It is very important to detect errors and resolve them in timely manner. In the DW ecology the data flows, which resemble a river system, the earlier, faster an error is detected, the better for problem solving. Thus, stop bad data at upperstream as soon as possible, otherwise it becomes more difficult to fix when it reaches downstream. Imagine that if errors were not detected during data loading and have lurked for several months. By the time the truth unfolds (error found), it is already too late. "*The rice had been cooked and then been consumed*". Data has been loaded into fact/dimension tables, keys have been generated, summary cubes have been refreshed, and reports already released, and have been rolled out online. – More troubles lie ahead! Our major concern here is: How to build timely error detection/warning lines as earlier as possible in the data upstream.

4.3.6 Tracing errors of origin – back tracking

Error tracing normally starts from downstream to upstream, that is going in an exactly opposite direction of the data flow travel in DW - by way of backtracking.

The presence of errors in the reports, quickly lead to finding of errors in measures, calculations and related cubes, from which also can be traced to their sources - the underlying tables. The origins of errors can also be traced back to the ETL processes, which should be examined closely, as it being the most frequently source of errors. In some cases, the errors are probably even derived from ODS.

Consider the characteristics of your DW environment and follow the chains of events. The best defense for QA is to extend your detection lines as far as possible in upstream of data flows; detect error as early as possible. Building your *Distant Early Warning line* is far better than scrambling to fight destructive odd in your own arrays.

Peeling back the onion layers – digging deeper for root causes

There appear to be numbers of the multiple layers have to be peeled in order to trace problem of origin in a multi-tiered system.

Let's take a look at the following chains of events on error detection and tracing. It is very interesting to see that it appears to go backwards against actual processing flows.

In order to trace source of origin in a multi-tiered system, multiple layers have to be peeled off one by one, layer by layer. Here is how search flow goes:

Error is first detected from the final OLAP analysis or reports by end-users.

1. Check the User interface

Application server side

- Formatting or data type
- Calling error
- Calling parameter
- Result set transport

Backend server side

Summary management/OLAP

- Measures, calculations, KPI definitions
- Query logic – stored procedures
- Virtual cubes – query definitions
- Immediate underline summary materialized views/cubes
- Refresh process
- The event log of refresh process batch
- Materialized view table Stale, error,
- Refresh fail?
- Nested mviews
- Refreshing path
- Materialized view/cube definitions and logic
- Missing data
- Joins, inner join, union or outer join
- Cornerstone or primary cubes

Core data

- Fact tables (key violation)
- Dimensions (uniqueness, duplication)
- ETL Loading
    - o ETL batch process log may give a clue
    - o Loading
    - o Transformation
    - o Extraction
    - o Incremental loading window
    - o Loading test, using the so-called "sandwich" type test (pre-image –loading – post image) which takes a snapshot as a pre-loading image, during loading, then during post-loading, and compares those images.

Source system

- Source snapshot or image within loading window
- Possible error from ODS (source systems)

A figure shows how to peel back the onion to uncover the hidden problem of origin in a multiple layered DW system.

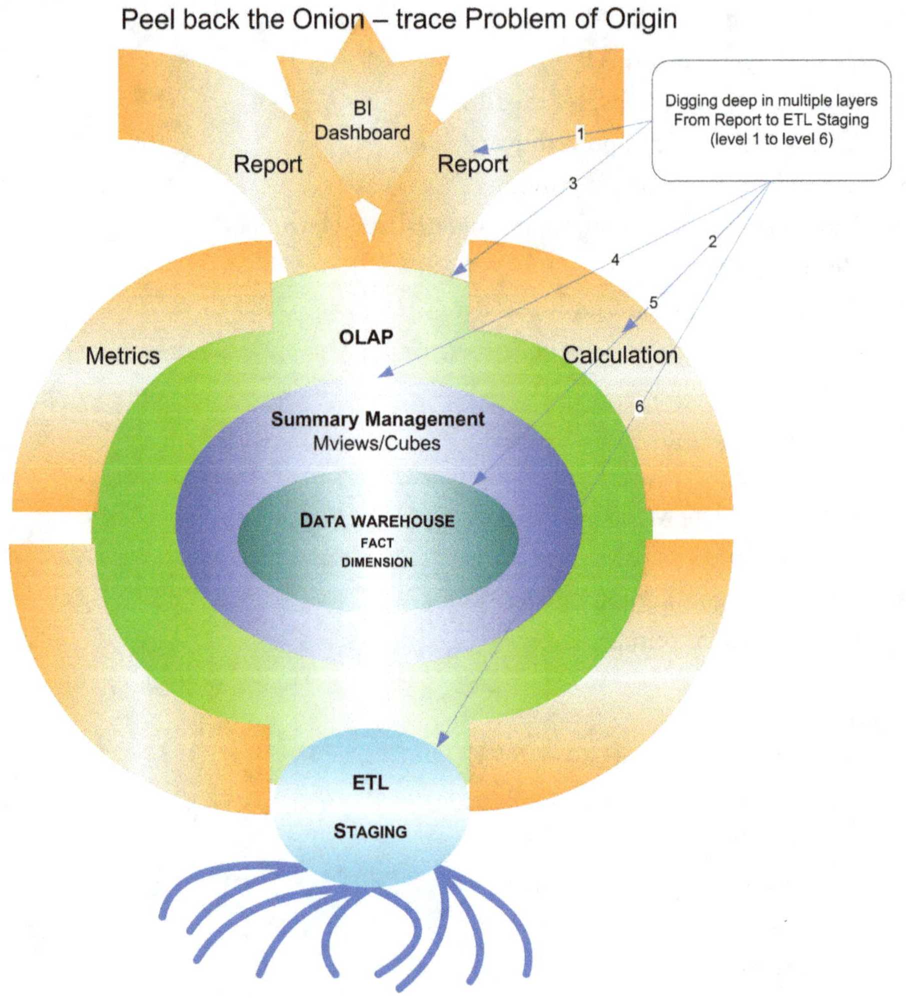

Figure 4-4.3-12 Onion

4.3.7 Dealing with dirty data

If a database has been contaminated by dirty data, what are the overall impacts on DW? It really depends on where it resides and how it's been used. If it lies at a major junction or joining path in the queries and has been frequently used (for example a major dimension), the impacts will be great. As its propagation effect through connected systems, it may contaminate all the reports/queries which referencing it. The propagation effects can be subtle and hard to be detected. It is difficult to pinpoint which is the culprit. All participants (joining tables) fall under suspicion.

How could data get so dirty?

The data may come from external sources, such as Web applications. Some web applications unfortunately lack data validation and permit non-restricted free entries. In consequence, massive dirty data flood into DW and causes great problems. Generated summary cubes look a bit odd; the numbers from reports look suspicious. People start wondering how come the numbers like that? Where are those numbers come from? As mater of fact, non-standard and inconsistent naming in dimensions is one of the major causes of sparse cubes which make hard to converge in aggregation.

Uniqueness

Very often, the same item goes under a variety of different names in databases. For example, same car maker may have multiple different names and spellings, such as "Ford Motor Company", "ford co.", ford, Ford Motor, FORD (those names may come from different ODS). In worst case one model or product item even has more than a dozen different names. And when such happen, these nonstandard values present problems in analysis reports such as generating swollen or sparse cubes with duplicated presentations. In order to prevent such problem, every object in dimension must be **uniquely defined**.

Company	Car Sold	Sales
Ford Motor Company	100	2,000,000
ford co.	12	260,000
Ford Motor		
FORD	5	150,000

It should be summarized like following:

Company	Car Sold	Sales
Ford Motor Company	117	2,410,000

Such problems can be traced back to DW initial design – missing sound logical modeling! All data domains, entity-relationship, attribute definitions that enforce data integrity and all data names, descriptions should be uniquely identified.

Properly designed ETL or mappings can solve problems mentioned above. That is: mapping all those blurring names into one and only one stardard name: like the table shown on the bottom.

- Dimensions describe the fact tables; to reflect the historic data scopes, timestamps should be added into the dimensions.
- Handle the slowly changing dimensions
- Versioning of dimension is necessary in case of tracking the dimension changes history.
- Build primary key in dimension with logical or business sense whenever possible. Build alias names perhaps in separate table, and link to the primary name

"Garbage in, garbage out" seems an inescapable reality, the messy, dirty data exists in DW, meanwhile there are urgent demands to extract and output data for business operations like email campaigns, one-to-one marketing and other promotions. Data must be cleaned in order to be useful. Team must therefore take actions to fix quality issues. This includes cleansing data, building necessary data dictionaries, function and procedure libraries to deal with frequent data parsing or conversion processes, dedupe fact and dimension tables and reconstructing unique keys. All these efforts are for just one single purpose: to get uniform, clean data, and ultimately regain business users' trust.

Fix defects in the data model

Problem: Integrity and consistency problems caused by inferior data modeling (logical modeling and physical modeling)

Solution: Refine the data model to enforce data integrity, maintain metadata, such as domans, entity-relationship, attributes and share those metadata and use it guide overall design/developments; reduce data redundancy and keep one piece of data in one place. Doing so can avoid a lot of pain down the road.

Fix and eliminate duplicates in user/customer information/dimension

Problem: Duplicate data in user/customer dimension

Solution: Use user names and email names to uniquely identify each user - eliminate duplication.

Fix city and state/province names

Problem: City and state/province names get messy duo to unrestricted free entries. Sometimes, a dozen different values actually refer to a single city or state/province name, for example, "wa", "wash", "Washington", if plus spelling errors you may get more than what you can think of.

Solution: Use postal code/zip code and the standard state/city name list (obtained from the postal services) to fix the state/province and city name.

Fix dirty name

Problem: In the early internet online registration, some users named themselves as they wish. This has introduced a lot of offending or dirty names, most commonly as "prick", "hell", "#$@%&%" which could not be used in email or promotional campaigns. You just can't send email and call somebody "Dear @#!#$%", ... even if that was how they named themselves. Other funny name such as "spunky big fat mom", not a decent name either when you greeting your dear customers.

Solution:

- Scan the entire database using key words and get collection of all offending or dirty words from the user names. Sometimes, such process involve sampling millions of usernames in order to create a reference table as a forbidden name list or a forbidden name dictionary.
- Scan whole user names. If you find a match with forbidden name table, then mark or tag it.
- During a data pull for email and promotional campaign, if user name has been tagged or marked, use a substitute such as 'Dear customer' to avoid offending word even it was originated from user's own input.

Such efforts are worthwhile, because they are like recovering placer gold from river gravel paydirt. By this way, you can recover insightful from pile of mess.

The following are major defense lines (check points) in quality control:

1. ODS (operational data source)
   Data entry, although source systems are most likey beyond the DW teams' control, through cooperation with source system team, some quality issue can be addressed and eventually resolved. An example would be building various supporting tables (lookup tables, list boxes, standard value/measure, value range check and associated procedures) which help to stop bad data entering the system up front.
2. **ETL.** Build a function or procedure libraries for data cleansing or conversions necessary for data standardization.
3. **Fact** tables. Tighten database integrity constraints, especially relationships with dimension tables.
4. **Dimension.** Standardize the dimension tables. A typical example is to obtain standard zip code system from US Post Office and integrate it into your location dimensions.
5. **Fix data that's already loaded.** This may seem a little strange at first. According to the characteristics of DW after all we know that DW basically is **invariable**, but the wrong is wrong in any case, it has to be resolved, this, of course, must be removed, the sooner, the better. Use surrogate key here may beneficial to locate bad section of data quickly then strip it out.
   How can we detect and strip problematic data from data objects and minimize less positive features without distorting rest of DW objects? Careful planning and thoughtful process are needed, including cleaning the data step by step, striping problematic data and refreshing DW systems. Correspondent processes are also needed to reconstruct keys, cascade delete or update and so on so forth. Some of them are nonreversible processes, therefore must be fully tested and should assure success before they are put into actions. More importantly, have a backup strategy.

6. **Parse useful data from the pile of mess.** Sometimes, useful data is mixed with or buried in unwanted mess. To get it, you should build functions, subroutines to parse, extract, strip and filter the useful data from bundled data mess.
7. **Use logging mechanism.** Track and trap errors in a manageable manner.

Example: See <Chapter Five Data warehouse Development>, the Section <ETL>

4.4 Resources, Teams and Skills

> *The clever combatant looks to the effect of combined energy, and does not require too much from individuals. Hence his ability to pick out the right men and utilize combined energy.*
>
> *—Sun Zi*

4.4.1 Knowledge – the intellectual assets of organizations

Knowledge flows in a circular fashion

Intellectual assets, namely the know-how and talent of dedicated people in the organizations are precious treasures, but these not like a gold reserve, which retains its initial value fairly stable no matter what. Instead, they are goin to move like running water in a reservoir or in a river system, constantly changing over time, going up and down, swinging between flood and drought.

Knowledge, skills, talents, experiences and solutions are primarily kept in human's brains. When people leave for other companies they take their knowledge with them. What is left for the organization? It depends. May be plenty or may be nothing. Check the areas such as the system documentation, metadata management/ maintenance system to find out.

A tribe has no written language – a place lack of documentation

It is not uncommon to find a place where there is lack of system documentations. This hurts organization in many ways. The lacking of documentation is costing you more than you think

- No documentation about system is just like studying the culture of a tribe that has no written language. Their stories are passed by way of legend, which makes them vulnerable to losing their history. In thousands year history, the human have tried so hard to get their messages out, they recorded their events and stories in every possible way, in every possible manner; even the primitive cavemen must scratch rock walls, draw the pictures or symbols and record something important for them and for their descendants. - Are we smarter than a caveman? If yes, please do documentation and do it well.

- Little is known of their IT history; little has been recorded about how their systems work. Where to look for solutions when there is a problem? How to make necessary changes to cope with business requirements?
- Newcomers and outside helpers such as consultants found themselves in a world that is totally strange to them and have to undergo a slow walk in dark tunnel.
- This costs time and money.
- Even a failed project (may cost them dearly) just gone without trace, it can't even offer any useful lessons for the organization and IT management due to lack of a systems documentation addressing key problems and issues.

> *Water shapes its course according to the nature of the ground over which it flows; the soldier works out his victory in relation to the foe whom he is facing.*
>
> *Therefore, just as water retains no constant shape, so in warfare there are no constant conditions.*
>
> *The five elements (water, fire, wood, metal, earth) are not always equally predominant; the four seasons make way for each other in turn. There are short days and long; the moon has its periods of waning and waxing.*
>
> —*Sun zi*

If we take words literally, then manpower just as water which retains no constant shape, tend not stay in one place for very long.

Knowledge retention in a dynamically changing environment

An old saying goes "*A fort is as rigid as iron made while soldiers flowing in and out as running water*".

Many organizations have a high turnover rate, people come and go, which causes instability in teams. There is fear that their intellectual assets will eventually be depleted. However, in fact, intellectual assets can be considered as renewable assets if you establish good team building methods, well-documented knowledge repositories and cross-training programs. Even if some people leave, the documentation process will trap their knowledge as catching gold from paydirt, which can then be shared by other members.

Documentation: Reflection of IT development history

The data warehouse, as a superstructure of IS, is a central hub of many systems built in an iterative development cycle. Good documentation is definitely treasured. Without it, the whole system would be unimaginable difficult to understand. But in reality, it is often difficult to do good documentation. In a dynamic, fast-paced development environment, you may not have enough time to do it. However, a very-focused documentation essential to overall system functionalities is a must. One picture for all is at least worth to try! A blueprint for overall system design is something you must have.

There might be system records establishing a history for the database development of particularly projects. Such information follows the body of the system architecture in clearly defined documents, and aids the member in establishing or confirming evolution trends. The lack of concrete documentation means that this is no insightful information can be employed to establish merit or value. The intellectual properties, if they belong to organization, should be well documented in order be shared and used for sake of business success.

Gold trapping pan - Metadata repository/Integrated documentation

In the old days, a gold miner used a trapping pan or riffle tray to trap placer gold. Similarly, metadata repository in development cycles will retain essential technical and information details. Many systems are documented through data modeling or version control tools. But well-defined documentation systems should also be able to incorporate various tools with traditional or informative written documents and links to tie them together. System documentation is just like getting gold from paydirt.

At the same time, documentation must demonstrate the future course of development by consolidating widespread technology streams, and to nurture the genesis of an organizations cultural character, which resulted from a remarkable period of absorptive creativity at the inception of the IT knowledge.

Total completion of projects should include both building the system and associated system documentation, which can server as a useful guide helping shorten learning paths and avoid confusions and mistakes. Under a good education environment, fresh force is very likely to get nursed and grow mature quickly. The overall documentation should serve as blueprint for all parties involved. For documentation detail, see Chapter Two 2.8 Metadata.

Promoting continuous learning

People learn a great deal from their works and their co-workers, a new approach or smart trick once proved success, most likely will be spread through an organization like a fever.

Good technical documentation used to find a common language to streamline communications and it will offer opportunities for influencing professional development and disciplines of participants. For newcomers, documentation can be a useful guide in this respect. The chance to deepen one's knowledge and to engage in cooperative effort through well-prepared documents is great.

Share ideas and knowledge. Develop team skills, and emphasize cross-training. Appreciate team's diversity; that is the way to go! In an environment where everybody guards his waterhole jealously in a drought Sahara Desert will not going to accept an "outsider", and therefore will not be a creative, healthy, culture-rich environment.

Complete System Documentation - Intellectual Knowledge Pool

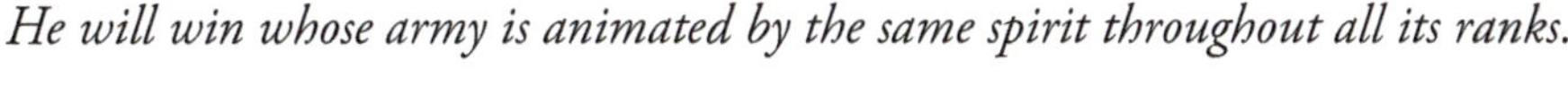

> *He will win whose army is animated by the same spirit throughout all its ranks.*
>
> *—Sunzi*

4.5 Security

> *The general who is skilled in defense hides in the most secret recesses of the earth (under the ninth earth); he who is skilled in attack flashes forth from the topmost heights of heaven (above the ninth heaven). Thus on the one hand we have ability to protect ourselves; on the other, a victory that is complete.*
>
> *—Sun Zi*

> *You can be sure of succeeding in your attacks if you only attack places which are undefended. You can ensure the safety of your defense if only hold positions that your enemy does not know what to attack.*
>
> *—Sun Zi*

Much has been written about the security. In this chapter, we will focus on DW architecture that is essential for addressing major security issues.

4.5.1 Threat

"Flies are eager to attack the eggs which have inviting cracks!" - Proverb

Security threats may come from any of possible sources, from internal or outside, from man-made to natural disasters. If there are cracks in a system, intruders will explore them and cause as much damage as possible. On the other hand, more often, human stupidity also cause operational errors and collateral damage through unbounded privilege escalation.

Keep in mind that today, many hackers – like tunnel rats roam free on internet. Given the chance, they can do the considerable damages through the holes and the cracks in system especially when there is a kind of "sewage network" (once let in, can go anywhere), not even the deepest hidden system can offer total protection from such attack. Today's world is more and more towards a cyber world, today's one of the biggest security threat is **cyber attack!**

The next world war likely to be "**cyber warfare**".

4.5.2 Establishing proactive strategies

Develop specific strategies and action plans against threats. Action items should include creating isolation and control for protected systems; patching security holes; building deep, multiple fortification lines in the system and providing protections for business such as Confidentiality, Integrity, Availability and Reliability.

4.5.3 Security counter measure and strategies

Security policies and keywords

Data, network, internet, backup and restore, account, password, and group policy
IP security, granularity privilege control, fine-grained access control, role based security, separation of production and development system, SQL injection prevention, view access.

Technologies to Secure Network Connectivity

Firewalls provide protection by blocking unwanted traffic

4.5.4 Architecture design has impact on security considerations

Firewalls can be breached, once this occurs, the hacker may have unlimited access to database core data unless there are additional layers serving as additional of fortification lines. Fortunately, more security measures can be deployed on such layered architectures.

Build defense line based on a multi-layers and multi-sectors (MLMS) strategy

A multi-layered solution, as already discussed, offers great security. Each layer can provide isolation to its core, thus make it hard to be penetrated. Each section or segment can provide isolation to other sections or segments, thus making it hard to spoil and disturb rest of sections or the whole system when things go wrong. A system is architected in such, like a double-shelled ship with many sealed chambers – one hole in a ship can't sink it.

See details in the Chapter Four <**Data warehouse Development Highlights**>, the Section 4.1 <Data Warehouse Platform>.

Granularity privilege

A multilayered architecture and strategy helps neutralize security threat. Based on a MLMS structure, apply the typical granularity privilege, with fine- grained access control in the databases according to the organization's functionalities, planning user groups. Assign appropriate privileges according their responsibilities. Using role-based privilege will help in privilege management. Avoid so-called "all or nothing" privilege assignments, which invites security troubles. The system's vulnerabilities are such that a bad apple can spoil the whole bunch. It is especially vulnerable to SQL Injection that encroaches on unexpectedly, through application in which dynamic SQL is used without fine-grained access control.

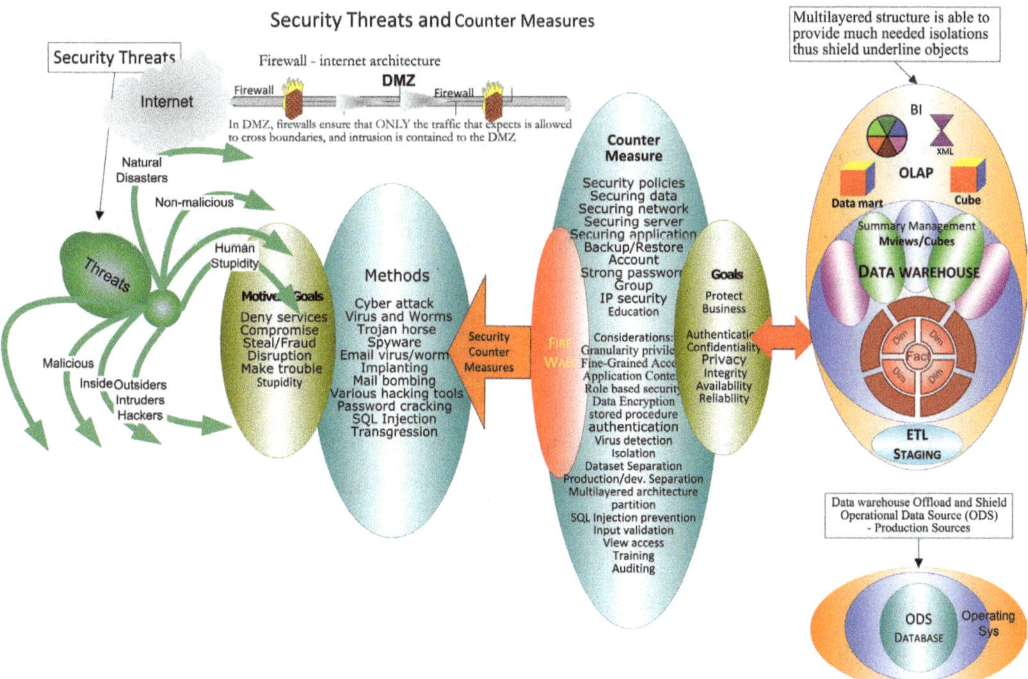

Filgure 4-4.5-15DwSecurityCounterMeasure

CHAPTER FIVE

DATA WAREHOUSE DEVELOPMENT CODE SAMPLES

- ❑ **5.1** Conceptual Modeling
- ❑ **5.2 Data warehouse Modeling**
- ❑ **5.3** ETL
- ❑ **5.4** Summarizing Data
- ❑ **5.5** OLAP
- ❑ **5.6** Report Preparation
- ❑ **5.7** Reporting Frame and its Supporting Library

Note: In this Chapter, all SQL codes, if not specified default will be Oracle PL/SQL or Oracle SQL.

5.1 Conceptual Modeling

The purpose of the conceptual/logical data model is to show how the data is organized and how the data is related in order to satisfy business requirements in a platform/database (environment) independent manner.

Enterprise data warehouse (EDW) model should be based on at least a virtual relational conceptual model which may physically become a staging database and form a core data repository. On top of it, multi-dimensional model for olap, cube, solutions will be defined. DW design involved overall DW environment and many steps. This is well illustrated in Figure DwArchiPhase

Please refer to Chapter Two Figure 2-2.8-24 DwArchiPhase

5.1.1 Schema and conceptual model

Following Figure shows a star schma for a popular example - sales analysis includes a fact entity which tie to a series of dimension such as time, customers, products, channels and promotions.

Star Schema Fact, Dimensions
Please refer to Chapter Two Figure 2-2.4-13 DwStarCube

For online advertising example, please see Chapter Two Figure 2-2.2-3 DwAdArch

Star Schemas

Star schema consists of fact table as center piece which tie to the dimension tables through the relationships (keys).

Snowflake Schemas

Star schema may be further extended into Snowflake schema which mormalize the dimensions in order to eliminate the redundancy, such as splitting a big dimension table into a group of related tables. Sometimes a group of tables may hang on the major dimension table forming a dimension cluster; very often, forming the hierachical levels reflecting the nature of the real business world. The hierachical levels in the dimensions often to be used as the aggregation paths during the drill-down analysis.

Please refer to Chapter Two Figure 2-2.4-9 Snowflakes

5.1.2 Data Warehousing Basic Tables

Fact Table

As a core data element in data warehouse, fact table should be designed as a clean, lean and simple object, besite the measures, most of columns would be key or numerical type, easy to be added in and easy for computings.

The key issue in design should be focused on cleaning the transaction/event table which is original state of fact table, removing the descriptive columns and put them into dimension tables or elsewhere then form a lean and simple fact table.

Dimension Tables

Dimension tables hold the keys referenced by fact tables. The most attributes in fact table have the relationships with the dimension tables. Use shared and standardized dimension design, which in turn will have important impacts on data warehouse and OLAP.

5.1.3 Project database size

There are many ways to project future database size, in general, we need first calculate a baseline from which database will grow. A baseline is an initial size of database including all objects. Next thing need to do is to multiply the sizes of baseline objects with some magic nember in order to predict future database size.

Hare is an example to populate the current database size as a baseline (In SQL Server T-SQL). The first thing first, create a table to hold baseline table size

```
CREATE TABLE [dbo].[sz1](
    [name] [sysname],
    [rows] [int],
    [reserved] [varchar](20),
    [data] [varchar](20),
    [index_size] [varchar](20),
    [unused] [varchar](20)
) ON [PRIMARY]
```

Next create a procedure using dynamic SQL (T-SQL in SQL Server 2005).
The procedure use system database (metadata) to get all database object names and use dynamic SQL to the works.

```
CREATE PROCEDURE [dbo].[usp_PopTableSize]
AS
DECLARE @QString NVARCHAR(4000)
DECLARE @schema_id int;
DECLARE @schemaname sysname;
DECLARE @object_id int;
DECLARE @tablename sysname;
DECLARE tables_cursor CURSOR
  FOR

  SELECT s.schema_id, s.name, t.object_id,t.name
  FROM sys.objects AS t
  JOIN sys.schemas AS s ON s.schema_id = t.schema_id
  WHERE t.type = 'U';
```

```
SET NOCOUNT ON
if exists (select * from dbo.sysobjects where id =
object_id(N'[dbo].[sz1]')
and OBJECTPROPERTY(id, N'IsUserTable') = 1)
TRUNCATE TABLE [dbo].[sz1]
OPEN tables_cursor;
FETCH NEXT FROM tables_cursor INTO @schema_id,@schemaname,
@object_id,@tablename;
WHILE (@@FETCH_STATUS <> -1)
BEGIN;
  SELECT @QString = 'insert into dbo.sz1 EXEC sp_spaceused '+'''['+
@schemaname +']'+ '.' +'['+ @tablename +']'''
print @qstring
  EXEC (@QString);
  FETCH NEXT FROM tables_cursor INTO @schema_id, @schemaname,
@object_id,@tablename;
END;
PRINT 'The size on all tables have been calculated.';
CLOSE tables_cursor;
DEALLOCATE tables_cursor;
SET NOCOUNT OFF
```

Then run the procedure above to populate data in table sz1
Next, use query calculate projected db size by multiple a magic number (factor) to each object in table sz1 such as rows or data size, index size. – I rather leave it to you.

5.2 Data warehouse Modeling

The purpose of the physical data model is to show how the data elements will be implemented and stored on the database as a means to meet the system process performance requirements such as process speed (partition for parallel), response times, and storages.

It also undergo the transformations from logical model to a more detailed, platform/ database dependent physical forms such as entity -> table, record -> row, attribute -> column, relationship -> foreign key, unique identifier -> primary key, etc.

The physical design of data warehouse normally includes the following areas:

- ❑ Fact Tables
- ❑ Dimensions

- ❑ Parallelism and Partitioning in Data Warehouses
- ❑ Indexes
- ❑ Integrity Constraints
- ❑ Materialized Views

5.2.1 Fact Tables

5.2.1.1 Define fact table

Frist of all, we need to define the measures as the business key performance indicators:
Mesures: QUANTITY _SOLD, AMOUNT _SOLD.
Dimension identifiers: Product code (PROD_ID), Customer Id (CUST_ID), TIME_ID, CHANNEL_ID, promotion id (PROMO_ID). Those dimension ids serve as forein keys link to dimension tables.
Granuality: sales per day, customer, channel, promotion, product.
Partition Granule quarter, Partition by range (quarter).

5.2.1.2 Create fact table

The common pattern of creation of fact table as the following (pseudo code, partition by quarter):

```
CREATE TABLE FACT TABLE NAME (For example: SALES_FACT)
( dimension A ID NAME     DATA TYPE ,
 dimension B ID NAME     DATA TYPE,

 dimension C ID NAME     DATA TYPE,
 dimension D ID NAME     DATA TYPE,
 ...
 dimension x ID NAME     DATA TYPE,
 timeid                  INTERGER, -- suggest using Julian date
 loading_batch_number    INTERGER, -- supporting column (loading
batch number)
 loading_DateTime        DATE,    --  supporting  column  (loading
datetime)
 measure A NAME     DATA TYPE,
 measure B NAME     DATA TYPE,
 ...
 measure X NAME     DATA TYPE
)
```

```
PARTITION BY RANGE (TIME_ID)
(PARTITION      SALES_FACT_Q1_1999      VALUES      LESS      THAN
(TO_DATE('1999-04-01', 'YYYY-MM-DD')),
 PARTITION      SALES_FACT_Q2_1999      VALUES      LESS      THAN
(TO_DATE('1999-07-01', 'YYYY-MM-DD')),
 PARTITION      SALES_FACT_Q3_1999      VALUES      LESS      THAN
(TO_DATE('1999-10-01', 'YYYY-MM-DD')),
 PARTITION      SALES_FACT_Q4_1999      VALUES      LESS      THAN
(TO_DATE('2000-01-01', 'YYYY-MM-DD')),
 PARTITION      SALES_FACT_Q1_2000      VALUES      LESS      THAN
(TO_DATE('2000-04-01', 'YYYY-MM-DD')),
 PARTITION      SALES_FACT_Q2_2000      VALUES      LESS      THAN
(TO_DATE('2000-07-01', 'YYYY-MM-DD')),
 PARTITION      SALES_FACT_Q3_2000      VALUES      LESS      THAN
(TO_DATE('2000-10-01', 'YYYY-MM-DD')),
 PARTITION      SALES_FACT_Q4_2000      VALUES      LESS      THAN
(TO_DATE('2001-01-01', 'YYYY-MM-DD'))
);
```

Online Advertising BI solution example

Please refer to Chapter Two Figure 2-2.4-12 DwAdFactDimension

5.2.2 Dimensions

5.2.2.1 Creating Dimensions

Create a dimension with primary key refrenced by fact tables, for example, create customer dimension and set customer key as its primary key which linked by the customer key in the fact tables. Relationship between dimension and fact is parent-child.

Add a dimension

The best practice is puting things as much as possible into design phase to avoid later change and patches in data model which is pain in the butt, but reality is not so ideal, patch in model is not uncommon. The following example shows how to add a dimension to a star schema:

Suppose we want to add a dimension called transaction type which describes the transation type in sales.

At first, create dimension table called transaction_type_dim with the following columns:

- o Transaction_type_id as primary key
- o Source_name tells data origination
- o Source_transaction_id: original transaction id in the source system which can be used as logical key.
- o End_date, start_date describe the transaction effect date
- o Status_code describe status such as valid, invalid, most resent or historic
- o Version_num describe the version in this dimension can be used to track historic changes.

```
CREATE TABLE transaction_types
(
TRANSACTION_TYPE_ID NUMBER NOT NULL,
TRANSACTION_TYPE_NAME VARCHAR2(255),
TRANSACTION_TYPE_CODE VARCHAR2(255),
TRANSACTION_TYPE_DESC VARCHAR2(255),
SOURCE_NAME VARCHAR2(100),
SOURCE_TRANSACTION_TYPE_ID NUMBER NOT NULL,
END_DATE DATE,
START_DATE DATE,
STATUS_CODE NUMBER,
VERSION_NUM NUMBER,
CREATE_DATE DATE,
UPDATE_DATE DATE,
CONSTRAINT transaction_types_pk primary key(transaction_type_id)
);
```

The following SQL statement alter fact table add the new dimension id column.

```
ALTER TABLE SALES_FACT ADD (TRANSACTION_TYPE_ID NUMBER);
```

Te following SQL statement alter fact table, add the database constraint which define the new dimension id column as foreign key tie to the new dimension table.

```
ALTER TABLE SALES_FACT ADD (
CONSTRAINT          SALES_FT_TRAN_TYPE_FK          FOREIGN          KEY
(TRANSACTION_TYPE_ID)
REFERENCES TRANSACTION_TYPES (TRANSACTION_TYPE_ID));
```

The following SQL statement creat bit-map index on the column we just added in fact table.

```
CREATE BITMAP INDEX SALES_FACT_TRAN_BIX ON SALES_FACT
(TRANSACTION_TYPE_ID) ;
```

Populate time dimension

The time dimension is one of the most common dimensions. Here is an example of creating a time dimension table using SQL Server T-SQL

First thing first, create a table and define the tim_id based on Julian date (convert calendar date julian date and vise versa).

```
if exists (select * from dbo.sysobjects where id =
object_id(N'[dbo].[dim_Time]') and OBJECTPROPERTY(id,
N'IsUserTable') = 1)
drop table [dbo].[dim_Time]
GO
CREATE TABLE [dbo].[dim_Time] (
    [time_id] [int] NOT NULL ,
    [the_date] [datetime] NOT NULL ,
    [the_day] [nvarchar] (20) NOT NULL ,
    [the_month] [nvarchar] (20) NOT NULL ,
    [the_year] [smallint] NOT NULL ,
    [day_of_month] [smallint] NOT NULL ,
    [week_of_year] [smallint] NOT NULL ,
    [month_of_year] [smallint] NOT NULL ,
    [quarter] [smallint] NOT NULL
) ON [PRIMARY]
GO
```

Here is an example of populating time dimension table in SQL Server using a stored procedure:

Note: use Julian day as primary key for time dimension table. The procedure populate time dimension based on given parameters: start date and end date.

```
CREATE PROCEDURE usp_PopTime @startDt datetime, @endDt datetime
```

```
as
declare
@vdate datetime, @cnt int
set @vdate = @StartDt
set @cnt = 1
while (@vdate <= @endDt)
begin
-- convet to Julian day
insert into dbo.Dim_Time
VALUES (convert(int,@vdate),@vdate, datename(dw,@vdate),
datename(month,@vdate), datepart(yyyy, @vdate),
datepart(dd,@vdate), datepart(week,@vdate), datepart(mm,@vdate),
datepart(q,@vdate))
set @vdate = @vdate +1
set @cnt = @cnt + 1
    if @cnt > 100000
    break
    else
    continue
end
GO
```

Finally, execute the procedure to populate time dimension table with 10 year span.

```
execute usp_PopTime @startDt = '1/1/2000' @endDt = '12/31/2010'
```

Note: Julian date
Many applications store dates in the Julian format, which is a 5 digit number, consisting of a 2 digit year and a 3 digit day-of-year number. It is more convinent in coverting calendar date to julian date and vise versa, because many system has built-in function, when you want to get time dimension key you don't have to lookup from the time dimension table.

5.2.2.2 Multiple Hierarchies

A dimension often has its hierarchical levels through the linkages with other related tables. For example customer dimension may link to a group of geographic-spatial related tables (such as region, country, state/province, county, postal code and associated latitude/logitute system) forming the hierachical levels, which serves as aggregation path during the analysises.

5.2.2.3 Hybrid structure

Dimension tables can become very complex, for example customer dimension may become fairly big and complex and it is not wise to use single table to hold all customer related information, a group of tables attached to a primary dimension table may be a necessary option and it mostly following the normalization rules and provide needed benefits and flexibilities. Some dimension tables may hook to a master dimension from which then tie to fact table – Snowflake architecture.

Please refer to Chapter Two Figure 2-2.4-10 SnowflakeDWtopo

5.2.3 Partition

Fact table holding the huge amount of data need to be patitioned in order to be processed or maintained.

Here's how it starts:

Dropping a Table Partition

First, disable constrain, drop partition, then enable constrain

```
ALTER TABLE sales_fact DISABLE CONSTRAINT sales_fact_con1;
ALTER TABLE sales_fact DROP PARTITTION sales_fact_q4_2000;
ALTER TABLE sales_fact ENABLE CONSTRAINT sales_fact_con1;
```

Remove data from partition

```
ALTER TABLE sales_fact DISABLE CONSTRAINT sales_fact_con11;
ALTER TABLE sales_fact TRUNCATE PARTITTION sales_fact_q4_2000;
ALTER TABLE sales_fact ENABLE CONSTRAINT sales_fact_con11;
```

Exchange Partitions

```
ALTER TABLE mytab EXCHANGE PARTITION p04 WITH my_table_04;
```

Adding a Partition:

Adding a Partition (sales_fact_q1_2003) to a Range-Partitioned Table (sales_fact)

```
ALTER TABLE sales_fact
ADD PARTITION sales_fact_q1_2003 VALUES LESS THAN ('01-APR-2003')
TABLESPACE tsx;
```

Moving Partitions

```
ALTER TABLE sales_fact MOVE PARTITION sales_fact_Q4_2000
TABLESPACE ts_2000 COMPRESS NOLOGGING;
```

5.2.3.6 Roll Summary

Rotating Data - Partition Based on 8-quarter Rolling Window

Figure 5-5.2-3 DwPartition_Quarter

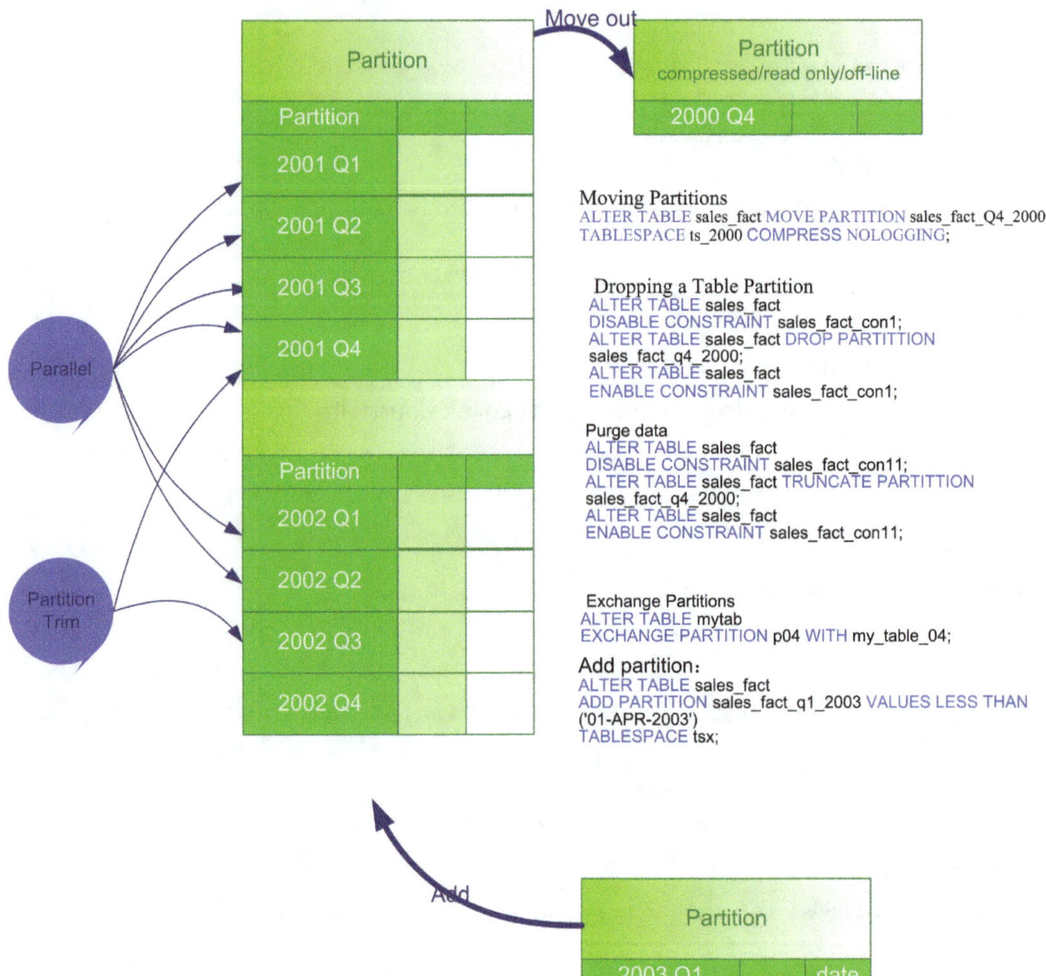

5.2.4 Indexes

Create bitmap index on the column transaction_type_id

```
CREATE BITMAP INDEX SALES_FACT_TRAN_BIX ON SALES_FACT
(TRANSACTION_TYPE_ID);
```

Use same way to create bitmap indexes for the followsing columns:
`CHANNEL _ID, CUST _ID, PROD _ID, and TIME _ID`

5.2.5 Materialized Views

A materialized view or indexed view is an important object in database that contains the result of a query, often used to create summary tables based on aggregations of a table and related dimensions or based on remote data replication.

Refresh materialized view

Refresh materialized views after the completion of the following data warehouse loading tasks:

- ➢ Data loading on fact and dimension tables
- ➢ Update indexes on data warehouse primary tables (fact and dimension) after loading.
- ➢ Completion of quality assurance and testing of loading sessions. Check loading session logs.

Nested Materialized Views

Based on the business requirements, choose the most frequently needed data sets; create materialized views which serve as base of OLAP. For example, the analysis based on monthly sales against channels are mosly required process, so build such materialized vivew and from which futher build a series of materialized views. Put these materialized views in the batch refresh jobs on which the expensive table joinings and computing can be completed during off-peak hours and set the solid foundation for OLAP analysises by providing fast response time. We consider those primary materialized views as cornerstone materialized views.

5.2.6.3.1 Create materialized views from fact/dimension tables

At first, create a materialized view directly from fact and dimension tables:
The new materialized view summarizes sales by (channels, calendar month and customer).

```
CREATE MATERIALIZED VIEW sum_sales_month_mv
BUILD DEFERRED
REFRESH FAST
ENABLE QUERY REWRITE
AS
SELECT     channel_id,     calendar_month_desc,     cust_id,
SUM(quantity_sold)     sum_quantity_sold,     SUM(amount_sold)
sum_amount_sold
FROM sales_fact s, times t
WHERE s.time_id = t.time_id
GROUP BY channel_id,calendar_month_desc,cust_id;
```

In order to implement fast refresh other materialized view which may depend on this materialized view, we need build materialized view log first.

```
CREATE MATERIALIZED VIEW LOG ON sum_sales_month_mv
WITH rowid
(channel_id,calendar_month_desc,cust_id,sum_quantity_sold,sum_a
mount_sold)
INCLUDING NEW VALUES;
```

These laid the ground work for bulding other new materialized views.

5.2.6.3.2 Create nested materialized view (summarize on channels, month)

A new materialized view will be created based on the materialized view (sum_sales_channel_month_mv).
This materialized view summarizes sales by channels, calendar month).

```
CREATE MATERIALIZED VIEW sum_sales_channel_month_mv
BUILD DEFERRED
REFRESH FAST
ENABLE QUERY REWRITE
AS
SELECT channel_id,
      calendar_month_desc,
      SUM(sum_quantity_sold) sum_quantity_sold,
      SUM(sum_amount_sold) sum_amount_sold
FROM sum_sales_month_mv
GROUP BY channel_id,calendar_month_desc;
```

Create materialized view (summarize on month)

```
CREATE MATERIALIZED VIEW sum_sales_all_month_mv
BUILD DEFERRED
REFRESH FAST
ENABLE QUERY REWRITE
AS
SELECT
      calendar_month_desc,
      SUM(sum_quantity_sold) sum_quantity_sold,
      SUM(sum_amount_sold) sum_amount_sold
FROM sum_sales_month_mv
GROUP BY calendar_month_desc;
```

5.2.6.3.3 Create nested mview (summarize on year, country)

The new mview summarizing sales by (calendar year, country) is created from sum_sales_country_mv.

```
CREATE MATERIALIZED VIEW sum_sales_country_mv
BUILD IMMEDIATE
REFRESH COMPLETE
ENABLE QUERY REWRITE
AS

SELECT  SUBSTR(s.calendar_month_desc,1,4)  year,  C.COUNTRY_ID
country,
      SUM(sum_amount_sold) sum_amount_sold
FROM sum_sales_month_mv s, customers c
WHERE s.cust_id=c.cust_id AND
     c.country_id IN ('US','UK','FR','ES','JP', 'AU' )
GROUP BY SUBSTR(s.calendar_month_desc,1,4), c.COUNTRY_ID;
```

5.2.6.3.4 Create nested mview (summarize on channels, month, country, city)

The new materialized view summarizing sales on (channels, calendar month, country and city).

```
CREATE MATERIALIZED VIEW sum_sales_chan_city_mv
BUILD DEFERRED
REFRESH FAST
ENABLE QUERY REWRITE
```

```
AS
SELECT channel_id,
       calendar_month_desc,  country_id, cust_city city,
       SUM(sum_quantity_sold) sum_quantity_sold,
       SUM(sum_amount_sold) sum_amount_sold
FROM sum_sales_month_mv s, customers c
WHERE s.cust_id = c.cust_id
GROUP BY channel_id,calendar_month_desc,country_id,cust_city;
```

5.2.6.3.5 The nested mviews form the tree structure

The following figure clearly shows that the cornerstone mviw on the top of fact table and support a set of dependent mviews forming a tree structure.

Tree structure of Materialized Views

Figure 5-5.2-4 Dw_Salesfact_mv

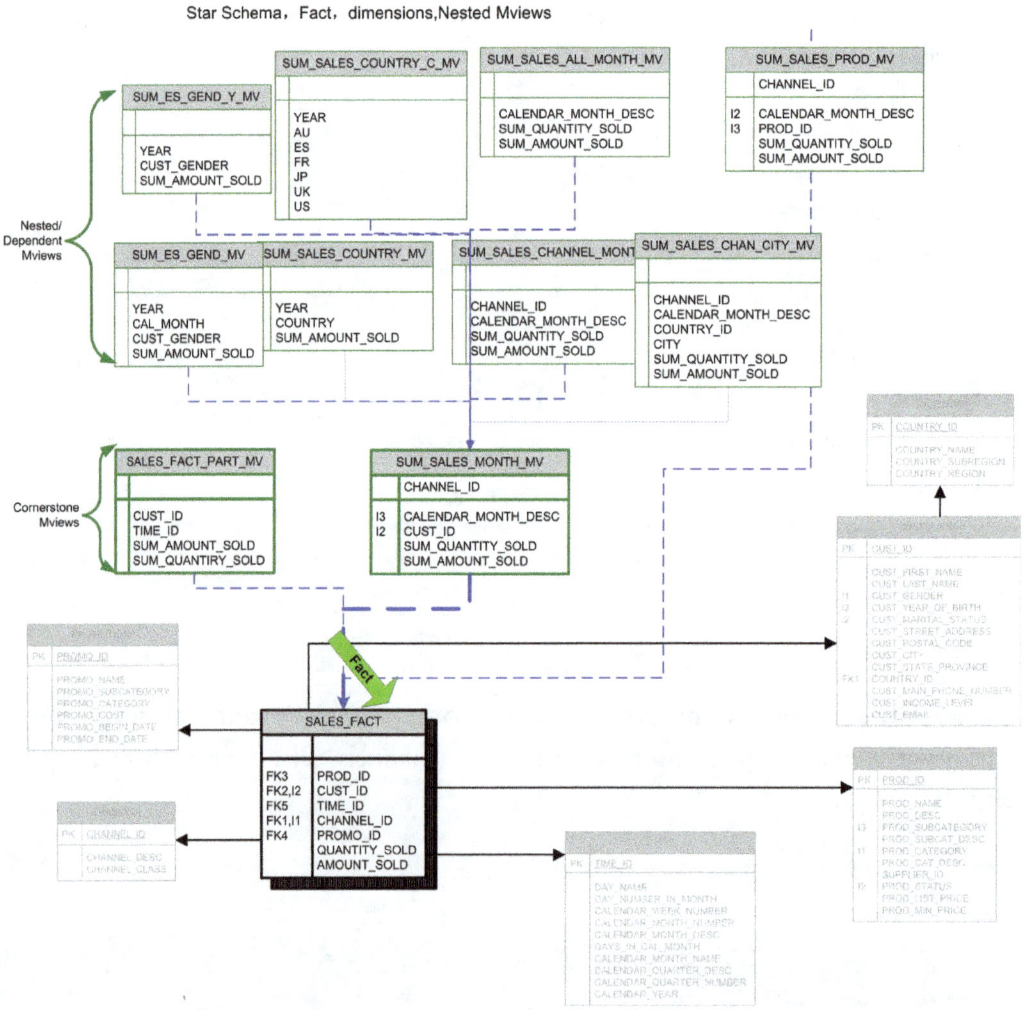

5.2.6.3.6 Utilizing the nested/cornerstone mviews

Use the primary mviews to substitute fact table and serve as the cornerstone of reporting/ analytical cube series will provide fast query speed at lower system costs. Use nested materialized views/cubes will reduce number of scans to fact table.

5.2.6.3.7 Find the optimal paths in the mview tree

Creation of mviews/cubes provides shortcut, enable quick and direct data access, thus save tremendous online execution time that most likely will be running repeatly.

Please refer to Chapter Two Figure 2-2.4-17 DwMvShortCut

5.2.6.4 Creating Materialized Views

Naming Materialized Views
Base-table name + aggregation level + _mv
For example: sum_**sales**_month_**mv**
Build Methods, Enabling Query Rewrite, Refresh

In SQL SERVER Indexed view is essentially same as materialized view.
Here is example of indexed view used for Search keywords in an online advertising BI application:

```
CREATE View [dbo].[vKeyword]
with schemabinding
As
Select
Publisher,SiteAlias,CampaignName,AdGroup,Category,Keyword,COUNT
_BIG(*) Cnt
From Keyword_ReferenceTable
Group by Publisher,SiteAlias,CampaignName,
AdGroup,Category,Keyword

create unique clustered index ux_vKeyword on vKeyword
(Publisher,SiteAlias, CampaignName,AdGroup,Category,Keyword)
```

Check if view has space - materialized

```
exec sp_spaceused 'vKeyword'
```

5.2.6.5 Create nested materialized view (summarize on channels, month)

Materialized View Logs

Materialized view logs are used to track table changes and enable fast refresh.
Here's how it starts:

5.2.6.5.1 Create materlialized view log on fact table

```
CREATE MATERIALIZED VIEW LOG ON SALES_FACT WITH SEQUENCE, ROWID
(prod_id,cust_id, time_id, channel_id,quantity_sold,
amount_sold)
INCLUDING NEW VALUES;
```

5.2.6.5.2 Create materlialized view log on dimension tables

```
CREATE MATERIALIZED VIEW LOG ON CHANNELS
WITH ROWID
(CHANNEL_ID,CHANNEL_DESC,CHANNEL_CLASS)
INCLUDING NEW VALUES;
```

Create mview log on time dimension

```
CREATE MATERIALIZED VIEW LOG ON TIMES
WITH ROWID
( TIME_ID,DAY_NAME,
 DAY_NUMBER_IN_MONTH,
 CALENDAR_WEEK_NUMBER,
 CALENDAR_MONTH_NUMBER,
 CALENDAR_QUARTER_DESC,
 CALENDAR_MONTH_NAME,
 CALENDAR_MONTH_DESC,
 CALENDAR_YEAR)
INCLUDING NEW VALUES;
```

5.2.6.5.3 Define an mview as fast refreshed

```
CREATE MATERIALIZED VIEW sum_sales_prod_time_mv
PARALLEL
BUILD DEFERRED
REFRESH FAST ON DEMAND
ENABLE QUERY REWRITE
AS
SELECT s.time_id, s.prod_id,
COUNT(*) count_grp,
SUM(s.amount_sold) sum_sales,
COUNT(s.amount_sold) count_sales,
SUM(s.quantity_sold) sum_quantity_sales,
COUNT(s.quantity_sold) count_quantity_sales
FROM sales_fact s
GROUP BY s.time_id, s.prod_id;
```

5.2.6.6 Create a fast refreshable mview for monthly sales

Create mview for monthly sales, which lay the ground work for other aggreagations or new mviews.

```
CREATE MATERIALIZED VIEW sum_sales_month_mv
BUILD DEFERRED
REFRESH FAST
ENABLE QUERY REWRITE
AS
SELECT channel_id,calendar_month_desc,cust_id,SUM(quantity_sold)
sum_quantity_sold, SUM(amount_sold) sum_amount_sold
FROM sales_fact s, times t
WHERE s.time_id = t.time_id
GROUP BY channel_id,calendar_month_desc,cust_id;
```

Create bitmap index on mviews

```
CREATE      BITMAP      INDEX      SALES_MONTH_MV_CHANNEL_BIX      ON
SUM_SALES_MONTH_MV (CHANNEL_ID)
NOLOGGING TABLESPACE EXAMPLE;
CREATE      BITMAP      INDEX      SALES_MONTH_MV_MONTH_BIX      ON
SUM_SALES_MONTH_MV (CALENDAR_MONTH_DESC)
NOLOGGING TABLESPACE EXAMPLE;
CREATE BITMAP INDEX SALES_MONTH_MV_CUST_BIX ON SUM_SALES_MONTH_MV
(CUST_ID)
NOLOGGING TABLESPACE EXAMPLE;
```

Using DBMS_MVIEW package to refresh mview in fast mode
Note: Second parameter '?' makes DBMS_MVIEW try fast refresh if possible otherwise do a complete refresh.

```
begin
DBMS_MVIEW.REFRESH('sum_sales_month_mv',  '?',  '',TRUE,  FALSE,
0,0,0, FALSE);
end;
```

NOTE: SECOND PARAMETER 'F' MAKES DBMS_MVIEW DO FAST REFRESH.

```
begin
DBMS_MVIEW.REFRESH('sum_sales_month_mv',  'F',  '',TRUE,  FALSE,
0,0,0, FALSE);
end;
```

5.2.6.7 Create a fast-refreshable mview for monthly product sales

```
CREATE MATERIALIZED VIEW sum_sales_prod_mv
BUILD DEFERRED
REFRESH FAST
ENABLE QUERY REWRITE
AS

SELECT channel_id,calendar_month_desc,prod_id,
SUM(quantity_sold) sum_quantity_sold,
SUM(amount_sold) sum_amount_sold
FROM sales_fact s, times t
WHERE s.time_id = t.time_id
GROUP BY channel_id,calendar_month_desc,prod_id;
```

Create bitmap index for mview

```
CREATE BITMAP INDEX SALES_PROD_MV_CHANNEL_BIX ON
SUM_SALES_PROD_MV (CHANNEL_ID)
NOLOGGING TABLESPACE EXAMPLE;
CREATE BITMAP INDEX SALES_PROD_MV_MONTH_BIX ON SUM_SALES_PROD_MV
(CALENDAR_MONTH_DESC)
NOLOGGING TABLESPACE EXAMPLE;
CREATE BITMAP INDEX SALES_PROD_MV_PROD_BIX ON SUM_SALES_PROD_MV
(PROD_ID)
NOLOGGING TABLESPACE EXAMPLE;
```

Using DBMS_MVIEW package to refresh mview (fast refresh)
Note: Second parameter '?' makes DBMS_MVIEW try fast refresh if possible otherwise do a complete refresh.

```
begin
DBMS_MVIEW.REFRESH('sum_sales_prod_mv', '?', '',TRUE, FALSE,
0,0,0, FALSE);
end;
```

NOTE: SECOND PARAMETER 'F' MAKES DBMS_MVIEW DO FAST REFRESH.

```
begin
DBMS_MVIEW.REFRESH('sum_sales_prod_mv', 'F', '',TRUE, FALSE,
0,0,0, FALSE);
end;
```

5.3 ETL

This chapter discusses the following topics:

- Mappings
- Mimic mapping from source to target by using view/mviews
- ETL Examples
- Methods of Extract-Transform-Load
- Data Standardization
- Data Cleansing
- Design your own ETL Tools
- Extraction
- Loading and Transformation

5.3.1 Mappings

Mapping describes target object and the conrespondent source objects on that a series operations may involved such as extract data from sources, transform data into required format, load data into target.

The views and materialized views can be used to mimic the mappings from sources to targets, - a very userful method during the development prototyping.

5.3.2 ETL Examples

5.3.2.1 At first, create a database link for a source.

```
CREATE DATABASE LINK SOURCE_DB
CONNECT TO source_db IDENTIFIED BY etl_opr
USING 'source_db';
```

5.3.2.2 From SQL PLUS run the following query and dumps the result into a file (in pseudo code).

```
SET echo off SET pagesize 0
SPOOL myfile_name.dmp
SELECT t1.column1 ||'|'|| t2.column2

FROM tab1 t1, tab2 t2
WHERE t1.col_id = t2.col_id
AND t1.column1= 'xname';
SPOOL off
```

5.3.2.3 Create a staging table (in pseudo code):

```
CREATE TABLE my_stg_tab NOLOGGING
AS
SELECT t1.column1, t2.column2
FROM tab1@source_db t1, column2@source_db t2
WHERE t1.col_id = t2.col_id
AND t1.column1='xname';

INSERT /*+ APPEND NOLOGGING PARALLEL */
INTO my_target_tab
SELECT col1_id, col2_id, col3_id, col4_id, col5, col6
FROM my_source_tab;
```

5.3.2.4 Load data into a table from a text file:

LOAD DATA
INFILE *my_target_tab.da*t
APPEND INTO TABLE *my_target_tab*
FIELDS TERMINATED BY "|"
(*COL1_ID, COL2_ID, COL3_ID, COL4_ID, COL5_ID, COL6*)

It can be loaded with the following command in UNIX:
$ sqlldr usr/password control=*my_target_tab.ctl* direct=true
SQLLDR DATA=*my_flat_file.dat* DIRECT=TRUE CONTROL=*my_flat_file.ctl*
LOAD INTO *my_target_tab*

5.3.2.5 Merge Operation Using SQL (pseudo code):

```
MERGE INTO my_dim_target_tab t
USING my_dim_target_tab_delta s
ON (t.col_id=s.col_id)
WHEN MATCHED THEN
UPDATE SET
t.col_x=s.col_x,
t.col_y=s.col_y
WHEN NOT MATCHED THEN
INSERT (my column list)
VALUES (my value list);
```

Here is an example of insert/update data loading in **SQL Server** using stored procedure. In the following example, the procedure update dimension table based on a staging table. See detail in 5.3.9.

Note: in pseudo code:

```
CREATE PROCEDURE usp_dimTable
AS
-- insert new
INSERT INTO dimTable (dim_pk, col1)
SELECT dim_pk, col1
FROM (
SELECT es.source_pk, es.col1, des.dim_pk
FROM sourceTable es
LEFT OUTER JOIN dimTable des
ON es.source_pk = des.dim_pk
) a
WHERE dim_pk IS NULL
-- update table when key match and column not match or column is null
UPDATE dimTable
SET col1 = es.col1
FROM sourceTable es
INNER JOIN dimTable des
ON es.source_pk = des.dim_pk
WHERE des.col1 IS NULL OR des.col1 != es.col1
```

About SQL query joinings

The joining is a major method to get related information from various tables, be familiar with it that will definitely help you to get right dataset qurickly in a clean maner. Here is the illustration showing the typical SQL joinings (in SQL Server T-SQL)

Figure 5-5.3-7 JoinSet

Join Sets – SQL Query

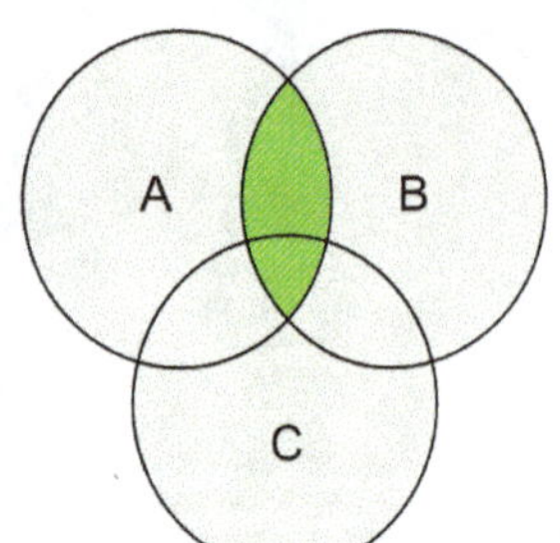

INNER JOIN
(A and B)

```
SELECT ?
FROM tableA JOIN tableB
ON tableA.key = tableB.key
```

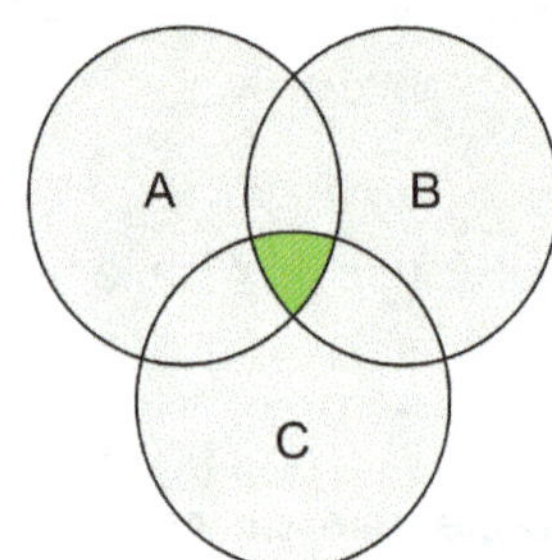

INNER JOIN
(A and B and C)

```
SELECT ?
FROM tableA JOIN tableB
ON tableA.key = tableB.key
JOIN tableC
ON tableA.key = tableC.key
```

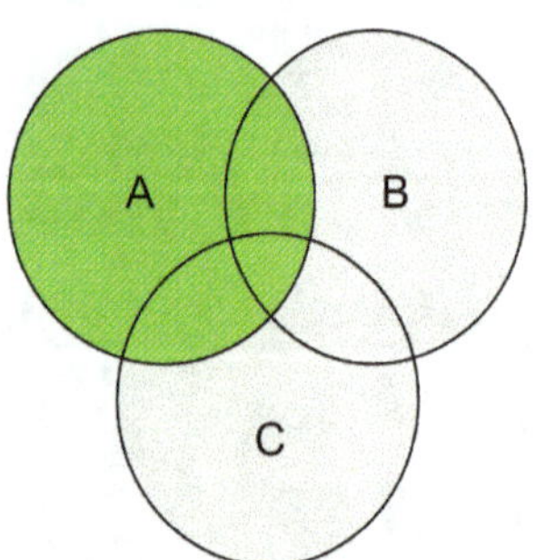

LEFT OUTER JOIN
A (full set) with B (matched set)

```
SELECT ?
FROM tableA
LEFT OUTER JOIN tableB
ON tableA.key = tableB.key
```

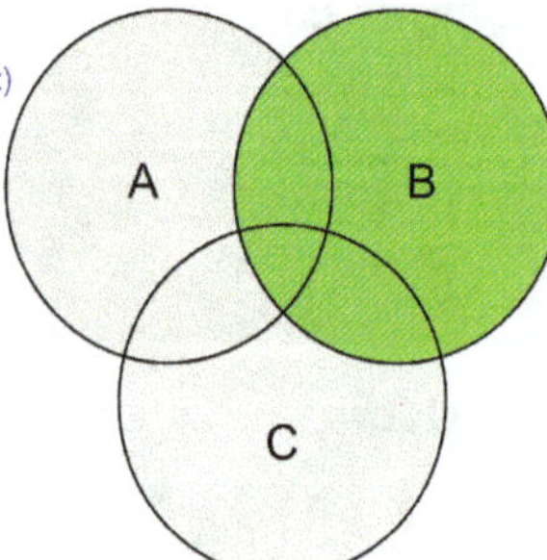

RIGHT OUTER JOIN
A (matched set) with B (full set)

```
SELECT ?
FROM tableA
RIGHT OUTER JOIN tableB
ON tableA.key = tableB.key
```

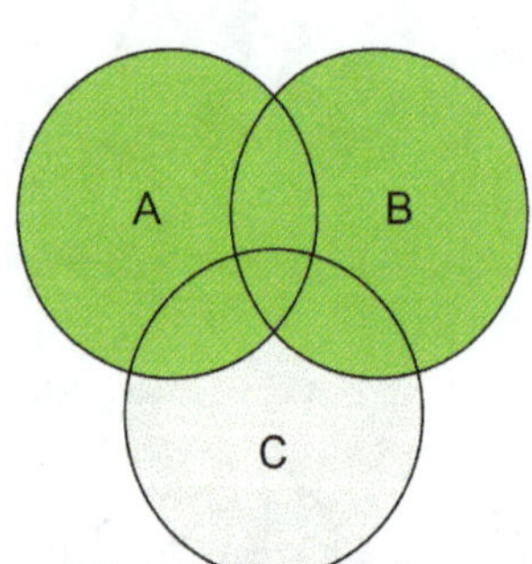

UNION
(A + B – duplicate)

```
SELECT ? FROM tableA
WHERE conditionA
UNION
SELECT ? FROM tableA
WHERE conditionB

===================

SELECT ? FROM tableA
WHERE ?
UNION
SELECT ? FROM tableB
WHERE ?
```

FULL OUTER JOIN
(A + B – duplicate)

```
SELECT ? FROM tableA
FULL OUTER JOIN tableB
ON tableA.key = tableB.key
```

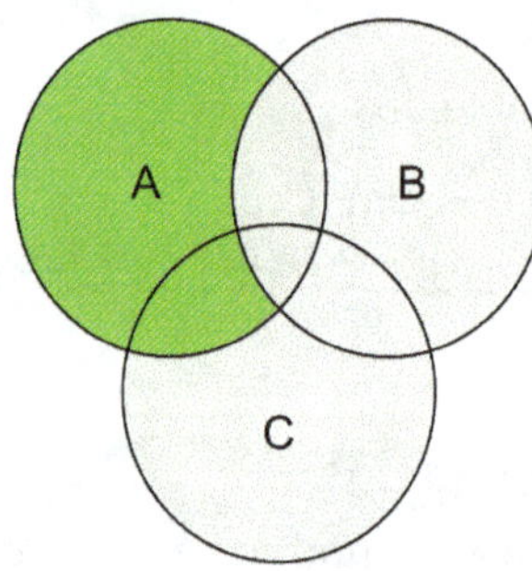

NOT IN
(A not in B)

```
SELECT ?
FROM tableA
WHERE col NOT IN
(SELECT col FROM tableB)
```

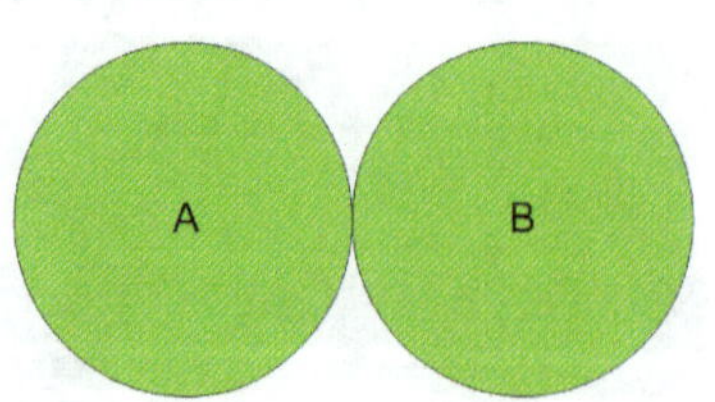

UNION ALL
(A + B)

```
SELECT ? FROM tableA
WHERE conditionA
UNION ALL
SELECT ? FROM tableA
WHERE conditionB

====================

SELECT ? FROM tableA
WHERE ?
UNION ALL
SELECT ? FROM tableB
WHERE ?
```

Note:
By default
A is dataset from tableA
B is dataset from tableB
C is dataset from tableC

5.3.3. Loading Types

There are multiple types such as indirect loading, direct loading or refreshing:
Indirect loading: through the intermediate files. Although it has lower efficincy comparing with other online access methords, it certainly has high availability and it can be done through staged operations (for example, extract data and dump data into the intermediate files first then load data at some convenint time later), which may not necessarily require both sources and target system open for access at same time (such requirement sometimes is not practical for some source systems).

Direct loading: though has high efficiency, it require that both source systems and target system open for access at same time, such methord are mostly applied on internal systems or target system (data warehouse); it is lucky to have ability or permission to access source systems directly.

Refreshing materialized views: it can automatically refresh mviews which have been defined through the mapping from sources to target system objects. Such type of loading need more developments that tightly coupling source and target objects.

5.3.4 Data Standardization

5.3.4.1 Build supporting library and objects

- standard dictionaries and code/name refrence tables
- subroutine and function library used for data conversion
- The mapping tables that map the various values into a uniform/standard values, such as alias names with their conrespondent standard name.

Such groundwork is essential for the data warehouse which has multiple disparate data sources.

5.3.4.2 Mapping table

In this example, every data item (such as “abc”, “f88”, ”ww”, “456”) come from various sources (A, B, C, D) will find the standard reference value (100 for example).
Create mapping tables to map various source values to data warehouse standard values

5.3.5 Data Cleansing

- Check errors such as spelling, value ranges; most these jobs can be done through comparing to the standard lookup tables.
- Processing Names and Addresses
- Building support tables or dicrionaries for names and addresses in order to help correcting errors. For example, by using state and zip/postal code may help determine wrong city name entries.

Example:

5.3.5.1 Using function replace () Covert ',' to '.'

select 'me@mwe,com' oldemail, replace ('me@mwe,com', ',', '.') newemail from dual;
Result: me@mwe,com   me@mwe.com

5.3.5.2 Using function replace ( ) trim imbedded space

select 'me@mwe .com' oldemail, replace ('me@mwe .com', ' ') newemail from dual;
Result: me@mwe .com   me@mwe.com

5.3.5.3 Using function validate email address format

The following function validates email address:

- check spae and tab
- check absence of '@'
- check pattern of something@something

```
FUNCTION          GETEMAILCHECKED
(p_email_id varchar2) RETURN number AS vstat number;
vemail varchar2(75);
BEGIN
-- check space, Tab only, check '%@%.%' pattern, check null
IF instr(p_email_id, ' ') > 0 or instr(p_email_id, '\t') > 0 THEN
RETURN 1;
ELSIF (p_email_id NOT LIKE '%@%.%') THEN
    RETURN 1;
ELSIF p_email_id is null THEN
    RETURN 1;
ELSE RETURN 0;
END IF;
END; -- Function GETEMAILCHECKED
```

5.3.5.4 Using function to Collapse 'space', Tab:

Create function collapse 'space', Tab from email address

```
FUNCTION GetEmailFixed
(p_email_id varchar2) RETURN varchar2 AS
vemail varchar2(75);
BEGIN
-- collapse space, Tab only.
vemail:=replace(replace(p_email_id,' '),'\t');
RETURN vemail;
END GetEmailFixed;
```

5.3.5.5 ETL Data Cleansing Process Flow

Figure 5-5.3-9 DwCleansingFlow

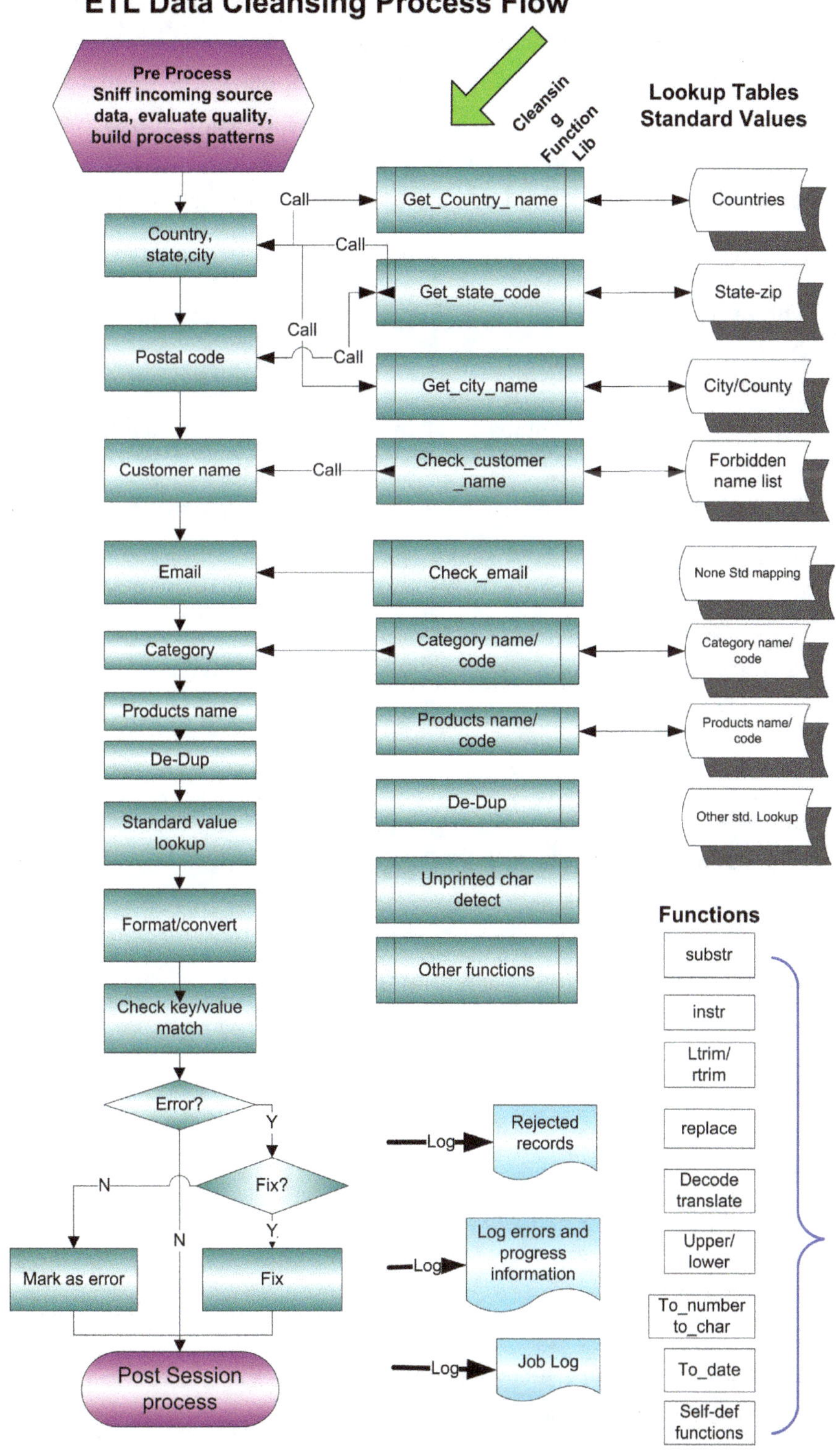

5.3.6 Design your dynamic date driven ETL(3DETL)

Use data-driven approach (DDDP) to create a 3DETL

The architectural model of the design provides a generic flexibility for various ETL coverage. The customization is done with ease. Additional information requirements (and the resulting queries) can be dynamically expanded as new requirements are identified through metadata. The entire customization mechanism means the standard product will rapidly become a business-specific tool in ETL. In another word, a single procedure able to import data from the given sources (servers, databases, tables) and load data into given target (sources, databases, tables) It can deal with the environment with multiple sources and targets databases.

How to achieve this? Here is an example (in the high level illustration).

First thing first,

Create a centralized (dedicated) database to handle all ETL works with following metadata:

- o Source Definition (servers, databases, tables, columns…)
- o Target Definition (servers, databases, tables, columns, keys…)
- o Mapping Specification
- o Mapping
- o Session (put mapping as ETL jobs)
- o Batch (schedules and executes data import/update processes)

Schema

- o Server/Database table: link source servers/databases and target servers/databases
- o sourceTable: source table list
- o stagingTable: staging table list
- o targetTable: target table list
- o sourceColumnTable: source table column/key list
- o targetColumnTable: target table column/key list
- o also using system database to track needed database objects

Procedures

The procedures read the metadata schema and execute jobs accordingly

- ➢ Import source definitions
- ➢ Fetch and capture metadata info such as table names, column list, primary key or unique key.
- ➢ Define targets
- ➢ Create target objects
- ➢ Create procedure using metadata and dynamic SQL
- ➢ Apply the database constrants

- ➢ Handle incremental update (determine delta).
- ➢ Log ETL processes

Mapping

Create mapping tables which control stream from sources to target and all necessary process stages. Including following transformation functions:

- o Server/database
- o Source table/Target table
- o Key column mapping – logical key/building key
- o Lookup
- o Filter
- o Key creation

Create import/update processes batch for the objects

- o DTS (Data Transformation Services)
- o Agent Job
- o Shedule
- o Post process job

Create monitoring processes and ETL job monitoring tables

- o Daily data feed log
- o Source/target table row counts
- o Views which track missing data

5.3.6.1 SQL Server T-SQL examples

The procedure actually load data from given server/database, it is indead a generic tool, there is no database object name (servers, databases, tables, and columns) specified in codes, the procedure get those names from metadata tables.

Call the procedure to import data from given server/databse in a dynamic fasion

```
USE MasterWhouseETL
DECLARE @ServerSource as sysname,
        @DBNameSource as sysname,
        @DBNameTarget as sysname
-- Call the procedure
exec [dbo].[usp_DailyImport]
        @ServerSource = 'EuroServer',
        @DBNameSource = 'DB1',
        @DBNameTarget = 'Warehouse1'
```

Call same procedure to import data from a different server/databse

```
USE MasterWhouseETL
DECLARE @ServerSource as sysname,
        @DBNameSource as sysname,
        @DBNameTarget as sysname
-- Call the procedure
exec DailyImport
        @ServerSource = 'USServer',
        @DBNameSource = 'DB3',
        @DBNameTarget = 'Warehouse3'
```

3DP has been proven very powerful and it works great!
The 3DETL is robust, flexible and extendable in addition of less maintenance and easy in deployments.
For major components of 3DETL, please see Chapter Four 4.2.4 Dynamic Data Driven ETL (3DETL) and Figure 4-4.2-8 EtlMasterComponent

Example: Dynamic ETL with distributed ODS and distributed staging areas
Case: ODS located in multiple serer/database, and all have similar schema/data structures.

Methods used:

- Use distributed staging area/db to holding loading data (staging schema may resemble source)
- Use an ETL database with metadata repository, dynamic procedures to achieve centralized control on data pulling
- Use views to combine database objects from staging areas/dbs forming integrated DW objects

The following diagram illustrates a centralized ETL control over source (distributed multiple server/databases) loading to multiple target server/database through a centralized metadata repositories and dynamic loading utilities (procedures). Because dynamic approach – metadata-driven ETL and dynamic SQL, this system has been successfully created and loaded data from a global distributed environment.

Please refer to Chapter Two Figure 4-4.2-10 MetaDataDrivenETL
Example
Please refer to Chapter Four diagram Figure 4-4.2-9 MasterETL which illustrates basic data schema for an ETL master database

The following flowchart shows ETL flow handling multiple data sources and destination databases dynamically.

Figure 5-5.3-9 DynamicETLFlow

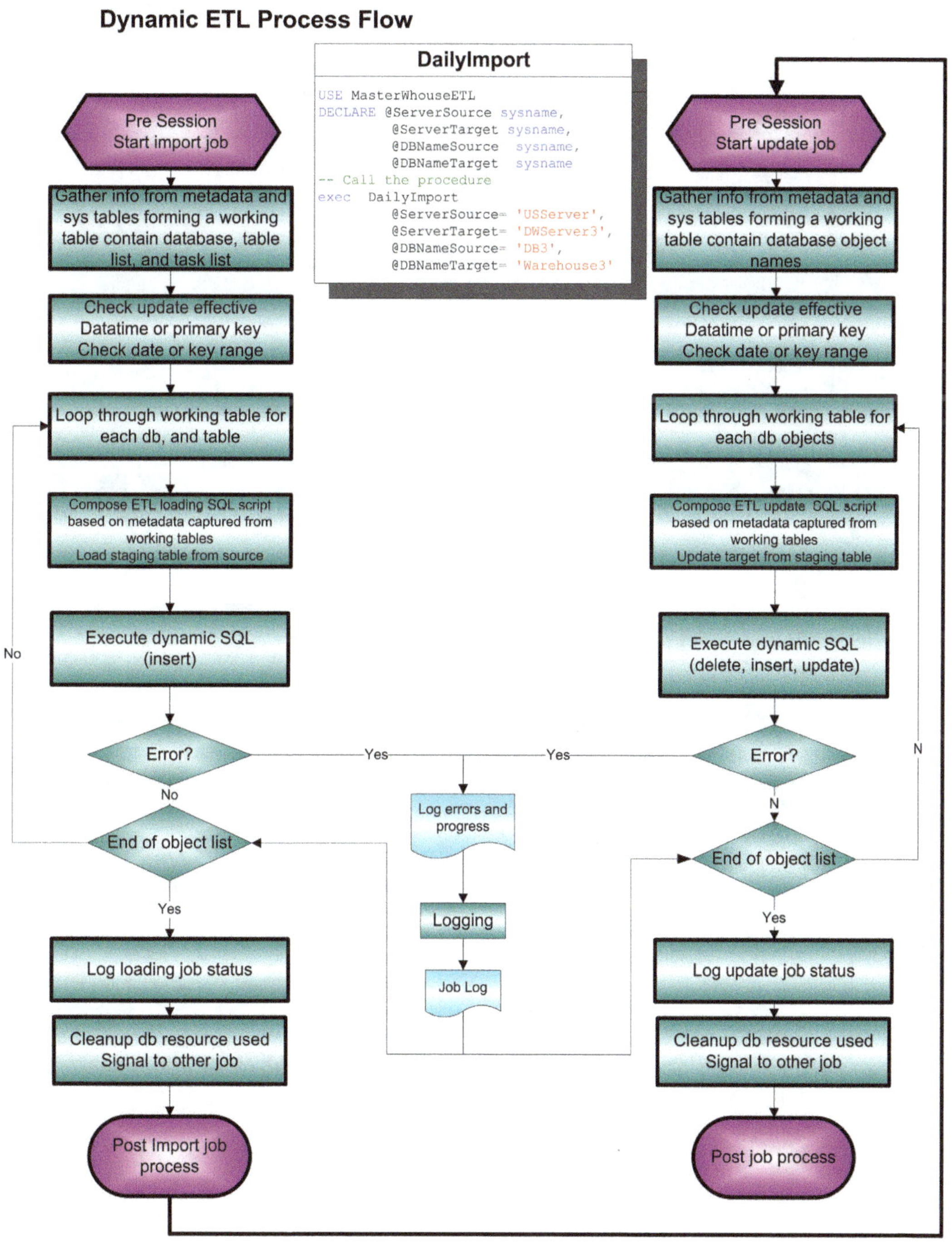

Dynamic ETL Process Flow

DailyImport

```
USE MasterWhouseETL
DECLARE @ServerSource sysname,
        @ServerTarget sysname,
        @DBNameSource  sysname,
        @DBNameTarget  sysname
-- Call the procedure
exec  DailyImport
        @ServerSource= 'USServer',
        @ServerTarget= 'DWServer3',
        @DBNameSource= 'DB3',
        @DBNameTarget= 'Warehouse3'
```

Pre Session Start import job

Gather info from metadata and sys tables forming a working table contain database, table list, and task list

Check update effective Datatime or primary key Check date or key range

Loop through working table for each db, and table

Compose ETL loading SQL script based on metadata captured from working tables Load staging table from source

Execute dynamic SQL (insert)

Error?

No

End of object list

Yes

Log loading job status

Cleanup db resource used Signal to other job

Post Import job process

Yes

Log errors and progress

Logging

Job Log

Pre Session Start update job

Gather info from metadata and sys tables forming a working table contain database object names

Check update effective Datatime or primary key Check date or key range

Loop through working table for each db objects

Compose ETL update SQL script based on metadata captured from working tables Update target from staging table

Execute dynamic SQL (delete, insert, update)

Error?

N

End of object list

Yes

Log update job status

Cleanup db resource used Signal to other job

Post job process

Dynamic ETL procedure

Figure 5-5.3-10 DynamicETLProcFlow

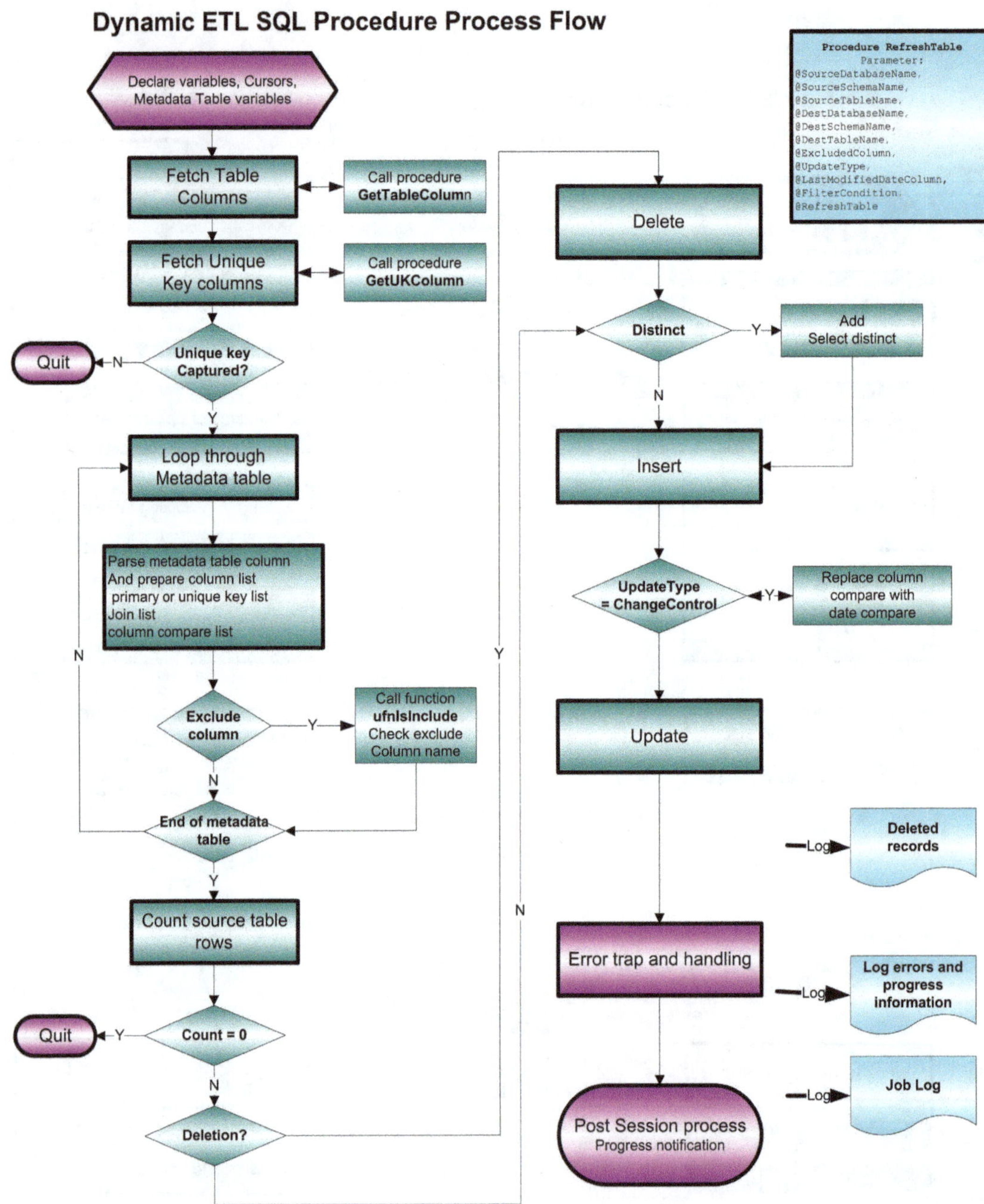

5.3.6.2 Code snippet

```
CREATE PROCEDURE [dbo].[DailyImportTables]
       @SRVSRC as sysname,
       @DBNameSRC as sysname,
       @DBNameDST as sysname,
       @LogMode int = null
AS
SET @SQLCMD2=N'truncate table
[@DBNameDST].[dbo].[@STAGETableName] Insert
[@DBNameDST].[dbo].[@STAGETableName] SELECT '
SET
@SQLCMD2=REPLACE(@SQLCMD2,'@STAGETableName',@STAGETableNa
me)
SET @SQLCMD2=REPLACE(@SQLCMD2,'@DBNameDST',@DBNameDST)
SET @SQLCMD2=@SQLCMD2 + N' FROM
@SRVSRC.@DBNameSRC.[dbo].[@LASTWHTBLNAME]'
SET @SQLCMD3 = N' Where @LastUpdateKeyField +
@LASTOffsetNumber > @MaxKeyValue '
SET
@SQLCMD3=REPLACE(@SQLCMD3,'@LastUpdateKeyField',@LastUpda
teKeyField)
SET
@SQLCMD3=REPLACE(@SQLCMD3,'@LASTOffsetNumber',@LASTOffset
Number)
SET
@SQLCMD3=REPLACE(@SQLCMD3,'@MaxKeyValue',@MaxKeyValue)
SET @SQLCMD2=@SQLCMD2 + @SQLCMD3
SET @SQLCMD2=REPLACE(@SQLCMD2,'@DBNameDST',@DBNameDST)
BEGIN
/* Skip code parse body - too long to read
{Code parse body}
*/
EXECUTE sp_executesql @SQLCMD2
END
```

5.3.6.3 Code snippet

```
CREATE PROCEDURE [dbo].[DailyUpdate]
        @SRVSRC as sysname,
        @DBNameSRC as sysname,
        @DBNameDST as sysname,
        @LogMode int = null
AS
```

Loop through table list, for each table

```
/* Skip code parse body
{Code parse body}
*/
```

Insert

```
SET @SQLCMD2=N'Insert [@DBNameDST].[dbo].@ProdTableName Select *
            From [@DBNameDST].[dbo].@STAGETableName where
@UpdateKeyField > @LastUpdateKey'
SET @SQLCMD2=REPLACE(@SQLCMD2,'@STAGETableName',@STAGETableName)
SET @SQLCMD2=REPLACE(@SQLCMD2,'@DBNameDST',@DBNameDST)
SET @SQLCMD2=REPLACE(@SQLCMD2,'@ProdTableName',@ProdTableName)
SET @SQLCMD2=REPLACE(@SQLCMD2,'@UpdateKeyField',@UpdateKeyField)
SET @SQLCMD2=REPLACE(@SQLCMD2,'@LastUpdateKey',@LastUpdateKey)
```

Log table load

```
/* Skip code parse body
{Code parse body}
*/
insert into dbo.TableDailyFeedLog (dbName, tableName,
BatchNumber,NumberOfDays,Cnt,InsCnt,
LastUpdate,RunDate,Err)
values(@dbNameDST,@ProdTableName,@BatchNumber,@NumberOfDa
ys,@Cnt,@InsCnt, @LastUpdate,getdate(),@Err)
```

5.3.6.3 Load file based on given file path, file name, and file type (Code snippet)

```
CREATE PROCEDURE [dbo].[LoadFile]
        @DBName as sysname = NULL,
        @HoldingDB as sysname = NULL,
        @TableName sysname = NULL,
        @ServerName sysname = NULL,
        @Path nvarchar(300),
        @FileName sysname,
        @FileType nvarchar(20)= NULL,
        @SheetName nvarchar(100) = NULL,
        @RefreshTable int = NULL,
        @BatchNum int = NULL,
        @SQLCMDPassback nvarchar(3000) output
AS
SET @SQLCMD1 = N'SELECT * INTO @HoldingDB.dbo.[@TableName]
FROM OPENROWSET (''Microsoft.Jet.OLEDB.4.0'',''Excel
8.0;Database=@Path\@FileName'',''SELECT * FROM
[@SheetName$]'')'
SET @SQLCMD1 = N'SELECT * INTO @HoldingDB.dbo.[@TableName]
FROM OPENROWSET (''MSDASQL'', ''Driver={Microsoft Text
Driver (*.txt; *.csv)};DBQ=@Path;'', ''SELECT * from
[@FileName]'');'
SET @SQLCMD1 = N'DELETE
[@ServerName].@dbName.dbo.[@TableName] INSERT INTO
[@ServerName].@dbName.dbo.[@TableName] SELECT * FROM
OPENROWSET (''MSDASQL'', ''Driver={Microsoft Text Driver
(*.txt; *.csv)};DBQ=@Path;'',''SELECT * from
[@FileName]'');'
SET @SQLCMD1=REPLACE(@SQLCMD1,'@DBName',@DBName)
SET @SQLCMD1=REPLACE(@SQLCMD1,'@TableName',@TableName)
SET @SQLCMD1=REPLACE(@SQLCMD1,'@ServerName',@ServerName)
SET @SQLCMD1=REPLACE(@SQLCMD1,'@HoldingDB',@HoldingDB)
SET @SQLCMD1=REPLACE(@SQLCMD1,'@Path',@Path)
SET @SQLCMD1=REPLACE(@SQLCMD1,'@FileName',@FileName)
SET @SQLCMD1=REPLACE(@SQLCMD1,'@SheetName',@SheetName)
/* Skip code parse body
{Code parse body}
*/
EXECUTE sp_executesql @SQLCMD1
RETURN
```

5.3.6.4 Fetch metadata such as column info. key definitions for given table, db, server name

In order to serve main ETL procedure (*RefreshTable*) in a modular fashion, a group of routines and functions must be defined thus form the subroutine/function library which includes the following:

- o *uspListDbTableColumn*
- o *uspGetUKColumn*
- o *uspGetUKColumn*
- o *ufnIsInclude*

Create stored procedure routines

```
CREATE procedure [dbo].[uspListDbTableColumn]
@table sysname ,@schemaName sysname = 'dbo'
,@dbname sysname = null, @servername sysname = null
as
declare @sqlstring nvarchar(3000)

 set @sqlstring = N'select t.name tableName, c.name
 columnName, ty.name datatype '
 if @dbname is null and @servername is null
 begin
     set @sqlstring = @sqlstring + N'
 from sys.tables t join sys.columns c on t.object_id =
 c.object_id
 join sys.schemas s on s.schema_id = t.schema_id
 join sys.types ty on ty.user_type_id = c.system_type_id
 where t.type = ''u''
 and t.name = ''@table'''
 end

 if @dbname is not null and @servername is null
 BEGIN
 IF NOT EXISTS (SELECT name FROM sys.databases WHERE name =
 @dbname)
 begin
     print 'database ' + @dbname + ' not exists'
     return
 end
 else
```

```
begin
    set @sqlstring = @sqlstring + N'
from @dbname.sys.tables t join @dbname.sys.columns c on
t.object_id = c.object_id
join sys.schemas s on s.schema_id = t.schema_id
join sys.types ty on ty.user_type_id = c.system_type_id
where t.type = ''u''
and t.name = ''@table'''
set @sqlstring = replace (@sqlstring, '@dbname',@dbname)
end

end
if @dbname is not null and @servername is not null
begin
IF NOT EXISTS (SELECT name FROM sys.servers WHERE name =
@servername)
begin
    print 'server ' + @servername + ' not exists'
    return
end
else
begin
    set @sqlstring = @sqlstring + N'
from @servername.@dbname.sys.tables t join
@servername.@dbname.sys.columns c on t.object_id =
c.object_id
join sys.schemas s on s.schema_id = t.schema_id
join sys.types ty on ty.user_type_id = c.system_type_id
where t.type = ''u''
and t.name = ''@table'''
set @sqlstring = replace (@sqlstring, '@dbname',@dbname)
set @sqlstring = replace (@sqlstring,
'@servername',@servername)
end
end
set @sqlstring = replace (@sqlstring, '@table',@table)
print @sqlstring
exec sp_executesql @sqlstring
return
```

Call this procedure to fetch table columns

```
execute [dbo].[uspListDbTableColumn]
 @table
 ='ProductInventory',@dbname=null,@schemaName='Production'
```

tableName	columnName	datatype
ProductInventory	ProductID	int
ProductInventory	LocationID	smallint
ProductInventory	Shelf	nvarchar
ProductInventory	Bin	tinyint
ProductInventory	Quantity	smallint
ProductInventory	rowguid	uniqueidentifier
ProductInventory	ModifiedDate	datetime

5.3.6.3.5 Fetch unique key for given table

```
CREATE PROCEDURE [dbo].[uspGetUKColumn]
   @SourceServer sysname=NULL
  ,@SourceDataBase sysname=NULL
    ,@SchemaName sysname ='dbo'
  ,@SourceTable sysname
AS
DECLARE @pkList TABLE (IndexName nvarchar(128), TableName
nvarchar(128), ColumnName nvarchar(128),key_ordinal
tinyint)
DECLARE @indexName nvarchar(128), @TableName1
nvarchar(128),@ColumnName nvarchar(128), @key_ordinal
tinyint, @PkL nvarchar(128)
, @initFlag tinyint, @SqlStmt nvarchar(max)
DECLARE cur1 CURSOR FOR
SELECT ColumnName FROM @pkList
WHERE TableName = @SourceTable ORDER BY key_ordinal
BEGIN
SET @SourceServer = '['+ISNULL(@SourceServer,@@servername)
+']'
SET @SourceDatabase = ISNULL(@SourceDatabase,db_name())
SET @initFlag = 0
```

```
IF @SourceServer IS NULL
BEGIN
SELECT @SqlStmt = N'SELECT   i.name AS IndexName,
    t.name AS TableName, c.name AS ColumnName,
ic.key_ordinal
FROM @SourceDataBase.sys.indexes AS i
INNER JOIN @SourceDataBase.sys.index_columns AS ic
    ON i.object_id = ic.object_id AND i.index_id =
ic.index_id
and i.is_unique = 1
join @SourceDataBase.sys.columns c on c.column_id =
ic.column_id
join @SourceDataBase.sys.tables t on t.object_id =
i.object_id and t.object_id = c.object_id
AND t.name = ''@SourceTable''
AND t.schema_id IN
(select schema_id from sys.schemas where name =
''@schemaName'')'
END
ELSE
BEGIN
SELECT @SqlStmt = N'SELECT   i.name AS IndexName,
    t.name AS TableName, c.name AS ColumnName,
ic.key_ordinal
FROM @SourceServer.@SourceDataBase.sys.indexes AS i
INNER JOIN @SourceServer.@SourceDataBase.sys.index_columns
AS ic
    ON i.object_id = ic.object_id AND i.index_id =
ic.index_id
and i.is_unique = 1
join @SourceServer.@SourceDataBase.sys.columns c on
c.column_id = ic.column_id
```

```
join @SourceServer.@SourceDataBase.sys.tables t on
t.object_id = i.object_id and t.object_id = c.object_id
AND t.name = ''@SourceTable''
AND t.schema_id IN
(select schema_id from sys.schemas where name =
''@schemaName'')'
END
IF @SourceServer IS NOT NULL
BEGIN
SET @SqlStmt = REPLACE(@SqlStmt,
'@SourceServer',@SourceServer)
END
SET @SqlStmt = REPLACE(@SqlStmt,
'@SourceDataBase',@SourceDataBase)
SET @SqlStmt = REPLACE(@SqlStmt,
'@SourceTable',@SourceTable)
SET @SqlStmt = REPLACE(@SqlStmt, '@SchemaName',@SchemaName)
print @SqlStmt
EXECUTE SP_EXECUTESQL @SqlStmt;
END
```

Call this procedure to fetch unique key columns

```
EXECUTE [dbo].[uspGetUKColumn]
  @SourceServer = NULL
  ,@SourceDataBase =NULL
  ,@schemaName = 'Production'
  ,@SourceTable = 'ProductInventory'
```

IndexName	TableName	ColumnName	Order
PK_ProductInventory_ProductID_LocationID	ProductInventory	ProductID	1
PK_ProductInventory_ProductID_LocationID	ProductInventory	LocationID	2

5.3.6.6 Create a function to indicate if column is included in column list

```
CREATE FUNCTION [dbo].[ufnIsInclude]
(@str1 nvarChar(128), @strList nvarchar(4000))
RETURNS int
AS
BEGIN
  DECLARE @ReturnValue int, @IsInclued int, @length int,
@startPos int, @endPos int
, @str0 nvarchar(max), @str01 nvarchar(4000);
       SET @Length = len(@strList);
       -- remove one space only
       set @str0 = replace(@strList,', ',',')
       set @str0 = replace(@str0,' ,',',')
   SELECT @endPos = CHARINDEX(@str1,@str0);
   IF @endPos = 0
   BEGIN
       SET @IsInclued = 0
       RETURN @IsInclued ;
   END
   ELSE
   BEGIN
       set @startpos = 1
       set @endpos = 1
   END

  WHILE @startPos +1 < @length
  BEGIN
   set @str0 = SUBSTRING(@str0, @startPos, @length -
@startPos + 1)
       set @endPos = charindex(',',@str0)
       if @endPos =0
       begin
```

```
            if @str1 = @str0
            begin
                SET @IsInclued = 1;
                break;
            end
            else
            begin
                SET @IsInclued = 0;
                break;
            end
        end
        set @str01 = SUBSTRING(@str0, 1,@endpos -1)
        IF @str1 = SUBSTRING(@str01,1, @endpos-1)
        BEGIN
            SET @IsInclued = 1;
            BREAK;
        END
    SET @startPos = @endpos +1 ;
  END;
  RETURN @IsInclued ;
END;
```

Call function to check if column name ModifiedDate exists in column list

```
SELECT [dbo].[ufnIsInclude] ('ModifiedDate',
'ProductID,LocationID,Shelf,Bin,Quantity,rowguid,Modified
Date')
```

It return 1 mean column name 'ModifiedDate' exists

```
SELECT [dbo].[ufnIsInclude] ('ModifiedDate', '
ProductID,LocationID,Shelf,Bin,Quantity,rowguid')
```

It return 0 mean column name 'ModifiedDate' not exists

The following procedure get metadata by self-fetch manner and use dynamic SQL update target table based on a staging table.

The following flow chart shows the procedure process flow, see figure DynamicETLProcFlow

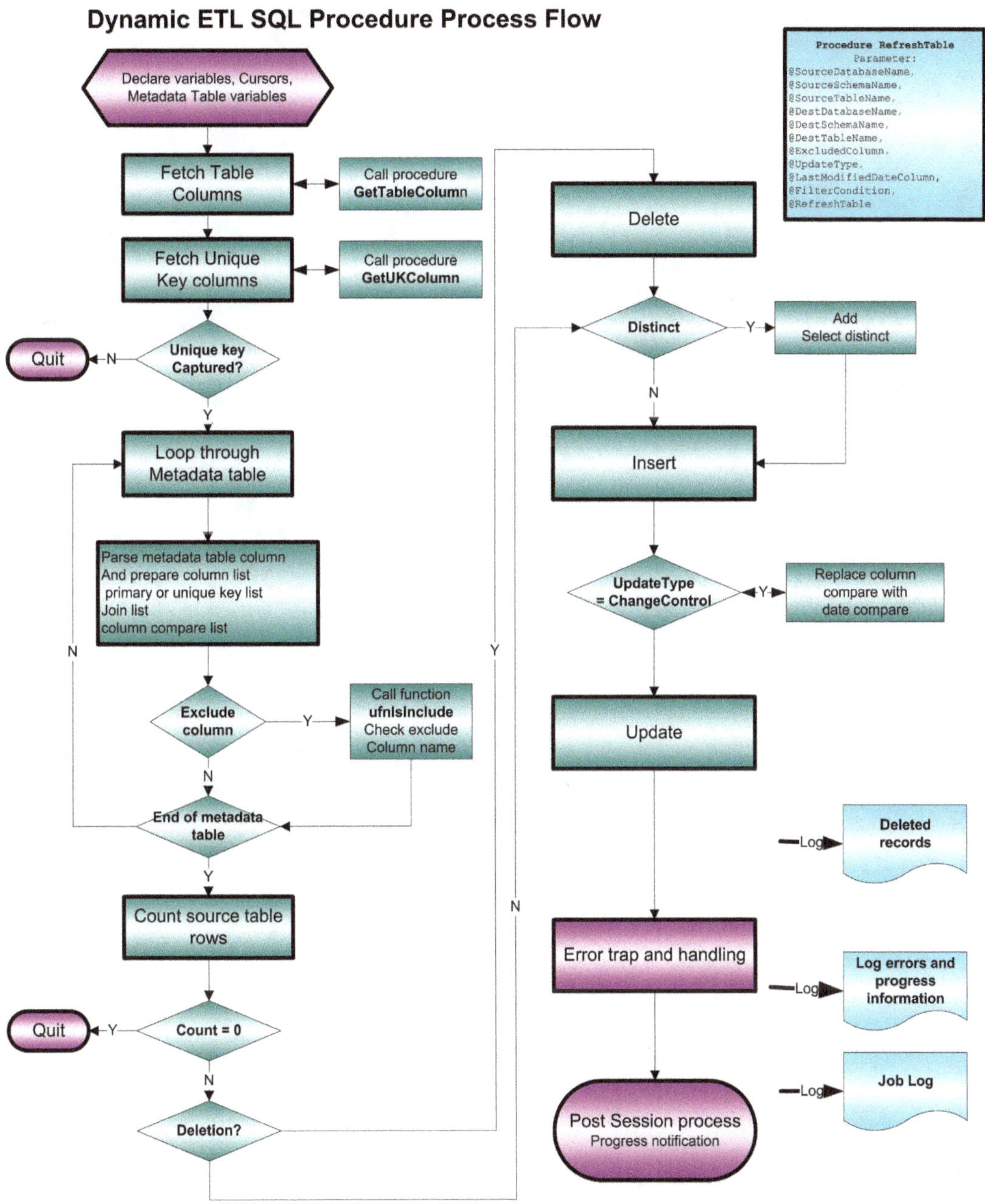

5.3.6.7 Main ETL procedure (It call function and routines described above)

```
CREATE PROCEDURE [dbo].[RefreshTable]
(               @SourceDatabaseName as sysname = NULL,
                @SourceSchemaName as sysname = 'dbo',
                @SourceTableName sysname = NULL,
                @DestDatabaseName as sysname = NULL,
                @DestSchemaName as sysname = 'dbo',
                @DestTableName sysname ,
                @ExcludedColumn varchar(2000) = NULL,
                @UpdateType nvarchar(200)= NULL,
                @LastModifiedDateColumn sysname =NULL,
                @FilterCondition nvarchar(2000) = NULL,
                @RefreshTable int = NULL
)
AS
/* ---------------------------------------
Incremental update table by compare column name between source and destinate table
parameter @UpdateType can be used 'DISTINCT DELETE ChangeControl'
parameter @ExcludedColumn can be used in column list 'col1, col2, col3, coln'
call by function [dbo].[ufnIsInclude] (@ColumnName, @ExcludedColumn)
-----------------------------------------------------------------------*/
set nocount on;
DECLARE @sqlstr nvarchar(max), @sqlstrDelete nvarchar(max),@sqlstrUpdate
nvarchar(max),@sqlstrUpdateRemote nvarchar(max), @Cnt int
,@initFlag int,@initFlag2 int,@initFlag3 int,@initFlag4 int,@sqlstr1 nvarchar(max), @sqlstrCountRow
nvarchar(max),@colName sysname
, @columnList nvarchar(max), @FullcolumnList nvarchar(max),@PkList nvarchar(max), @RequiredColList
nvarchar(3000),@WhereList nvarchar(max)
,@RowCount bigint, @JoinList nvarchar(max), @WhereJoinList nvarchar(max), @WhereJoinList_Insert
nvarchar(max)
,@UpdateList nvarchar(max),@ColumnCompareList nvarchar(max),@TableName sysname, @UpdateErrList
nvarchar(max),@ColList nvarchar(max)
,@Err int,@ErrorNumber int, @ErrorMessage varchar(255),@ErrMessage nvarchar(max), @ErrorMess
nvarchar(max),@BatchNum int
,@sColumnList varchar(max),@InsertColumnList varchar(max), @Table_Deleted sysname,
@DeleteOutputList varchar(max), @NL char(2)
DECLARE @TemplateColumnTable TABLE
([TableName] sysname,[ColumnName] sysname,[Datatype] sysname,[IndexName] varchar(400),[Key_ordinal]
int,IsPk smallint)
DECLARE @TemplateColumnList TABLE
([TableName] sysname,[ColumnName] sysname,[Datatype] sysname)
DECLARE @TemplatePKColumn TABLE
([IndexName] varchar(400),[TableName] sysname,[ColumnName] sysname,[Key_ordinal] int)
DECLARE
        @ColumnName [varchar](255),       @DataType [varchar](255),@PrimaryKey [int],
        @RequiredValue [int],
        @TransformRule [varchar](255), @TransformCode [varchar](255),@TransformCodeCatch
[varchar](255)
DECLARE curTemplateColumnTable CURSOR FOR
        SELECT tableName, columnName, dataType, IsPk FROM @TemplateColumnTable
        SET @initFlag = 0; SET @initFlag2 = 0; SET @initFlag3 = 0; SET @initFlag4 = 0; SET
@NL=char(13)+char(10);

IF @ExcludedColumn IS NOT NULL
print 'there are excluded columns'

SET @Table_Deleted = @DestTableName + '_Deleted'

        INSERT INTO @TemplateColumnList
        EXECUTE [dbo].[uspListDbTableColumn]
        @table = @DestTableName
        ,@dbname = @DestDatabaseName
        ,@schemaName = @DestSchemaName

        INSERT INTO @TemplatePKColumn
        EXECUTE [dbo].[uspGetUKColumn]
        @Sourcetable = @DestTableName
        ,@SourceDatabase = @DestDatabaseName
        ,@SchemaName = @DestSchemaName

IF @@ROWCOUNT = 0
```

```
BEGIN
        PRINT 'There is no unique key defined in Destination table ' + @DestTableName
                        RETURN
END
INSERT INTO @TemplateColumnTable
        SELECT t.tableName, t.ColumnName,t.DataType,i.indexName, i.Key_ordinal
        , IsPk = case
        when i.ColumnName is not null then 1 else 0 end
        FROM @TemplateColumnList t left outer join @TemplatePKColumn i on t.TableName = i.TableName
        and t.ColumnName = i.ColumnName

select * from @TemplateColumnTable

-- Loop through column table

        OPEN curTemplateColumnTable
        FETCH NEXT FROM curTemplateColumnTable INTO    @TableName,@ColumnName,@DataType,@PrimaryKey
        WHILE (@@FETCH_STATUS <> -1)
        BEGIN
                IF @initFlag = 0
                BEGIN
                        -- first column
                        -- first column is pk
                        IF @initFlag2 = 0 and @PrimaryKey =1
                        BEGIN
                                SET @PkList = '['+@ColumnName+']'
                                SET @JoinList = 's.['+@ColumnName+']' + ' = ' + 't.['+@ColumnName+']'
                                SET @WhereJoinList = 's.['+@ColumnName+']' + ' IS NULL '
                                SET @WhereJoinList_Insert = 't.['+@ColumnName+']' + ' IS NULL '
                                SET @initFlag2 = 1
                        END
                        -- first column is required value
                        IF @initFlag3 = 0 and @RequiredValue =1
                        BEGIN
                                SET @RequiredColList = '['+@ColumnName+']'
                                SET @WhereList = '['+@ColumnName+']' + ' IS NULL '
                                SET @UpdateErrList = ' +case when isnull( ' +'['+@ColumnName+']' +
' ,'''')='''' then ''' +'['+@ColumnName+']' + ' is blank; '' else '''' end '
                                SET @initFlag3 = 1
                        END

                        -- COLUMN LIST
                                SET @FullColumnList = '['+@ColumnName+']'
                                IF (@ExcludedColumn IS NULL) OR (@ExcludedColumn IS NOT NULL AND
[dbo].[ufnIsInclude] (@ColumnName, @ExcludedColumn) =0)
                                BEGIN
                                SET @ColumnList = '['+@ColumnName+']'
                                SET @DeleteOutputList = 'DELETED.'+'['+@ColumnName+']'
                                END
                                SET @initFlag = 1
                END
                ELSE
                -- not first column
                BEGIN
                        -- first pk
                        IF @initFlag2 = 0 and @PrimaryKey =1
                        BEGIN
                                SET @PkList = '['+@ColumnName+']'
                                SET @JoinList = 's.['+@ColumnName+']' + ' = ' + 't.['+@ColumnName+']'
                                SET @WhereJoinList = 's.['+@ColumnName+']' + ' IS NULL '
                                SET @WhereJoinList_Insert = 't.['+@ColumnName+']' + ' IS NULL '
                                SET @initFlag2 = 1
                        END
                        ELSE
                        BEGIN
                                IF @PrimaryKey =1
                                BEGIN
                                        SET @PkList = @PkList + ',' +'['+@ColumnName+']'
                                        SET @JoinList = @JoinList + ' AND ' + 's.['+@ColumnName+']' + ' =
' + 't.['+@ColumnName+']'
```

```
                                        SET @WhereJoinList = @WhereJoinList + ' OR ' +
's.['+@ColumnName+']' + ' IS NULL '
                                        SET @WhereJoinList_Insert = @WhereJoinList_Insert + ' OR ' +
't.['+@ColumnName+']' + ' IS NULL '
                                END
                        END
                        -- first required (non null)
                        IF @initFlag3 = 0 and @RequiredValue =1
                        BEGIN
                                SET @RequiredColList = '['+@ColumnName+']'
                                SET @UpdateErrList = ' +case when isnull( ' +'['+@ColumnName+']' +
' ,'''')='''' then ''' +'['+@ColumnName+']' + ' is blank; '' else '''' end '
                                SET @WhereList = '['+@ColumnName+']' + ' IS NULL '
                                SET @initFlag3 = 1
                        END
                        ELSE
                        BEGIN
                        IF @RequiredValue =1
                                BEGIN
                                        SET @RequiredColList = @RequiredColList + ',' +
'['+@ColumnName+']'
                                        SET @UpdateErrList = @UpdateErrList + ' +case when isnull( '
+'['+@ColumnName+']' + ' ,'''')='''' then ''' +'['+@ColumnName+']' + ' is blank; '' else '''' end '
                                        SET @WhereList = @WhereList + ' OR ' + '['+@ColumnName+']' + ' IS
NULL '
                                END
                        END

                        IF LEN(@TransformCode) > 2
                        BEGIN
                                SET @TransformCodeCatch = @TransformCode
                                SET @ColumnName = @TransformCode
                                SET @ColumnList = @ColumnList + ',' +@ColumnName
                        END
                        ELSE
                        BEGIN
                                SET @ColName = @ColumnName
                                SET @FullColumnList = @FullColumnList + ',' +'['+@ColumnName+']'
                                IF (@ExcludedColumn IS NULL) OR (@ExcludedColumn IS NOT NULL AND
[dbo].[ufnIsInclude] (@ColumnName, @ExcludedColumn) =0)
                                BEGIN
                                        SET @ColumnList = @ColumnList + ',' +'['+@ColumnName+']'
                                        SET @DeleteOutputList = @DeleteOutputList + ',' +
'DELETED.'+'['+@ColumnName+']'
                                END
                                IF @PrimaryKey =0
                                BEGIN
                                        IF (@initFlag4 = 0 AND @ExcludedColumn IS NULL) OR (@initFlag4 = 0
AND @ExcludedColumn IS NOT NULL AND [dbo].[ufnIsInclude] (@ColumnName, @ExcludedColumn) =0)
                                        BEGIN
                                                SET @UpdateList = '['+@ColumnName+']' + ' = ' +
's.['+@ColumnName+']'
                                                SET @ColumnCompareList = 't.['+@ColumnName+']' + ' <> ' +
's.['+@ColumnName+']'
                                                SET @initFlag4 = 1
                                        END
                                        ELSE
                                        IF (@initFlag4 = 1  AND @ExcludedColumn IS NULL) OR (@initFlag4 =
1 AND @ExcludedColumn IS NOT NULL AND [dbo].[ufnIsInclude] (@ColumnName, @ExcludedColumn) =0)
                                        BEGIN
                                                SET @UpdateList = @UpdateList + ',' + '['+@ColumnName+']' +
' = ' + 's.['+@ColumnName+']'
                                                SET @ColumnCompareList = @ColumnCompareList + ' OR ' +
't.['+@ColumnName+']' + ' <> ' + 's.['+@ColumnName+']'
                                        END
                                END
                        END
                END

        FETCH NEXT FROM curTemplateColumnTable INTO @TableName,      @ColumnName,@DataType,@PrimaryKey
```

```
        END
        CLOSE curTemplateColumnTable
        DEALLOCATE curTemplateColumnTable

print '@pklist: ' + @PkList
print '@ColumnList: ' +@ColumnList
print '@JoinList: ' + @JoinList
print '@WhereJoinList: ' + @WhereJoinList
print '@WhereJoinList_Insert: ' + @WhereJoinList_Insert
print '@UpdateList: ' + @UpdateList
print '@ColumnCompareList: ' + @ColumnCompareList
print '@WhereList: ' + @WhereList
PRINT '@DeleteOutputList = ' + @DeleteOutputList
print '@UpdateErrList: ' +@UpdateErrList;

BEGIN TRY
-- refresh target table
                        SET @sqlstr1 = '';
                        -- create TARGET DELETE scripts
                        SET @sColumnList = replace(@ColumnList, '[','s.[')
print '@sColumnList: ' + @sColumnList

-- count rows from sourece table if source table empty quit process
SET @sqlstrCountRow = N'SELECT @Rowcount = COUNT(*) FROM
@SourceDatabaseName.@SourceSchemaName.[@SourceTableName] '
                        SET
@sqlstrCountRow=REPLACE(@sqlstrCountRow,'@SourceDatabaseName',@SourceDatabaseName)
                        SET
@sqlstrCountRow=REPLACE(@sqlstrCountRow,'@SourceTableName',@SourceTableName)
                        SET
@sqlstrCountRow=REPLACE(@sqlstrCountRow,'@SourceSchemaName',@SourceSchemaName)
print @sqlstrCountRow
                        EXECUTE SP_EXECUTESQL @sqlstrCountRow, N'@Rowcount int output', @Rowcount
output
print ' @RowCount = ' + convert(varchar(30), @RowCount) + ' @@ROWCOUNT= ' + convert(varchar(30),
@@RowCount)

IF @ROWCount = 0
BEGIN
        PRINT 'Source Table is empty ' + @SourceTableName + ' quit process.'
        RETURN
END

-- check if is instructed for delete
IF CHARINDEX('DELETE',@UpdateType) > 0
BEGIN

-- delete rows
                        SET @sqlstr1 = N'
                        DELETE FROM [@DestDatabaseName].@DestSchemaName.[@DestTableName]
                        FROM [@DestDatabaseName].@DestSchemaName.[@DestTableName] t
                        LEFT OUTER JOIN [@SourceDatabaseName].@SourceSchemaName.[@SourceTableName] s
                                ON @JoinList WHERE (@WhereJoinList)'
print 'delete Script:'+@sqlstr1
                        SET @sqlstr1=REPLACE(@sqlstr1,'@DestDatabaseName',@DestDatabaseName)
                        SET @sqlstr1=REPLACE(@sqlstr1,'@SourceDatabaseName',@SourceDatabaseName)
                        SET @sqlstr1=REPLACE(@sqlstr1,'@SourceSchemaName',@SourceSchemaName)
                        SET @sqlstr1=REPLACE(@sqlstr1,'@DestSchemaName',@DestSchemaName)
                        SET @sqlstr1=REPLACE(@sqlstr1,'@DestTableName',@DestTableName)
                        SET @sqlstr1=REPLACE(@sqlstr1,'@SourceTableName',@SourceTableName)
-- keeep sequence right
                        SET @sqlstr1=REPLACE(@sqlstr1,'@WhereJoinList',@WhereJoinList)
                        SET @sqlstr1=REPLACE(@sqlstr1,'@JoinList',@JoinList)
print 'Delete Script:'+@NL+@sqlstr1

BEGIN TRANSACTION
                        EXECUTE SP_EXECUTESQL @sqlstr1;
COMMIT TRANSACTION
                        SET @RowCount = @@ROWCOUNT;
```

```
print convert(varchar(30), @RowCount) + ' rows deleted'

END
-- insert into #temp table
IF CHARINDEX('DISTINCT',@UpdateType) > 0
BEGIN

                    SET @sqlstr1 =N'
                    INSERT INTO [@DestDatabaseName].@DestSchemaName.[@DestTableName] (@ColumnList)

                    SELECT DISTINCT @sColumnList
                    FROM [@SourceDatabaseName].@SourceSchemaName.[@SourceTableName] s
                    LEFT OUTER JOIN [@DestDatabaseName].@DestSchemaName.[@DestTableName] t
                           ON @JoinList
                    WHERE (@WhereJoinList_Insert) ';
END
ELSE
BEGIN
       SET @sqlstr1 = N'
                    INSERT INTO [@DestDatabaseName].@DestSchemaName.[@DestTableName] (@ColumnList)

                    SELECT @sColumnList
                    FROM [@SourceDatabaseName].@SourceSchemaName.[@SourceTableName] s
                    LEFT OUTER JOIN [@DestDatabaseName].@DestSchemaName.[@DestTableName] t
                           ON @JoinList
                    WHERE (@WhereJoinList_Insert) ';
END

                    IF @FilterCondition IS NOT NULL
                    BEGIN
                    SET @sqlstr1 = @sqlstr1+N' AND ' + '(' + @FilterCondition +') '
                    END

print 'insert Target Script:'+@sqlstr1
                    SET @sqlstr1=REPLACE(@sqlstr1,'@DestDatabaseName',@DestDatabaseName)
                    SET @sqlstr1=REPLACE(@sqlstr1,'@SourceDatabaseName',@SourceDatabaseName)
                    SET @sqlstr1=REPLACE(@sqlstr1,'@SourceSchemaName',@SourceSchemaName)
                    SET @sqlstr1=REPLACE(@sqlstr1,'@DestSchemaName',@DestSchemaName)
                    SET @sqlstr1=REPLACE(@sqlstr1,'@DestTableName',@DestTableName)
                    SET @sqlstr1=REPLACE(@sqlstr1,'@SourceTableName',@SourceTableName)
                    SET @sqlstr1=REPLACE(@sqlstr1,'@WhereJoinList_Insert',@WhereJoinList_Insert)
                    SET @sqlstr1=REPLACE(@sqlstr1,'@JoinList',@JoinList)
                    SET @sqlstr1=REPLACE(@sqlstr1,'@sColumnList',@sColumnList)
                    SET @sqlstr1=REPLACE(@sqlstr1,'@FilterCondition',ISNULL(@FilterCondition, ' '))
                    SET @sqlstr1=REPLACE(@sqlstr1,'@ColumnList',@ColumnList)
print 'Insert Target Script:'+@NL+@sqlstr1

       BEGIN TRANSACTION
                    EXECUTE SP_EXECUTESQL @sqlstr1;
                    SET @RowCount = @@ROWCOUNT;

-- update. Use ChangeControl if parameter @UpdateType indicate usage
                    IF @LastModifiedDateColumn IS NOT NULL AND
CHARINDEX('ChangeControl',@UpdateType) > 0
                    -- use only changecontrol (LastModifiedDate) to compare
                    BEGIN
                           SET @ColumnCompareList = N's.' + @LastModifiedDateColumn + N' > t.' +
@LastModifiedDateColumn
                    END
                    ELSE
                    BEGIN
                           IF @LastModifiedDateColumn IS NOT NULL
                                  BEGIN
                                  PRINT 'Use ' +       @LastModifiedDateColumn
                                  END
                    END

IF CHARINDEX('DISTINCT',@UpdateType) > 0
BEGIN
       SET @sqlstrUpdate = N'
```

```
                    UPDATE @DestDatabaseName.@DestSchemaName.[@DestTableName]
                    SET @UpdateList
                    FROM @DestDatabaseName.@DestSchemaName.[@DestTableName] t
                    JOIN (SELECT DISTINCT @ColumnList FROM
@SourceDatabaseName.@SourceSchemaName.[@SourceTableName] ) s
                          ON @JoinList WHERE (@ColumnCompareList)';
END
ELSE
BEGIN
      SET @sqlstrUpdate = N'
                    UPDATE @DestDatabaseName.@DestSchemaName.[@DestTableName]
                    SET @UpdateList
                    FROM @DestDatabaseName.@DestSchemaName.[@DestTableName] t
                    JOIN @SourceDatabaseName.@SourceSchemaName.[@SourceTableName] s
                          ON @JoinList WHERE (@ColumnCompareList)';
END
print 'Update Target Script:'+@sqlstrUpdate
                    SET @sqlstrUpdate=REPLACE(@sqlstrUpdate,'@DestDatabaseName',@DestDatabaseName)
                    SET
@sqlstrUpdate=REPLACE(@sqlstrUpdate,'@SourceDatabaseName',@SourceDatabaseName)
                    SET @sqlstrUpdate=REPLACE(@sqlstrUpdate,'@SourceSchemaName',@SourceSchemaName)
                    SET @sqlstrUpdate=REPLACE(@sqlstrUpdate,'@DestSchemaName',@DestSchemaName)
                    SET @sqlstrUpdate=REPLACE(@sqlstrUpdate,'@DestTableName',@DestTableName)
                    SET @sqlstrUpdate=REPLACE(@sqlstrUpdate,'@SourceTableName',@SourceTableName)
                    SET @sqlstrUpdate=REPLACE(@sqlstrUpdate,'@JoinList',@JoinList)
                    SET @sqlstrUpdate=REPLACE(@sqlstrUpdate,'@ColumnList',@ColumnList)
                    SET
@sqlstrUpdate=REPLACE(@sqlstrUpdate,'@ColumnCompareList',@ColumnCompareList)
                    SET @sqlstrUpdate=REPLACE(@sqlstrUpdate,'@UpdateList',@UpdateList)
print 'Update Script:'+@NL+@sqlstrUpdate
                    EXECUTE SP_EXECUTESQL @sqlstrUpdate;
                    SET @RowCount = @@ROWCOUNT;

COMMIT TRANSACTION
END TRY
   BEGIN CATCH
   ROLLBACK TRANSACTION
print @ErrorNumber
print @ErrorMessage
 -- error handling routine here
   END CATCH
RETURN
```

5.3.6.7.1 Usages:

This procedure can be called with following parameters:

```
execute [dbo].[RefreshTable]
            @SourceDatabaseName = 'AdventureWorks',
            @SourceSchemaName ='Production',
            @SourceTableName = 'tes_TempProductInventory',
            @DestDatabaseName = 'AdventureWorks',
            @DestSchemaName ='Production',
            @DestTableName = 'tes_ProductInventory',
            @ExcludedColumn = 'ModifiedDate',
            @UpdateType= 'DELETE DISTINCT test',
            @LastModifiedDateColumn ='ModifiedDate',
            @FilterCondition = NULL,
            @RefreshTable = NULL
```

It generates and executes the following SQL code: without specify UpdateType as 'ChangeControl' procedure doing compare each column to determine update.

```
Delete Script:
                    DELETE FROM [AdventureWorks].Production.[tes_ProductInventory]
                    FROM [AdventureWorks].Production.[tes_ProductInventory] t
                    LEFT OUTER JOIN [AdventureWorks].Production.[tes_TempProductInventory] s
                          ON s.[ProductID] = t.[ProductID] AND s.[LocationID] = t.[LocationID]
WHERE (s.[ProductID] IS NULL OR s.[LocationID] IS NULL )
Insert Target Script:
                    INSERT INTO [AdventureWorks].Production.[tes_ProductInventory]
([ProductID],[LocationID],[Shelf],[Bin],[Quantity],[rowguid])
```

```
                    SELECT DISTINCT
s.[ProductID],s.[LocationID],s.[Shelf],s.[Bin],s.[Quantity],s.[rowguid]
                    FROM [AdventureWorks].Production.[tes_TempProductInventory] s
                    LEFT OUTER JOIN [AdventureWorks].Production.[tes_ProductInventory] t
                          ON s.[ProductID] = t.[ProductID] AND s.[LocationID] = t.[LocationID]
                    WHERE (t.[ProductID] IS NULL OR t.[LocationID] IS NULL )
Update Script:
                    UPDATE AdventureWorks.Production.[tes_ProductInventory]
                    SET [Shelf] = s.[Shelf],[Bin] = s.[Bin],[Quantity] = s.[Quantity],[rowguid] =
s.[rowguid]
                    FROM AdventureWorks.Production.[tes_ProductInventory] t
                    JOIN (SELECT DISTINCT
[ProductID],[LocationID],[Shelf],[Bin],[Quantity],[rowguid] FROM
AdventureWorks.Production.[tes_TempProductInventory] ) s
                          ON s.[ProductID] = t.[ProductID] AND s.[LocationID] = t.[LocationID]
WHERE (t.[Shelf] <> s.[Shelf] OR t.[Bin] <> s.[Bin] OR t.[Quantity] <> s.[Quantity] OR t.[rowguid]
<> s.[rowguid])

execute [dbo].[RefreshTable]
             @SourceDatabaseName = 'AdventureWorks',
             @SourceSchemaName ='Production',
             @SourceTableName = 'tes_TempProductInventory',
             @DestDatabaseName = 'AdventureWorks',
             @DestSchemaName ='Production',
             @DestTableName = 'tes_ProductInventory',
             @ExcludedColumn = 'ModifiedDate',
             @UpdateType= 'DELETE DISTINCT ChangeControl test',
             @LastModifiedDateColumn ='ModifiedDate',
             @FilTerCondition = NULL,
             @RefreshTable = NULL
```

This procedure call use parameter UpdateType= ChangeControl and LastModifiedDateColumn = 'ModifiedDate' so that procedure compare modifieddate to determine update.

```
Delete Script:
                    DELETE FROM [AdventureWorks].Production.[tes_ProductInventory]
                    FROM [AdventureWorks].Production.[tes_ProductInventory] t
                    LEFT OUTER JOIN [AdventureWorks].Production.[tes_TempProductInventory] s
                          ON s.[ProductID] = t.[ProductID] AND s.[LocationID] = t.[LocationID]
WHERE (s.[ProductID] IS NULL OR s.[LocationID] IS NULL )
Insert Target Script:
                    INSERT INTO [AdventureWorks].Production.[tes_ProductInventory]
([ProductID],[LocationID],[Shelf],[Bin],[Quantity],[rowguid])
                    SELECT DISTINCT
s.[ProductID],s.[LocationID],s.[Shelf],s.[Bin],s.[Quantity],s.[rowguid]
                    FROM [AdventureWorks].Production.[tes_TempProductInventory] s
                    LEFT OUTER JOIN [AdventureWorks].Production.[tes_ProductInventory] t
                          ON s.[ProductID] = t.[ProductID] AND s.[LocationID] = t.[LocationID]
                    WHERE (t.[ProductID] IS NULL OR t.[LocationID] IS NULL )
Update Script:
                    UPDATE AdventureWorks.Production.[tes_ProductInventory]
                    SET [Shelf] = s.[Shelf],[Bin] = s.[Bin],[Quantity] = s.[Quantity],[rowguid] =
s.[rowguid]
                    FROM AdventureWorks.Production.[tes_ProductInventory] t
                    JOIN (SELECT DISTINCT
[ProductID],[LocationID],[Shelf],[Bin],[Quantity],[rowguid] FROM
AdventureWorks.Production.[tes_TempProductInventory] ) s
                          ON s.[ProductID] = t.[ProductID] AND s.[LocationID] = t.[LocationID] WHE
(s.ModifiedDate > t.ModifiedDate)
```

5.3.7 Data Extraction

5.3.7.1 Data Extraction

Change Data Capture will be done by using the following methords:

- o Time stamps (insert/update datetime)
- o Partition
- o Using minus query with comparison of data
- o Triggers
- o Materialized view log or stream LCR (Logical change Record)
- o Transaction log

5.3.7.2 Extract data into files

- o Use SQL*Plus extract data and dump into text files
- o Use OCI or Pro*C extract data
- o Use Oracle Export Utility
- o Use Oracle Utl_File
- o Remote data replication or snapshot
- o Transaction log reader

5.3.7.3 Example of using SQL*Plus extract file:

Example A:

The UNIX file invokes Oracle SQL Plus and run a SQL file from which extract data from database into file:

```
# runsqlfil
# run a sql file
echo $0
# pass sql file name as parameter
sqlfil=$1
# get password from a secure place
pass1=/export/home/etl/Informatica/PowerCenter/passetl
# invoke a SQL*Plus session
sqlplus -s <<EOF
@$pass1
@$sqlfil
EOF
```

Note: between <<EOF and EOF is SQL*Plus session. @$pass1 is a password file; @$sqlfil is SQL file.

Sqlfil is a SQL FILE contains SQL queries like the following: (in following example, '|' has been used as delimiter to separate fields.

```
SELECT t1.column1 ||'|'|| t2.column2
FROM table1 t1, table2 t2
WHERE t1.col_id = t2.col_id
AND t1.column1= 'xname';
```

Example B:
The UNIX file invokes Oracle SQL Plus and set the format for output flat file run a SQL file which extract data from database and output file to operating system (UNIX):

```
# runsqlflatfil
# run sql file and generate flat file format
#echo $0
# pass sql file name as parameter
sqlfil=$1
# get password from a secure place
pass1=/export/home/etl/Informatica/PowerCenter/passetl

# invoke a SQL*Plus session and setup output format
sqlplus -s <<EOF
@$pass1
SET NEWPAGE 0
SET SPACE 0
SET LINESIZE 1024
SET PAGESIZE 0
SET ECHO OFF
SET FEEDBACK OFF
SET HEADING OFF
SET MARKUP HTML OFF SPOOL OFF
@$sqlfil
EOF
```

Note: between <<EOF and EOF is SQL*Plus session. @$pass1 is a password file; @$sqlfil is SQL file.

Example C:
The UNIX file read the SQL file list from a file and kickoff all of them such as file above which invokes Oracle SQL Plus and set the format for output flat file and extract data from database and output file to operating system (UNIX):

Here's how it starts:

```
# kicksqljob1
# kick off sql query file from given file name
# pass file name as parameter
# fil=$1
# compose output file name
outfil="/export/home/etl/prog1/outfil_$1.out"
# remove files
rm $outfil
# loop through sql list
for i in `cat sqlfil_$1.lst`
do
runsqlflatfil $i >> $outfil
done
```

5.3.8.4 Extact data from the different databases

SQL SERVER Integration Services (SSIS) and Oracle Gateway can be used to establish links between different databases, those are important tools for data integration. Let's look at an example from SQL SERVER – linked servers:

From following example, we use linked server create a link from SQL Server to Oracle, extract data from Oracle database. In this example, SQL Server as target database server, meanwhle Oracle as source databae server.

1. At beginning, add a linked server by execute system stored procedure sp_addlinkedserverfrom SQL SERVER:
exec sp_addlinkedserver 'orayewtree', 'Oracle', 'MSDAORA', 'yewtree'

Note:
linked server name as orayewtree
'MSDAORA' is OLE DB for Oracle
'yewtree' is an Orale database

2. Create logg in by execute another system procedure sp_addlinkedsrvlogin:
exec sp_addlinkedsrvlogin 'orayewtree', false, NULL, 'firtree', 'FIRTREE1'

Note: 'firtree' and 'FIRTREE1' are Oracle user name and password

3a. After creation of linked server, use following SQL query against the linked server:

pseudo code:
SELECT * FROM *linkedserver_name..schemaname.table_name*

SQL query:
SELECT * FROM orayewtree..FIRTREE.RPT_MAIN

3b. We can create a table function from SQL SERVER 2000 to help the linked server access:

CREATE FUNCTION fn_oracledb1_rpt_main (@rpt_id INT)
RETURNS TABLE
AS RETURN (SELECT * FROM orayewtree..FIRTREE.RPT_MAIN WHERE rpt_id = @rpt_id)
then we can call this function from SQL SERVER 2000 and get data from the external database, for example, extract the record (id is 10) from table called RPT_MAIN under schema Pinetree in Oracle database called firtree:
SELECT * FROM fn_oracledb1_rpt_main(10)

5.3.8 Loading and Transformation

5.3.8.1 Import file into database

Syntax:
Imp user/password **parfile**=parameter file name

Example:
UNIX command file
# import table
# parameter: parameter file name with path
parfl=$1
imp usr/passwd parfile=$parfl

The parameter file describe import process
#import table par file
table name: OTHERMEMBERS_SN
file path(only the export file can be used)

FILE=/u04/export/otherbird.dmp
FROMUSER=gold_finch
TOUSER=chickadee
TABLES=(OTHERBIRDS)

5.3.8.2 Use Oracle SQL loader

Using control file, data file and command file.
Control file describe loading process.
Example A:
Control File: loadtab_emaildom.ctl
load data
infile 'output5.txt'
DISCARDFILE 'output5.dsc'
DISCARDMAX 99999
APPEND
into table email_dom
fields terminated by '|'
(email_id)

load file into database

UNIX File loadtabl:
# loadtabl
# load data into table from a flat file
loadtab_ctl=$1
sqlldr userid=usr/passwd **control**=$loadtab_ctl **log**=loadtabl.log

Example B:
Control File: loadtab_sub.ctl:
load data
infile '/$SRC/s_to_lower.txt'
into table s_unsubl
fields terminated by '|'
(key1, email_id)

5.3.8.3 Data Transformation

- o use CREATE TABLE AS SELECT …to form a staging table (study the email domains: extract distinct, the rest of email address part after '@' and convert it to lower case:
- o Use SQL CREATE TABLE AS SELECT is a powerful SQL which can do mass transformations:

```
create table email_dom NOLOGGING as
SELECT distinct lower(substr(email_id,instr(email_id,'@',1,1),length(email_id)+1 - instr(email_id,'@',1,1))) email_id
FROM email_dom_tmp
```

5.3.8.4 Key lookup

Data warehouse loading always involved with key loopup process, for example in dimension table loading we must compare the key between source and target to see if the record exist in the target table in order to determine possible process shuch as insert or update. During the fact table loading, we must get key from related dimension table first then insert record into fact table with those keys.

The following examples describe how to use defined functions to do key lookup (in the examples, we use dynamic SQL):

Example A:
At first, define a function, which accept dimension table name, primary key column name, match condition as parameters and return primary key from dimension table.

```
CREATE OR REPLACE FUNCTION GET_DIM_KEY2
(p_tab_name IN VARCHAR2,p_key_column_name IN
VARCHAR2,p_match IN VARCHAR2)
RETURN NUMBER IS
q_string VARCHAR2(4000);

v_key_value number default null;
BEGIN
q_string:= 'SELECT ' ||p_key_column_name ||
      ' FROM '|| p_tab_name ||
      ' WHERE ' || p_match;

-- DBMS_OUTPUT.PUT_LINE(q_string);
EXECUTE IMMEDIATE    q_string INTO v_key_value;
RETURN v_key_value;
EXCEPTION
   WHEN NO_DATA_FOUND THEN
    RETURN NULL;
END;
/
```

Usage: Use dimension table (products), primary key column, and match condition as parameters call function and find related primary key value:

In the real usage, you can use column variable call function.

```
SELECT GET_DIM_KEY2('products', 'prod_id', 'prod_name =
'||'''Cat F''' || ' AND supplier_id = 168 ') FROM DUAL;
```

Use customer dimension table(custormers), primary key column and match condition as parameters call function and find primary key:

```
SELECT GET_DIM_KEY2('customers', 'cust_id',
 'cust_first_name = '||'''Ab''' ||
 ' AND cust_last_name = '||'''Eve''' ||
 ' AND cust_postal_code = 58488 ')
FROM DUAL;
```

Example B:

At first, define a function, which accept dimension table name, primary key column name, match value as parameters and return primary key from dimension table.

```
CREATE OR REPLACE FUNCTION GET_DIM_KEY
(p_tab_name IN VARCHAR2
,p_key_column_name IN VARCHAR2
,p_match_key IN VARCHAR2
,p_match_value IN VARCHAR2)
 RETURN varchar2 IS
q_string VARCHAR2(4000);
v_key_value varchar2(20) default null;
BEGIN
q_string:= 'SELECT ' ||p_key_column_name ||
      ' FROM '|| p_tab_name ||
      ' WHERE '||p_match_key ||' = '||p_match_value;
EXECUTE IMMEDIATE q_string INTO v_key_value ;
--DBMS_OUTPUT.PUT_LINE(q_string||'    key    value    is:
'||v_key_value);
RETURN v_key_value;
EXCEPTION
   WHEN NO_DATA_FOUND THEN
    RETURN NULL;
END;
/
```

Usage:
Use dimension table (channels), primary key column, and match value as parameters call function and find related primary key value:

In the real usage, you can use column variable call function.

```
SELECT         GET_DIM_KEY('channels',         'channel_id',
'channel_desc','''Direct Sales''')
FROM DUAL;
```

5.3.8.5 Load data into a dimension table – SQL Server T-SQL Exsample

Here is an example of insert/update data loading in **SQL Server** using stored procedure. In the following example, the procedure update dimension table (dim_EventStatus) based on a staging table (EvntStatus_staging):

```
CREATE PROCEDURE Ins_EventStatus
AS
-- insert new
INSERT INTO dbo.EventStatus (EventStatus_pk, EventStatus, LastUpdate)
SELECT dimEventStatus_pk, EventStatusName, LastUpdate
FROM (
SELECT     es.EventStatus_pk,     es.EventStatusName,     es.LastUpdate,
des.EventStatus_pk AS dimEventStatus_pk, des.EventStatus
FROM dbo.EventStatus_staging es
LEFT OUTER JOIN dbo.EventStatus des
ON es.EventStatus_pk = des.EventStatus_pk
) a
WHERE dimEventStatus_pk IS NULL

-- update table when key match and StatusName not match or statusName is
null
UPDATE dbo.EventStatus
SET EventStatus = es.EventStatusName
FROM dbo.EventStatus_staging es
INNER JOIN dbo.EventStatus des
ON es.EventStatus_pk = des.EventStatus_pk
WHERE     des.EventStatus     IS     NULL     OR     des.EventStatus     !=
es.EventStatusName
```

5.3.8.6 Parse data – SQL Server T-SQL Example

In order to get useful data from seems unuserful data block or mess, parse function or utilities have to be created.

Here is an example which how useful dataset such as domain names, page names have been extracted through parsing an internet logging records.

```
/* exec dbo.refreshDomainPages -------*/
INSERT INTO [DomainPages] SELECT
domainName=SUBSTRING(LogMessage,(CHARINDEX('http://',LogM
essage)+7),((CHARINDEX('/', LogMessage,8))-8))
,domainPage = SUBSTRING(LogMessage,(CHARINDEX('http://',
LogMessage)+7),(LEN(LogMessage)-7))
FROM dbo.WeblogR
WHERE LogMessage like 'http://%'
and SUBSTRING(LogMessage,(CHARINDEX('http://', LogMessage)
+ 7), (LEN(LogMessage)- 7))
 not in
(SELECT DomainPage FROM [DomainPages])
```

LogMessage
http://mydomain/myMainRedPagevvvvvv
http://mydomain/myMainBluePagevvvvvv
http://hisdomain/myMainYellowPagevvvvvv
http://whodomain/myMainGreenPagevvvvvv

domainName	domainPage
mydomain	mydomain/myMainRedPagevvvvvv
mydomain	mydomain/myMainBluePagevvvvvv
hisdomain	hisdomain/myMainYellowPagevvvvvv
whodomain	whodomain/myMainGreenPagevvvvvv

Parse information from URL - SQL Server T-SQL Example
Case: when you search in Google using key words ('pacific yew', 'wild mushroom'...)
Parse URL string based on key such as '#hl=', 'source=', 'q=', 'aqi=' and '&', function CHARINDEX returns position in string when found.

```
SELECT
domainName=SUBSTRING(ClickThroughURL,(CHARINDEX('http://'
,ClickThroughURL)+7),((CHARINDEX('/',
ClickThroughURL,8))-8))
,#hl2 = CASE
WHEN CHARINDEX('#hl=', ClickThroughURL)= 0 THEN NULL
WHEN CHARINDEX('#hl=', ClickThroughURL) >0 AND
CHARINDEX('&', ClickThroughURL,CHARINDEX('#hl=',
ClickThroughURL)) =0
THEN SUBSTRING(ClickThroughURL,(CHARINDEX('#hl=',
ClickThroughURL) + 4)
 , LEN(ClickThroughURL) - (CHARINDEX('#hl=',
ClickThroughURL)+4))
ELSE
SUBSTRING(ClickThroughURL,(CHARINDEX('#hl=',
ClickThroughURL) + 4)
 , CHARINDEX('&', ClickThroughURL,CHARINDEX('#hl=',
ClickThroughURL)) - (CHARINDEX('#hl=',
ClickThroughURL)+4))
END
,source = CASE
WHEN CHARINDEX('source=', ClickThroughURL)= 0 THEN NULL
WHEN CHARINDEX('source=', ClickThroughURL) >0 AND
CHARINDEX('&', ClickThroughURL,CHARINDEX('source=',
ClickThroughURL)) =0
THEN SUBSTRING(ClickThroughURL,(CHARINDEX('source=',
ClickThroughURL) + 7)
 , LEN(ClickThroughURL) - (CHARINDEX('source=',
ClickThroughURL)+7))
ELSE
```

```
SUBSTRING(ClickThroughURL,(CHARINDEX('source=',
ClickThroughURL) + 7)
 , CHARINDEX('&', ClickThroughURL,CHARINDEX('source=',
ClickThroughURL)) - (CHARINDEX('source=',
ClickThroughURL)+7))
END
,q = CASE
WHEN CHARINDEX('q=', ClickThroughURL)= 0 THEN NULL
WHEN CHARINDEX('q=', ClickThroughURL) >0 AND CHARINDEX('&',
ClickThroughURL,CHARINDEX('q=', ClickThroughURL)) =0
THEN SUBSTRING(ClickThroughURL,(CHARINDEX('q=',
ClickThroughURL) + 2)
 , LEN(ClickThroughURL) - (CHARINDEX('q=',
ClickThroughURL)+2))
ELSE
SUBSTRING(ClickThroughURL,(CHARINDEX('q=',
ClickThroughURL) + 2)
 , CHARINDEX('&',ClickThroughURL,CHARINDEX('q=',
ClickThroughURL)) - (CHARINDEX('q=', ClickThroughURL)+2))
END
,aq = CASE
WHEN CHARINDEX('aq=', ClickThroughURL)= 0 THEN NULL
WHEN CHARINDEX('aq=', ClickThroughURL) >0 AND CHARINDEX('&',
ClickThroughURL,CHARINDEX('aq=', ClickThroughURL)) =0
THEN SUBSTRING(ClickThroughURL,(CHARINDEX('aq=',
ClickThroughURL) + 3)
 , LEN(ClickThroughURL) - (CHARINDEX('aq=',
ClickThroughURL)+3))
ELSE
SUBSTRING(ClickThroughURL,(CHARINDEX('aq=',
ClickThroughURL) + 3)
```

```
 , CHARINDEX('&',ClickThroughURL,CHARINDEX('aq=',
ClickThroughURL)) - (CHARINDEX('aq=', ClickThroughURL)+3))
END
,aqi = CASE
WHEN CHARINDEX('aqi=', ClickThroughURL)= 0 THEN NULL
WHEN CHARINDEX('aqi=', ClickThroughURL) >0 AND
CHARINDEX('&', ClickThroughURL,CHARINDEX('aqi=',
ClickThroughURL)) =0
THEN SUBSTRING(ClickThroughURL,(CHARINDEX('aqi=',
ClickThroughURL) + 4)
 , LEN(ClickThroughURL) - (CHARINDEX('aqi=',
ClickThroughURL)+4))
ELSE
SUBSTRING(ClickThroughURL,(CHARINDEX('aqi=',
ClickThroughURL) + 4)
 , CHARINDEX('&',ClickThroughURL,CHARINDEX('aqi=',
ClickThroughURL)) - (CHARINDEX('aqi=',
ClickThroughURL)+4))
END
,oq = CASE
WHEN CHARINDEX('oq=', ClickThroughURL)= 0 THEN NULL
WHEN CHARINDEX('oq=', ClickThroughURL) >0 AND CHARINDEX('&',
ClickThroughURL,CHARINDEX('oq=', ClickThroughURL)) =0
THEN SUBSTRING(ClickThroughURL,(CHARINDEX('oq=',
ClickThroughURL) + 3)
 , LEN(ClickThroughURL) - (CHARINDEX('oq=',
ClickThroughURL)+3))
ELSE
SUBSTRING(ClickThroughURL,(CHARINDEX('oq=',
ClickThroughURL) + 3)
 , CHARINDEX('&',ClickThroughURL,CHARINDEX('oq=',
ClickThroughURL)) - (CHARINDEX('oq=', ClickThroughURL)+3))
```

```
END
,fp = CASE
WHEN CHARINDEX('fp=', ClickThroughURL)= 0 THEN NULL
WHEN CHARINDEX('fp=', ClickThroughURL) >0 AND CHARINDEX('&',
ClickThroughURL,CHARINDEX('fp=', ClickThroughURL)) =0
THEN SUBSTRING(ClickThroughURL,(CHARINDEX('fp=',
ClickThroughURL) + 3)
 , LEN(ClickThroughURL) - (CHARINDEX('fp=',
ClickThroughURL)+3))
ELSE
SUBSTRING(ClickThroughURL,(CHARINDEX('fp=',
ClickThroughURL) + 3)
 , CHARINDEX('&',ClickThroughURL,CHARINDEX('fp=',
ClickThroughURL)) - (CHARINDEX('fp=', ClickThroughURL)+3))
END
FROM URL_searchSample;
```

URL string

Search keyword	**ClickThroughURL**
Pacific yew	http://www.google.com/#hl=en&source=hp&q=pacific+yew&aq=f&aqi=g10&oq=&fp=a048890d3c90c6fc
spruse	http://www.google.com/#hl=en&source=hp&q=spruse&aq=f&aqi=g-s10&oq=&fp=a048890d3c90c6fc
Wild mushroom	http://www.google.com/#hl=en&q=wild+mushroom&aq=f&aqi=g10&oq=wild+mushroom&fp=a048890d3c90c6fc
Drift wood	http://www.google.com/#hl=en&q=drift+wood&aq=&aqi=g-s5g1g-s3g1&oq=drift+wood&fp=a048890d3c90c6fc

Parsed results

domainName	#hl2	source	q	aq	aqi	oq	fp
www.google.com	en	hp	pacific+yew	f	g10		a048890d3c90c6f
www.google.com	en	hp	spruse	f	g-s10		a048890d3c90c6f

5.3.9 ETL Main Process Flow

Figure shows how control flows from the main ETL to the associated routines. As you can see, the it normally start from dimension loading prior to all other objects such as fact table loading because system need to get key in order to update fact tables. It may also involving processing staging tables in staging area if there is such need. Writing recors into the log files also is necessary for purpose of tracking ETL jobs.

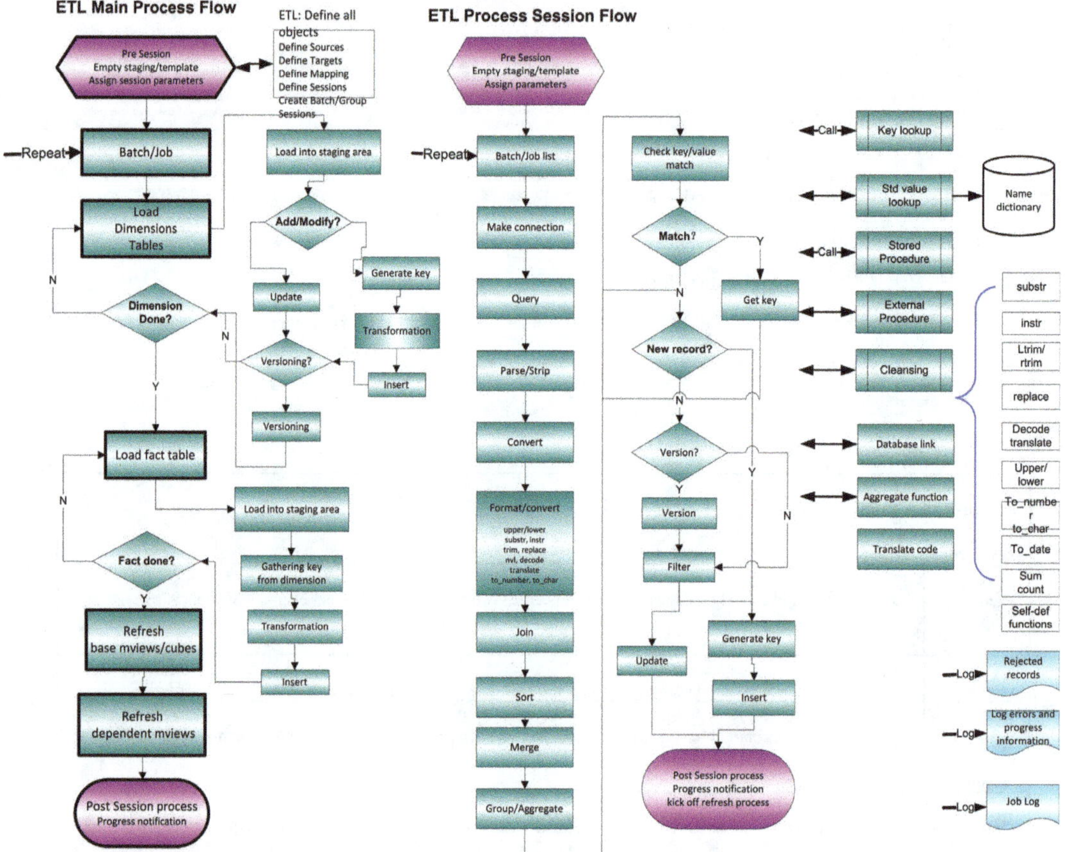

Figure 5-5.3-11 DwEtlMainProcessFlow

5.4 Summarizing Data

This chapter discusses the following topics:

- ❑ 5.4.1 Build OLAP Frame
- ❑ 5.4.2 Summary Preparation
- ❑ 5.4.3 Report Preparation
- ❑ 5.4.4 Refreshing the materialized views
- ❑ 5.4.5 Monitoring Database Refresh
- ❑ 5.4.6 Manage Mview Highlight

5.4.1 Build OLAP Framework

5.4.2 Summary Preparation

- ➢ Loading the detail data
- ➢ Updating or rebuilding the indexes on the detail data
- ➢ Performing quality assurance tests on the data

5.4.3 Generate/Refresh Mviews – the foundation of Report Preparation

A well-defined materialized view series should look like a tree with the stacked embedded materialized view, serving as the foundation or base for reporting system. A great deal can be accomplished by defining just a few core-materialized views/cubes, which serve as the alternate of monstrous fact table.

The mviews oftern play important roles in reporting, prepared mivews will be called directly instead of running the repeated queries on the execution time thus gain the following advantages:

- Reduce the expensive joining and aggregation computing operations,
- Reduce the number of scans against data warehouse fact table,
- Reduce response time greatly
- Efficient.
- Improve security greatly; user group can only access data from their mviews accordingly so that accessing underline tables (or other user group's data) can be avoided.

Defining such foundamenal mviews is a major task in the reporting systems design and developments. In this chapter we will frequently use some of these mviews such as Sum_sales_month_mv which already has done most necessary jonings and aggragations operations, in fact, it sometimes substitute the fact table as a quick shortcut.

5.4.4 Refreshing the materialized views

Use DBMS_MVIEW package

Note: second parameter 'C' makes the complete refresh.

```
begin
DBMS_MVIEW.REFRESH('sum_sales_month_mv',   'C',   '',TRUE,
FALSE, 0,0,0, FALSE);
end;
```

Note: second parameter '?' make the pakage try a fast refresh if possible otherwise do a complete refresh.

```
begin
DBMS_MVIEW.REFRESH('sum_sales_month_mv',   '?',   '',TRUE,
FALSE, 0,0,0, FALSE);
end;
```

Note: second parameter 'F' make the fast refresh.

```
begin
DBMS_MVIEW.REFRESH('sum_sales_month_mv',   'F',   '',TRUE,
FALSE, 0,0,0, FALSE);
end;
```

After refreshing the primary mview, we can start to refresh following dependent mviews.

```
begin
DBMS_MVIEW.REFRESH('sum_sales_channel_month_mv', '?',
'',TRUE, FALSE, 0,0,0, FALSE);
end;
begin
DBMS_MVIEW.REFRESH('sum_sales_county_mv', '?', '',TRUE,
FALSE, 0,0,0, FALSE);
end;
begin
DBMS_MVIEW.REFRESH('sum_sales_chan_city_mv', '?',
'',TRUE, FALSE, 0,0,0, FALSE);
end;
```

Use complete refresh during the first time refresh, second parameter'?' let database system decide which refresh method will be used (fast or complete).

```
begin
DBMS_MVIEW.REFRESH('sum_sales_all_month_mv', '?', '',TRUE,
FALSE, 0,0,0, FALSE);
end;
```

The following DBMS_MVIEW package will make fast refresh.

```
begin
DBMS_MVIEW.REFRESH('sum_sales_all_month_mv', 'F', '',TRUE,
FALSE, 0,0,0, FALSE);
end;
```

5.4.5 Monitoring Data Warehouse Refresh

5.4.5.1 DBMS_MVIEW

DBMS _MVIEW provides three different types of refresh operations:

- o DBMS _MVIEW.REFRESH - Refresh one or more materialized views.
- o DBMS _MVIEW.REFRESH _ALL _MVIEWS - Refresh all materialized views.
- o DBMS _MVIEW.REFRESH _DEPENDENT - Refresh all dependent mmaterialized views

5.4.5.2 Monitoring a Refresh

From sys view check refreshing status

```
SELECT * FROM V$SESSIO _LONGOPS;
```

To look at the progress of jobs, use:

```
SELECT * FROM DBA _JOBS _RUNNING;
```

Checking the Status of a Materialized View

Create the dedicated vews to monitor refresh status

Create a view and list all valid mviews:

```
CREATE VIEW mview _valid _list _v AS
SELECT MVIEW _NAME, STALENESS, LAST _REFRESH _TYPE, COMPILE _STATE
FROM USER _MVIEWS
WHERE COMPILE _STATE = 'VALID' ORDER BY COMPILE _STATE;
SELECT * FROM mview _valid _list _v;
```

Create a view and list all invalid mviews:

```
CREATE VIEW mview_none_valid_list_v AS
SELECT MVIEW_NAME, STALENESS, LAST_REFRESH_TYPE, COMPILE_STATE
FROM USER_MVIEWS
WHERE COMPILE_STATE != 'VALID' ORDER BY COMPILE_STATE;
SELECT * FROM mview_none_valid_list_v;
```

Create a view and grouping the mview compiling status:

```
CREATE VIEW mview_state_v AS
SELECT COMPILE_STATE, COUNT(*) COMP_STATE_CNT
FROM USER_MVIEWS GROUP BY COMPILE_STATE;
SELECT * FROM mview_state_v;
```

Compile Mview

```
ALTER MATERIALIZED VIEW [materialized_view_name] COMPILE;
```

Create views for checking the status of materialized views including summary, not valid, valid.

5.4.6 Mview highlights

- Using Materialized Views with Partitioned Tables
- Keep in sync with underline tables.
- Design better (simpler and faster) refreshing path
- Reduce the passes of scanning fact table

In summary, there are two type of refreshing mview, complete refresh and fast refresh, use fast refresh instead of complete refresh whenever possible because it take less time to finish, but in the real world, there are always some restrictions on fast refresh especially if there is a complex query used. If you find there are chain of mview with only complete refresh available, try to break it by embedding an intermediate table which would be built by complex query and incremental update operations then use it as a base for supporting fast refresh. You may get much better overall performance.

Star Schema, Fact, dimensions, Mviews, views
Please refer to figure 5-5.2-4 Dw_Sales_factMv

5.5 OLAP

5.5.1 SQL and Aggregation Functions

SQL aggregation including ROLLUP, CUBE, GROUPING, GROUPING SETS

5.5.2 Analyzing data Across Multiple Dimensions

As has been discussed in <The Great Pyramit> in Chapter Two, Data warehouse is a multi-layer architecture, where upper layers contain high concentrations of information, while lower layers contain more detailed. OLAP is the process of creating paths from bottom to the paramount top of this very pyramid.

Analyzing data across multiple dimensions is a major methord used in OLAP.

Please refer to figure 5-5.2-4 Dw_Sales_factMv

5.5.3 SQL Aggregate flow

There are rich set of SQL aggregation functions and operations froming the aggregate flows during summarization and query processes.

5.5.4 SQL for Aggregation Functions

5.5.4.4 Customer Analysis - GROUP BY (year, gender)

At first, generate a mivew group by gender from a monthly summary mivew for a specific country.

```
CREATE MATERIALIZED VIEW sum_es_gend_mv
BUILD DEFERRED
REFRESH FAST
ENABLE QUERY REWRITE
AS
SELECT  SUBSTR(s.calendar_month_desc,1,4) year,
  s.calendar_month_desc cal_month, c.CUST_GENDER,
      SUM(sum_amount_sold) sum_amount_sold
FROM sum_sales_month_mv s, customers c
```

```
WHERE s.cust_id=c.cust_id AND
     c.country_id = '52778' AND
     SUBSTR(s.calendar_month_desc,1,4) ='2000'
GROUP BY SUBSTR(s.calendar_month_desc,1,4),
 s.calendar_month_desc, c.CUST_GENDER;
```

Use DBMS_MVIEW package refresh the mview defined above:

```
begin
DBMS_MVIEW.REFRESH('sum_es_gend_mv', '?', '',TRUE, FALSE,
0,0,0, FALSE);
end;
```

Very often, users need use Office tools for further analysis, the following show how to define a crosstab from Microsoft ACCESS database which link to the Oracle backend database:

```
TRANSFORM Sum (SUM_AMOUNT_SOLD) AS TotalSUM_AMOUNT_SOLD
SELECT YEAR, CAL_MONTH
FROM SH_SUM_ES_GEND_MV
GROUP BY YEAR, CAL_MONTH
PIVOT CUST_GENDER;
```

crosstab_sum_es_gend_mv			
YEAR	**CAL_MONTH**	**F**	**M**
2000	2000-01	27290.29	14375.65
2000	2000-02	21338.46	19564.42
2000	2000-03	18601.76	17735.15
2000	2000-04	11347.94	16957.05
2000	2000-05	17596.29	17558.7
2000	2000-06	15809.31	14824.14
2000	2000-07	11541.28	24613.12
2000	2000-08	14736.68	29407.78
2000	2000-09	12104.57	42946.58
2000	2000-10	14179.53	26851.57
2000	2000-11	22413.49	30562.03
2000	2000-12	19747.66	40756.29

From Microsoft Office Excel, create Pivot table and specify mview (sum_sales_es_gend_mv) in Oracle as externel source.

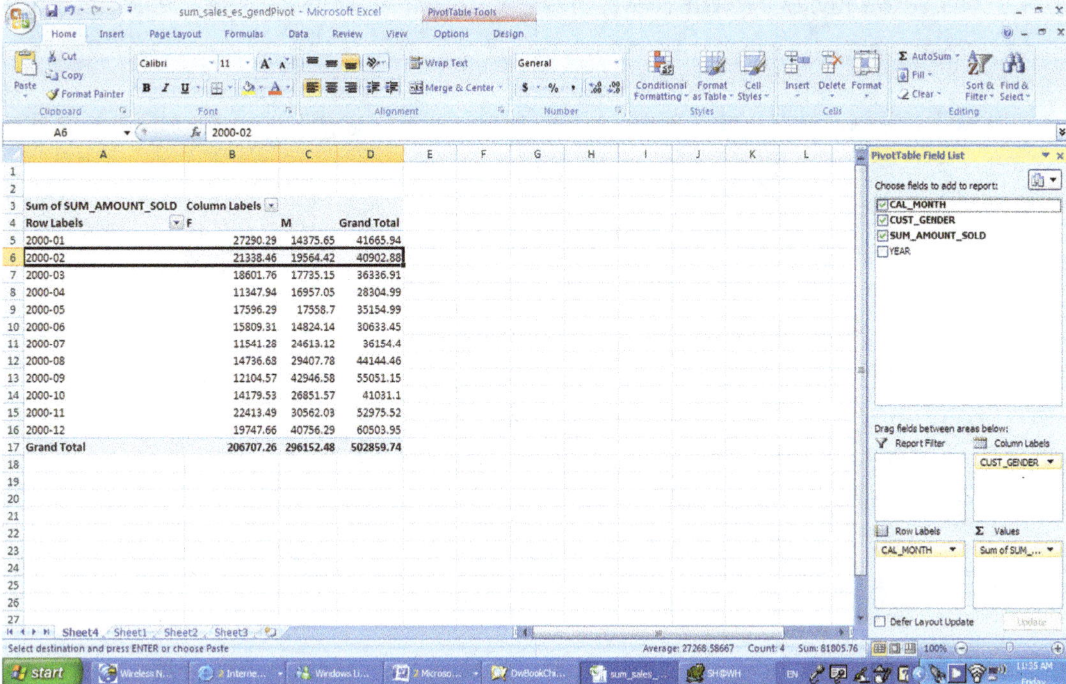

Sum of SUM_AMOUNT_SOLD	Column Labels		
Row Labels	F	M	Grand Total
2000-01	27290.29	14375.65	41665.94
2000-02	21338.46	19564.42	40902.88
2000-03	18601.76	17735.15	36336.91
2000-04	11347.94	16957.05	28304.99
2000-05	17596.29	17558.7	35154.99
2000-06	15809.31	14824.14	30633.45
2000-07	11541.28	24613.12	36154.4
2000-08	14736.68	29407.78	44144.46
2000-09	12104.57	42946.58	55051.15
2000-10	14179.53	26851.57	41031.1
2000-11	22413.49	30562.03	52975.52
2000-12	19747.66	40756.29	60503.95
Grand Total	206707.26	296152.48	502859.74

5.5.4.5 GROUP BY (month, contries)

At first, create mview (group by year, country) from a monthly sales summary mview.

```
CREATE MATERIALIZED VIEW sum_sales_6country_mv
BUILD IMMEDIATE
REFRESH COMPLETE
ENABLE QUERY REWRITE
AS
SELECT year, CO.COUNTRY_ISO_CODE country,
     SUM(sum_amount_sold) sum_amount_sold
FROM sum_sales_country_mv s, countries co
WHERE s.country=co.country_id AND
    co.country_iso_code IN ('US','GB','FR','ES','JP',
'AU' )

 GROUP BY year, co.COUNTRY_iso_code;
```

Next, based on mview created above, create a crosstab view using DECODE function showing summary sales for each contry.

```
CREATE OR REPLACE VIEW sum_sale_country_v AS
SELECT *
 FROM (SELECT year,
       sum(decode(COUNTRY, 'AU',sum_amount_sold)) AU,
       sum(decode(COUNTRY, 'ES',sum_amount_sold)) ES,
       sum(decode(COUNTRY, 'FR',sum_amount_sold)) FR,
       sum(decode(COUNTRY, 'JP',sum_amount_sold)) JP,
          sum(decode(COUNTRY, 'GB',sum_amount_sold)) GB,
       sum(decode(COUNTRY, 'US',sum_amount_sold)) US

      FROM sum_sales_6country_mv
       GROUP BY ROLLUP(year) );
```

YEAR	AU	ES	FR	JP	GB	US
1999	856929.35	440535.99	859035.11	1724980.36	1508110.49	11856749.16
2000	896291.71	502859.74	886244.61	1621977.2	1552223.06	13120594.21
	1753221.06	943395.73	1745279.72	3346957.56	3060333.55	24977343.37

The following SQL statement create a crosstab mview using DECODE function as a physical summary cube about summary sales for each contry.

```
CREATE MATERIALIZED VIEW SUM_SALES_COUNTRY_C_MV
BUILD IMMEDIATE REFRESH COMPLETE
ENABLE QUERY REWRITE
AS SELECT *
FROM (SELECT SUBSTR(s.calendar_month_desc,1,4) YEAR,
     SUM(DECODE(CO.COUNTRY_ISO_CODE,
'AU',sum_amount_sold)) AU,
     SUM(DECODE(CO.COUNTRY_ISO_CODE,
'ES',sum_amount_sold)) ES,
```

The view and mview above can achieve the same result, the difference is that view is used as virtual while mview is used as physical one for fast access.

In the following example, define a crosstab from ACCESS database based on an mview in the backend Oracle database for further analysises by using Mircosoft Office Tools:

```
TRANSFORM Sum(SUM_AMOUNT_SOLD) AS SUM_AMOUNT_SOLDOfSum
SELECT YEAR
FROM SH_SUM_SALES_6COUNTRY_MV
GROUP BY YEAR
PIVOT COUNTRY;
```

CrossTab_Sum_sales_6country_mv						
YEAR	**AU**	**ES**	**FR**	**GB**	**JP**	**US**
1999	856929.35	440535.99	859035.11	1508110.49	1724980.36	11856749.16
2000	896291.71	502859.74	886244.61	1552223.06	1621977.2	13120594.21

From Office Excel, create a Pivot table and specify a mview (sum_sales_6contry_mv) in Oracle as data source.

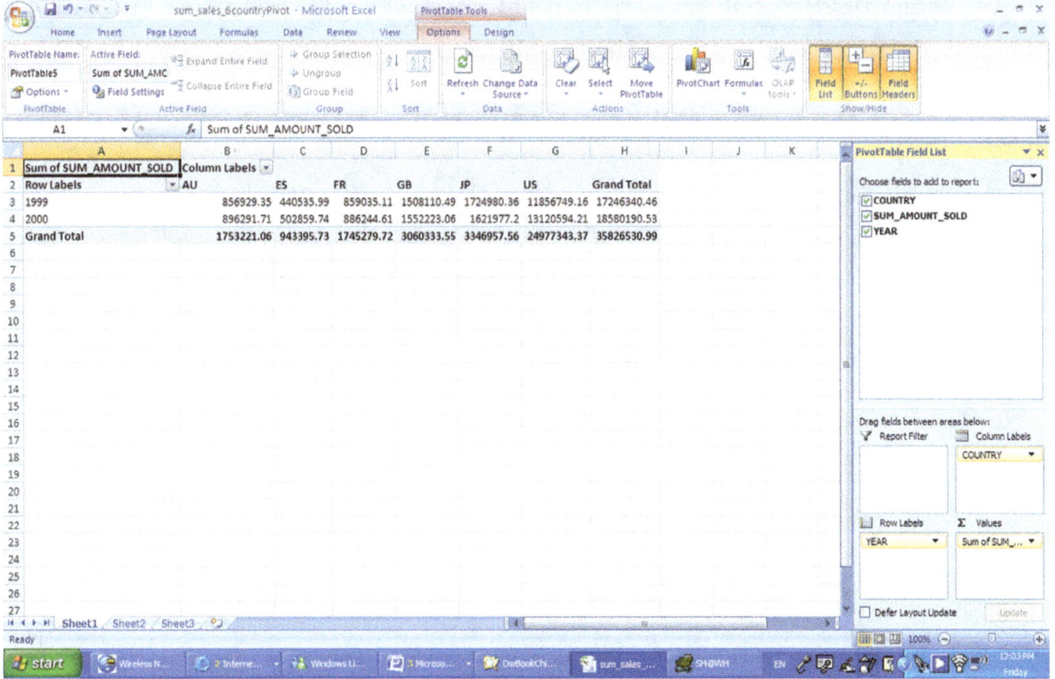

5.5.5 SQL and Analytical Functions

5.5.5.0 Data warehouse SQL Analysis Flow

Data Warehouse SQL Analytic Flow – Oracle

5.5.5.1 Top five RANK over sales by country, city

Using RANK function to get top five sales (by country, city) from monthly sales mview:

```
SELECT * FROM
(SELECT country_id, city,
       TO_CHAR(SUM(sum_amount_sold), '9,999,999,999')
sum_amount_sold,

       RANK() OVER (ORDER BY SUM(sum_amount_sold) DESC ) AS
CITY_RANK
FROM sum_sales_chan_city_mv
WHERE calendar_month_desc='2000-11'
GROUP BY country_id, city)
WHERE CITY_RANK <= 5;
```

COUNTRY_ISO_CODE	CITY	SUM_AMOUNT_SOLD	CITY_RANK
JP	Yokohama	97,926	1
US	San Mateo	69,862	2
US	Evinston	40,721	3
US	Frederick	34,883	4
US	Hiseville	34,479	5

5.6 Report Preparation

5.6.1 From Backend to Front end

5.6.1.1 Use Office Tools as your front end for further data analysises

Microsoft Office tools become popular tools in the business data processes/presentations as well as your front end analysis tools. From ACCESS database and Excel, you can define the crosstab, or pivot table, and all of these tables can be linked to backend databases through ODBC or OLE connections. All the materialized views/summary cubes can be accessed by end users through Office Tools for further data analysises.

Excel has become a popular reporting/analysis tool for end users. In Excel, one of the useful features is pivot table which can be used to quickly summarize data as well as analyze and display it using calculation methods and formats that you choose. It is especially useful when we tie it to backend databases or OLAP cubes through the data external source definitions.

5.6.2 The Highlights of Reports Creations

- Get Summary – Crosstab – Cubes – Pivot Table
- Materialized views/Summary cubes and rollup/drill down
- Pre-Process for OLAP
- User (Query) Navigation
- Create functions for report queries
- Create procedures for report queries
- Report Delivery
- XML
- Create Package and Report Tracking/Logging system

5.6.3 Drill down Multi-dimensional data

Drill down in the Multi-dimensional Cubes – Three dimensions (customers, channels, and times)

Figure 5-5.6-19 DwCubeDrill

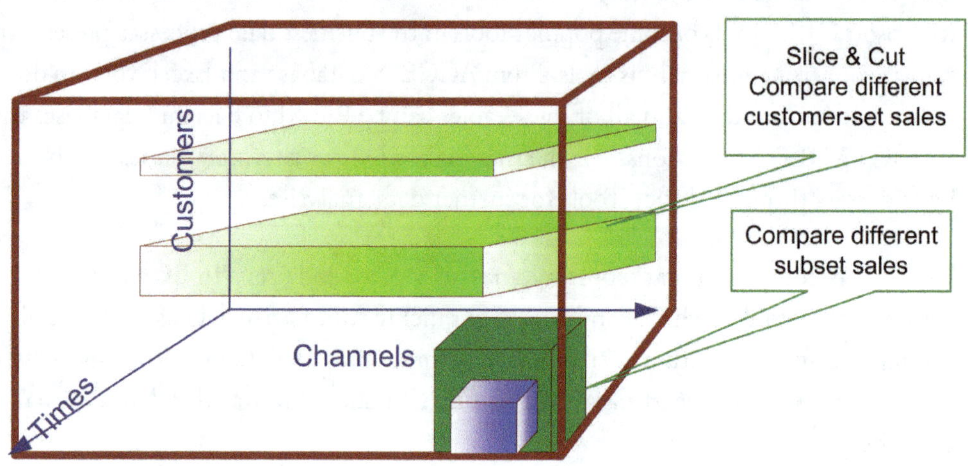

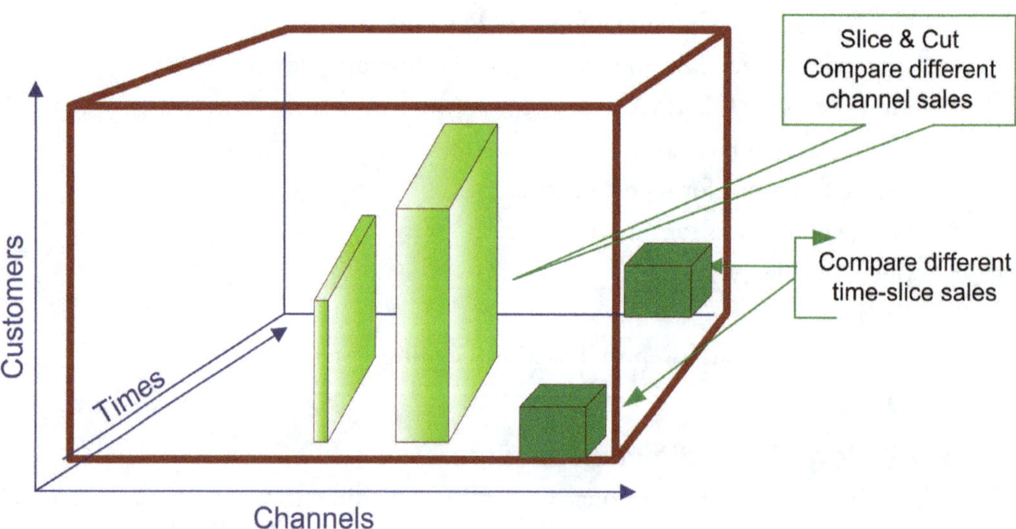

Cube drill down by data example:

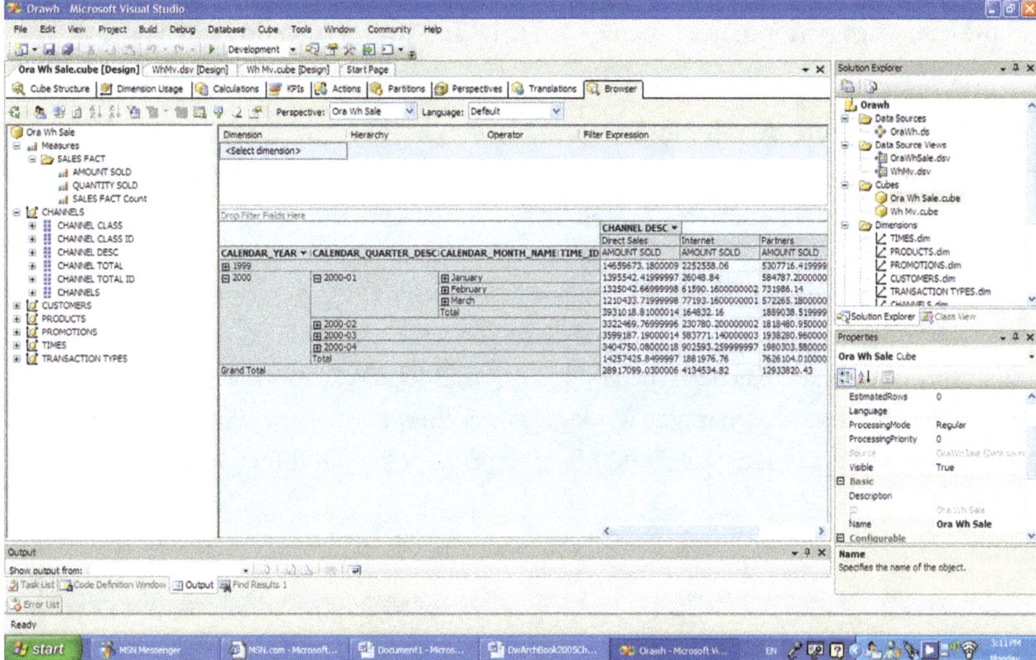

5.6.4 Pre-Process for OLAP

Pre-processing is one of the important stages for OLAP applications. It will simplify the usages of OLAP tools and make it more efficient.

So what is pre-process? What else are involved in this stage? Actually, creating summary materialized views/ cubes through the aggregations and calculations and refresh them in order to keep them in sync with underline tables, all those are pre-processes for OALP.

A well-defined summary cube series forming a tree structure by which the refresh paths must to be figured out in order to streamline the whole processes and make them faster and easier.

Make fast refresh, As has been described in 5.4.6 <Mview highlights> this chapter, one of the options to optimize the refresh path is to use fast refresh as much as possible, when there is a refresh chain with only comlete refreshes, try to break it and tame it to be fast refreshabled.

Skeletonize Using mviews/cubes to boost the performance has been described in Chapter Two, Section 2.13 <Multi-dimensional Cube>, By skeletonizing the cubes (contain only keys and measures) especially those intermedidate cubes, all aggregate operations will against a skeleton cube instead of a fat one during the pre-calculation, it may finally gain fat (join the dimension to get descriptions) only when deliver to users. It works better for those case when performance becomes real issue and the most reports can be pre-defined.

5.6.5 SQL Server Analysis Services

SQL Server Analysis Services (SSAS) been used here shows several basic methods and techniques simplified examples, especially in cube designs and processes.

SSAS can process data from various data sources such as SQL Server, Oracle…
The first thing to do is specify source from SSAS source view, in this example, sales data from Oracle database has been specified as external source. Cubes and dimensions can be defined with interactive manner. Work on source view and form a star/snowflake schema by link forein keys in fact table (sales_fact) to primary keys in dimension tables.

Source view

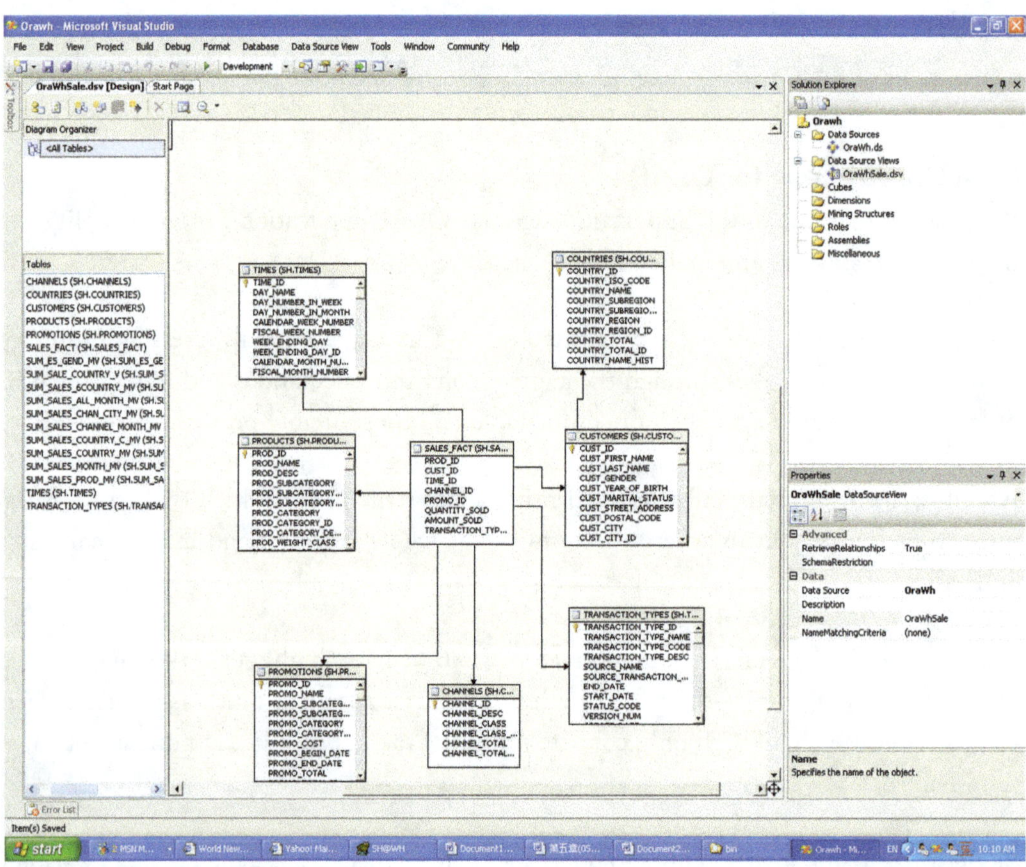

Cubes and dimensions can be defined by specifying fact table and dimension tables. Define cube view based on source view created:

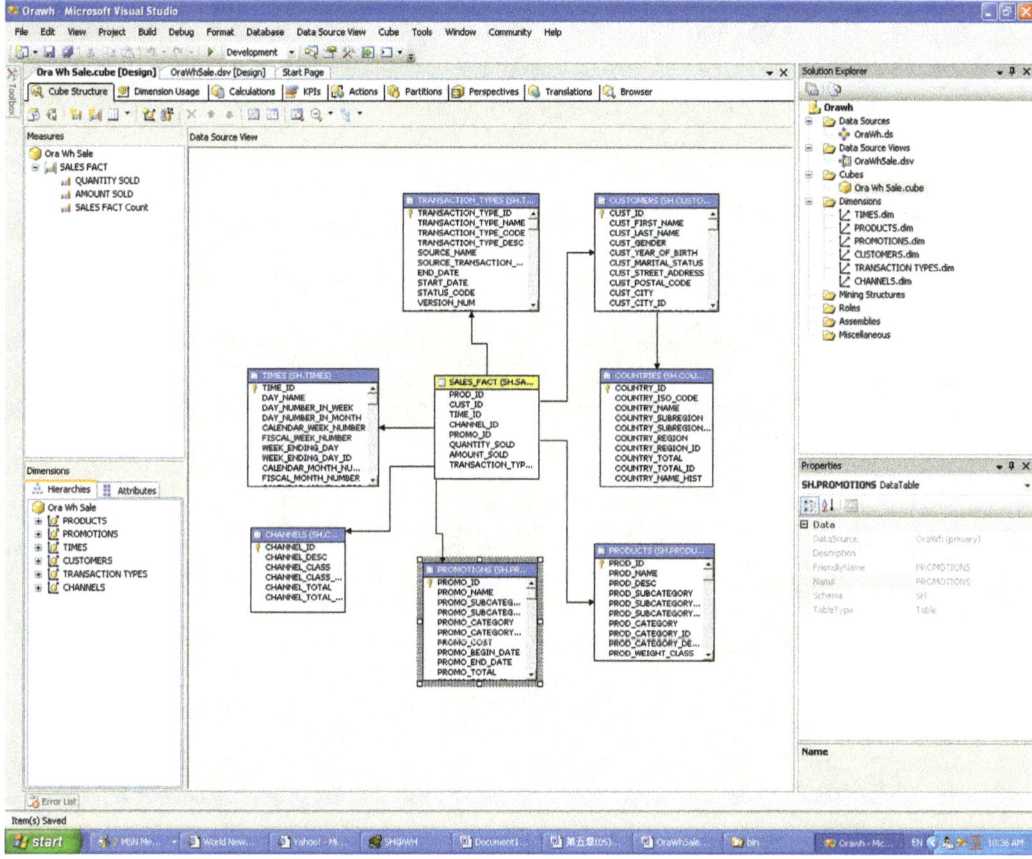

In this example, a monthly sales data from source database has been specified as external source. Work on source view and form a star/snowflake schema by linking forein key in fact table (sum_sales_fact_mv) to primary key in dimension tables.

Source view created based on reporting schema:

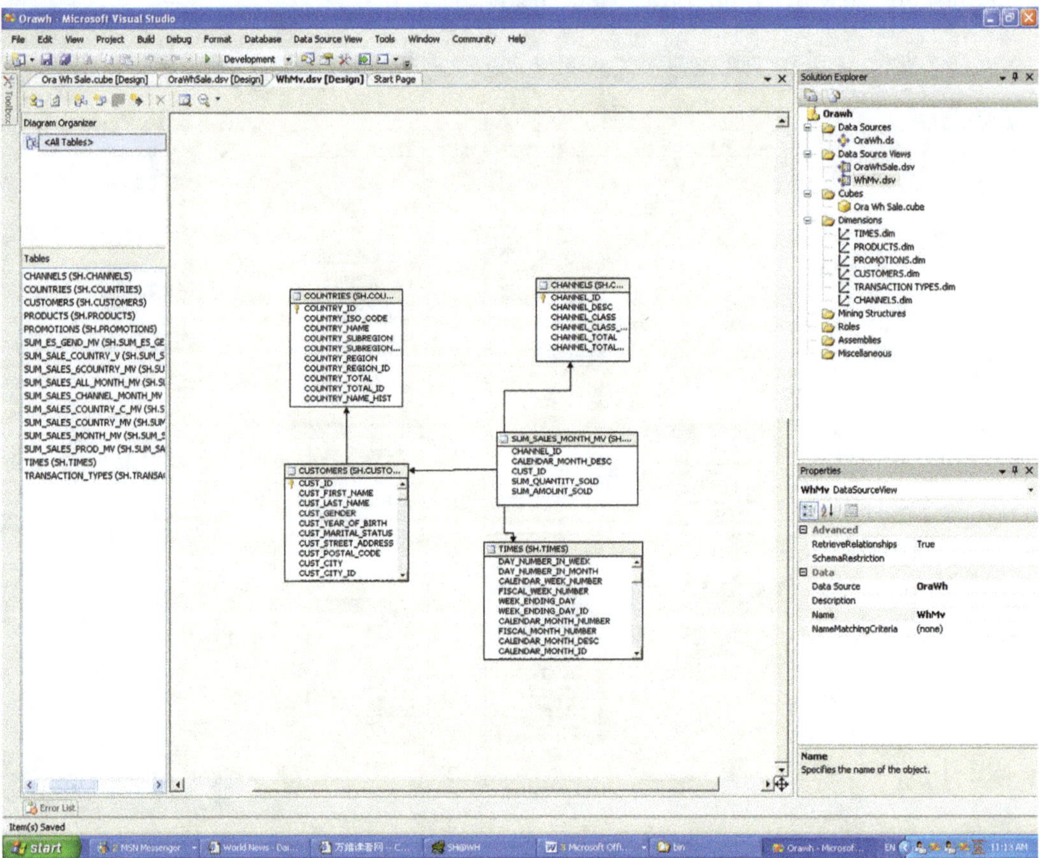

A cube definitions specifying a fact table, dimension tables and linking types; such as star, snowflake and parent-child relationship. After building cubes successfully, we can process cubes, analize data against cubes by drill down in the dimensions and drill through into details. Cubes also can be accessed through Excel Pivot table.

The following diagram shows a cube architecture which consist of a fact for sales (SUM_SALES_MONTH) tie to time and channel dimension tables through star connection, tie to customer/country dimension through snowflake connection. The following cube is used to analyze monthly sales as a much simplified example.

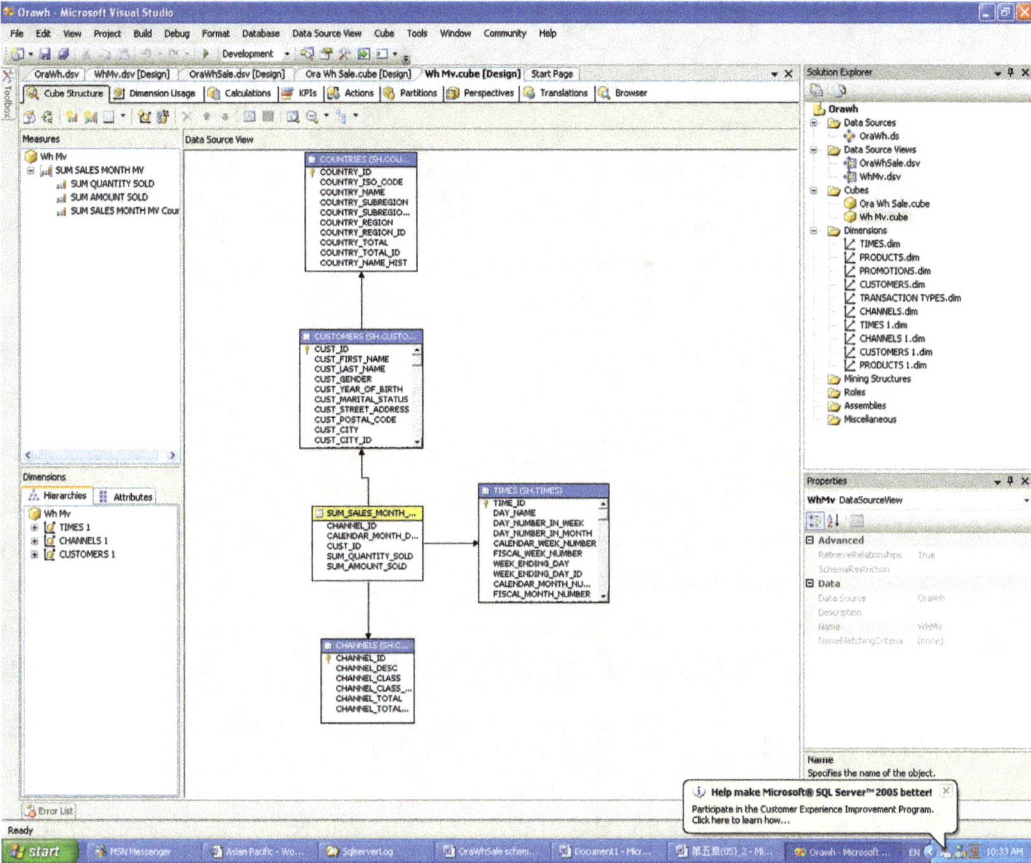

The following diagram shows how the cube is browsed. On left pane shows dimensions and measures, upper portion shows all the dimensions serve as filters, such as channels, customer, and time. User can drag and drop these dimensions into the cube matrix bellow then form the new calculations based on analysis needs.

The cube view shows drill down by customer/country such as from country to states/provinces.

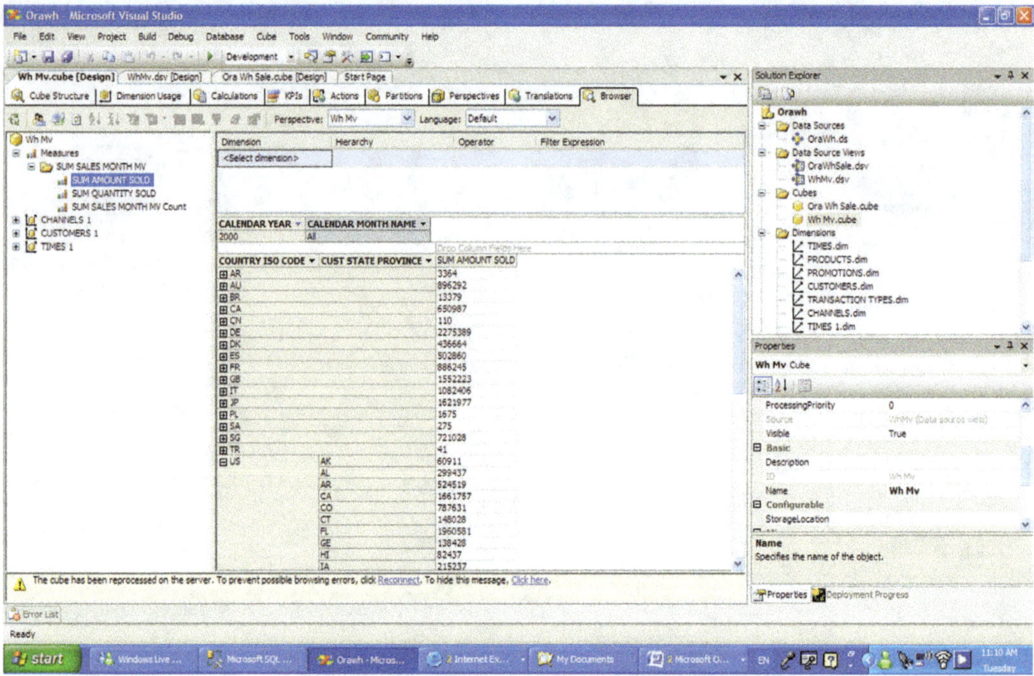

Excel often been used as OLAP Cube interface and analisis results delivery tools. The left side is a pivot table used for drill down analysis/process; right side shows all dimensions and measures which user can drag and drop into pivot table matrix for necessary calculations and/or analysis.

First, Create pivot table from Excel pointing to OLAP cube as source
Drag and drop measures and dimensions into pivot table

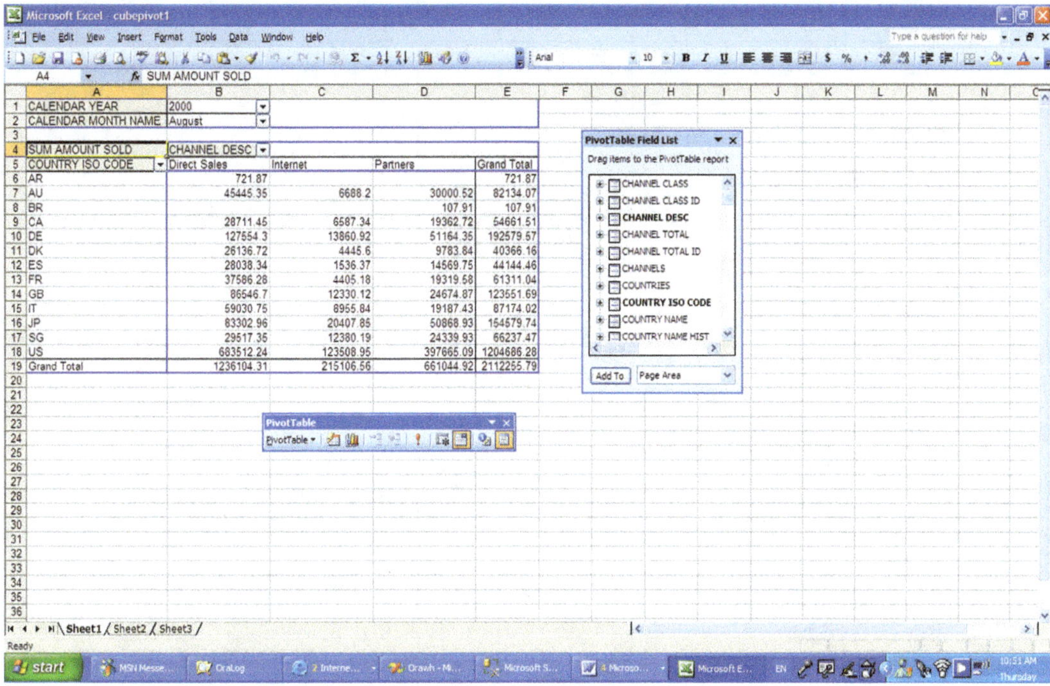

CALENDAR YEAR	2000			
CALENDAR MONTH NAME	August			
SUM AMOUNT SOLD	CHANNEL DESC			
COUNTRY ISO CODE	Direct Sales	Internet	Partners	Grand Total
AR	721.87			721.87
AU	45445.35	6688.2	30000.52	82134.07
BR			107.91	107.91
CA	28711.45	6587.34	19362.72	54661.51
DE	127554.3	13860.92	51164.35	192579.57
DK	26136.72	4445.6	9783.84	40366.16
ES	28038.34	1536.37	14569.75	44144.46
FR	37586.28	4405.18	19319.58	61311.04
GB	86546.7	12330.12	24674.87	123551.69
IT	59030.75	8955.84	19187.43	87174.02
JP	83302.96	20407.85	50868.93	154579.74
SG	29517.35	12380.19	24339.93	66237.47
US	683512.24	123508.95	397665.09	1204686.28
Grand Total	1236104.31	215106.56	661044.92	2112255.79

MDX (Multiple Dimension Expression) often used to query against cube.

In cube example *Sales*

```
WITH MEMBER
[Measures].[AMOUNT] AS [Measures].[AMOUNT SOLD],
FORMAT_STRING = "#"
SELECT {[Measures].[AMOUNT]} on columns,
non empty {[CHANNELS].[CHANNEL DESC].members} on rows
FROM [Ora Wh Sale]
```

	AMOUNT
All	45985454
Direct Sales	28917099
Internet	4134535
Partners	12933820

```
WITH MEMBER
[Measures].[AMOUNT] AS [Measures].[AMOUNT SOLD],
FORMAT_STRING = "#"
SELECT non empty {[CHANNELS].[CHANNEL DESC].members} on
columns,
non empty {[CUSTOMERS].[COUNTRY ISO CODE].members} on rows
FROM [Ora Wh Sale]
WHERE [Measures].[AMOUNT]
```

	All	Direct Sales	Internet	Partners
All	45985454	28917099	4134535	12933820
AR	8708	6341	2350	17
AU	1753221	1156523	140810	455888
BR	18463	13997	1366	3100
CA	1248672	711001	113825	423846
CN	1931	1260	671	(null)
DE	4401717	3198200	305295	898222
DK	882402	576994	65815	239593
ES	943396	614127	73242	256027
FR	1745280	1222495	107654	415131
GB	3060334	2113382	201865	745087
IT	2197580	1518162	170496	508922
JP	3346958	1927432	339576	1079949
PL	8366	4435	2001	1930
SA	275	(null)	275	(null)
SG	1389494	683441	187399	518654
TR	1314	956	41	317
US	24977343	15168354	2421854	7387135

```
WITH MEMBER
[Measures].[AMOUNT] AS [Measures].[AMOUNT SOLD],
FORMAT_STRING = "#"
SELECT
non empty {[CHANNELS].[CHANNEL DESC].members}on columns,
non empty {[CUSTOMERS].[CUST STATE PROVINCE].members} on
rows
FROM [Ora Wh Sale]
WHERE ([Measures].[AMOUNT],[United States of America],[CA])
```

	All	Direct Sales	Internet	Partners
All	24977343	15168354	2421854	7387135
CA	3218973	2106890	267961	844123

In a BI application example - *CourseStartCube*
Get cource registed summaries for all peple reporting to a given manager (whose PersonId is 112233),
{[Manager Hierarchy] is a dimension of parent-child type.

```
SELECT
 NON EMPTY { [Registration Date].[year].members } on columns,
 NON EMPTY {[Manager Hierarchy].&[112233].children} on rows
 FROM CourseStartCube
WHERE ( [Measures].[Registered] )
```

Add a linked server pointing to LOAP cube

```
-- add linked server
EXEC sp_addlinkedserver
  @server='CourseDwServer',

  @srvproduct='',
  @provider='MSOLAP',
  @datasrc=' CourseDwServer',
  @catalog='CourseStartCube'
```

Query OLAP cube through linked server above from SQL Server

```
SELECT * FROM OPENQUERY(CourseDwServer,
'select
  NON EMPTY {[Measures].members} on columns,
  NON EMPTY { [Class Start Date].[year].members } on rows
 from CourseStartCube')
```

Create a procedure returning the drillthrough result with people report to a given manager (whose PersonId is passed as parameter), {[Manager Hierarchy] is a dimension of parent-child type.

```
CREATE procedure usp_mdx_get_Children @PersonId int
as
declare
@qstring nvarchar(4000),
@qSelectString nvarchar(4000)
set @qSelectString =
'DRILLTHROUGH
select
  NON EMPTY { [Measures].[Registered] } on columns,
  NON EMPTY { ( [Manager Hierarchy].&[' +
convert(varchar(20),@PersonId) +'] ) } on rows
 from CourseStartCube
where ( [2004] )'
```

```
set @qstring = 'SELECT * FROM OPENQUERY(CourseDwServer, '
+ ''''+ @qSelectString + ''')'
print @qstring
exec sp_executesql @qstring
return
```

The following SQL statement calls the procedure and return drillthrough details for all the people reporting to a manager with giveng PersonId.

```
declare @personId INT
exec usp _mdx _get _Children @PersonId = 11223344
```

5.7 Report Frameworks

The whole report framework is consists of a number of reporting components and utilities including function library and procedure library which can be assembled into various functional groups based on business application needs; the data schemas and structures to support overall user access controls and to hold report group usages; finally the packages to manage or coordinate all report components to form the centralized report system and execute them in a destined manner.

Dynamic SQL provides powerful functionalities such as accepting user input and parameters then execute them accordingly. As for dynamic SQL, the database objects such as tables and columns can be treat as virtual, thus help to design and compile the programs while related database objects may not present at developing time.

The functions and procedures use PL/SQL and dynamic SQL are able to handle analytical requests dynamically.

A report framework is consist with the following modules:

- ❑ Generating XML Data from the Database
- ❑ Report Function Library
- ❑ Report Procedure Library
- ❑ Report Frame and its Supporting Schema
- ❑ Table functions

5.7 Reporting Frame and Its Supporting Library

This chapter describes how we build the frame and its components and then integrate everything together in order to support reporting and analysis.

Figure 5-5.7-19 DwReportFrame

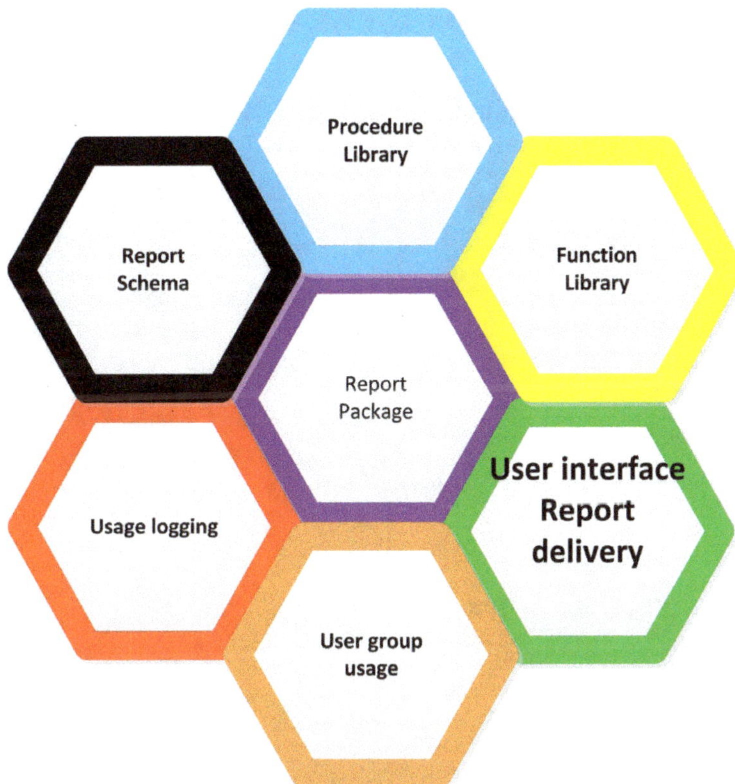

5.7.1 Generating XML Data

Extensible Markup Language (XML) is a very flexible text format derived from SGML. It was designed to describe data.

XML document can become a shared construct, which bridge the disparate systems through its cross-enterprise, cross-platform formatting. There are SQLX standard functions and packages for generating XML data from relational content:

The follwing shows how to use user-defined function to generate XML :

5.7.1.0 Generating XML Using SQLX Functions

FUNCTION Get_query_xml - It accept SQL string and return result as XML data

FUNCTION get_query_xml_withRowTag - It accepts SQL string and tag string returning XML data:

PROCEDURE Put_query_xml - It takes SQL query string as input parameter and ouput in XML format.

PROCEDURE Put_query_xml_withRowTag - It takes SQL query string and tag string as input parameters and ouput result in XML format.

5.7.1.1 FUNCTION Get_query_xml

5.7.1.1.1 Create the function which will accept SQL qury string and return result as XML data:

```
CREATE OR REPLACE FUNCTION Get_query_xml(q_string in
varchar2) RETURN CLOB
IS
ctx2 number;
xmldoc CLOB;
page NUMBER := 0;
xmlpage boolean := true;
refcur SYS_REFCURSOR;
BEGIN
OPEN refcur FOR q_string;
ctx2 := DBMS_XMLGEN.newContext( refcur);
dbms_lob.createtemporary(xmldoc, TRUE);
xmldoc := DBMS_XMLGEN.getXML(ctx2,DBMS_XMLGEN.NONE);
DBMS_XMLGEN.closeContext(ctx2);
return xmldoc;
END;
/
```

5.7.1.1.2 Call the function with the parameters:

```
select get _query _xml('select * from sum _sales _country _mv')
from dual;
```

5.7.1.1.3 The function returns the XML result as following:

In SQL*Plus:

```
SQL> select get _query _xml('select * from sum _sales _country _mv')
from dual;
```

```
GET_QUERY_XML('SELECT*FROMSUM_SALES_COUNTRY_MV')
-----------------------------------------------------
<?xml version="1.0"?>
<ROWSET>
 <ROW>
 <YEAR>1998</YEAR>
 <COUNTRY>AU</COUNTRY>
 <SUM_AMOUNT_SOLD>3367263.65</SUM_AMOUNT_SOLD>
 </ROW>
 <ROW>
 <YEAR>1998</YEAR>
 <COUNTRY>ES</COUNTRY>
 <SUM_AMOUNT_SOLD>8332515.8</SUM_AMOUNT_SOLD>

GET_QUERY_XML('SELECT*FROMSUM_SALES_COUNTRY_MV')
-----------------------------------------------------
 </ROW>
 <ROW>
 <YEAR>1998</YEAR>
 <COUNTRY>FR</COUNTRY>
 <SUM_AMOUNT_SOLD>20397560.7</SUM_AMOUNT_SOLD>
 </ROW>

 <ROW>
 <YEAR>1998</YEAR>
 <COUNTRY>JP</COUNTRY>
 <SUM_AMOUNT_SOLD>2569544.95</SUM_AMOUNT_SOLD>
 </ROW>
...
<ROWSET>
```

5.7.1.2 FUNCTION get_query_xml_withRowTag

5.7.1.2.1 Create the function accept SQL string and tag string return result as XML data:

```
CREATE OR REPLACE FUNCTION get_query_xml_withRowTag
 (q_string in varchar2 ,p_RowTag in varchar2 default null)
 RETURN CLOB
 IS
ctx number;xmldoc CLOB;page NUMBER := 0;xmlpage boolean :=
true;
refcur SYS_REFCURSOR;
BEGIN
OPEN refcur FOR q_string;
ctx := DBMS_XMLGEN.newContext( refcur);
dbms_lob.createtemporary(xmldoc, TRUE);
IF NOT(p_RowTag IS NULL) THEN
DBMS_XMLGEN.setRowTag(ctx, p_RowTag);
END IF;
xmldoc := DBMS_XMLGEN.getXML(ctx,DBMS_XMLGEN.NONE);
DBMS_XMLGEN.closeContext(ctx);
return xmldoc;
END;
/
```

5.7.1.2.2 Call the fuction with parameters

```
select     get_query_xml_withRowTag('select     *     from
sum_sales_country_mv', 'country report')
 from dual;
```

5.7.1.3 PROCEDURE Put_query_xml

5.7.1.3.1 Create the procedure thatl take SQL query string as parameter and ouput result in XML format.

```
CREATE  OR  REPLACE  PROCEDURE  Put_query_xml  (q_string  IN
varchar2,result OUT CLOB)
IS
qryCtx DBMS_XMLGEN.ctxHandle;
BEGIN
qryCtx := dbms_xmlgen.newContext(q_string);
-- set the row header to be REPORT
```

```
-- set the row header to be REPORT
DBMS_XMLGEN.setRowTag(qryCtx, 'REPORT');
result := DBMS_XMLGEN.getXML(qryCtx);
DBMS_XMLGEN.closeContext(qryCtx);
END;
/
```

5.7.1.3.2 Following PL/SQL Call the procedure and get result in XML format:

```
DECLARE
q_string1 VARCHAR2(2000); result CLOB;
BEGIN
q_string1:= 'select * from sum_sales_country_mv';
put_query_xml(q_string1, result);
INSERT INTO temp_clob_tab VALUES(result);
COMMIT;
END;
```

5.7.1.3.3 List the query result

```
select * from temp _clob _tab;
```

5.7.1.4 PROCEDURE Put_query_xml_withRowTag

Create a procedure that take SQL query string and tag string as parameters and ouput result in XML.

```
CREATE OR REPLACE PROCEDURE Put_query_xml_withRowTag
(q_string IN VARCHAR2,result OUT CLOB,p_RowTag IN VARCHAR2
DEFAULT NULL)
IS
qryCtx DBMS_XMLGEN.ctxHandle;
BEGIN
qryCtx := dbms_xmlgen.newContext(q_string);
IF NOT(p_RowTag IS NULL) THEN
-- set the row header
DBMS_XMLGEN.setRowTag(qryCtx, p_RowTag);
END IF;
result := DBMS_XMLGEN.getXML(qryCtx);
DBMS_XMLGEN.closeContext(qryCtx);
END;
/
```

Create a table with a clob column to store XML data

```
CREATE TABLE clob_tmp(result CLOB);
```

Following PL/SQL Call the procedure and get result in XML format:

```
DECLARE
q_string1    VARCHAR2(2000);    result    CLOB;    v_RowTag
varchar2(30);
BEGIN
v_RowTag:= 'REPORT';
q_string1:= 'select * from sum_sales_country_mv';
put_query_xml_withRowTag(q_string1, result,v_RowTag);
DISPATCH_RPT.put_query_xml_withRowTag(q_string1,
result,v_RowTag);
INSERT INTO clob_tmp VALUES(result);
COMMIT;
END;
```

5.7.1.5 PROCEDURE CHAN_MON_SALE

The procedure takes country_id and month as parameters and produces the result in XML.

```
CREATE OR REPLACE PROCEDURE CHAN_MON_SALE
(p_country_id IN VARCHAR2, p_month IN VARCHAR2)
IS
q_string1 VARCHAR2(2000);
result CLOB;
v_RowTag varchar2(30);
vprog errlog.PROG%type:= 'chan_mon_sale';
err_msg errlog.ERR_MSG%type;
err_num errlog.ERR_NUM%type;
BEGIN
v_RowTag:= 'Chan_CountrySale';
q_string1:= 'SELECT channel_desc, country_id,  TO_NUMBER
(TO_CHAR(SUM(sum_amount_sold),          ''999999999999''))
SUM_AMOUNT_SOLD '||
' FROM sum_sales_month_mv s, customers c, channels ch '||
' WHERE s.cust_id=c.cust_id AND
     s.channel_id= ch.channel_id AND
     ch.channel_desc IN (''Direct Sales'', ''Internet'')
AND
```

```
    s.calendar_month_desc='||''''||p_month||''''||' AND
    country_id IN ( '|| ''''||p_country_id||''''||') '||
' GROUP BY CUBE(channel_desc, country_id) ';

-- get the result in xml
put_query_xml_withRowTag(q_string1, result,v_RowTag);
-- save the result
INSERT INTO clob_tmp VALUES(result);
COMMIT;
EXCEPTION
  WHEN OTHERS  THEN
    NULL; -- SOME ERROR HANDLING
END;
/
```

The following PL/SQL Call the procedure and get result in XML format:

```
DECLARE
q_string1   VARCHAR2(2000);   result   CLOB;   v_RowTag
varchar2(30);
BEGIN
v_RowTag:= 'REPORT';
q_string1:= 'select * from sum_sales_country_mv';
put_query_xml_withRowTag(q_string1, result,v_RowTag);
INSERT INTO clob_tmp VALUES(result);
COMMIT;
END;
```

5.7.1.5.3 Call the procedure with the following parameters:

```
BEGIN chan_mon_sale('52789','2000-09'); END;
BEGIN chan_mon_sale('52779','2000-09'); END;
```

5.7.1.6 XML PROCEDURE CHAN_COUNTRY_SALE_XML

5.7.1.6.1 Create a procedure.

The procedure takes country_id and month as parameters and produices the result in XM.

```
CREATE OR REPLACE PROCEDURE CHAN_COUNTRY_SALE_XML
(p_country_id IN VARCHAR2,p_month IN VARCHAR2,result IN OUT
CLOB)
IS
q_string1 VARCHAR2(4000);v_RowTag varchar2(30);
BEGIN
v_RowTag:= 'Chan_CountrySale';
q_string1:= 'SELECT channel_desc, country_id,
      TO_NUMBER(TO_CHAR(SUM(sum_amount_sold),
''999999999999'')) SUM_AMOUNT_SOLD
 FROM sum_sales_month_mv s, customers c, channels ch
 WHERE s.cust_id=c.cust_id AND   s.channel_id=
ch.channel_id AND
     ch.channel_desc IN (''Direct Sales'', ''Internet'')
AND
     s.calendar_month_desc='||''''||p_month||''''||' AND
     country_id IN ( '|| ''''||p_country_id||''''||')
 GROUP BY CUBE(channel_desc, country_id) ';
-- call the procedure to get the result in XML format
put_query_xml_withRowTag(q_string1, result,v_RowTag);
--Do something about returned xml result
EXCEPTION
WHEN OTHERS    THEN
    NULL; -- SOME ERROR HANDLING
END;
/
```

5.7.1.6.2 Following PL/SQL Call the procedure and get result in XML format:

```
DECLARE
result CLOB;p_country_id countries.country_id%type;
p_month channels.channel_desc%type;
BEGIN
p_country_id:= '52779';
p_month:= '2000-09';
chan_country_sale_XML(p_country_id,p_month,result);
INSERT INTO clob_tmp VALUES(result);
COMMIT;
END;
/
```

5.7.2 Create Report Function Library

This section provides the examples of where you might use PL/SQL to build function library in a dynamic fashion.

The following function groups accept call with parameters (such as time period, country list, channels, postal code) and return the result set (usually correspondent SQL statement). The functions use PL/SQL and dynamic SQL, which provides flexibility and enables you to build and process SQL statements "on the fly" at run time.

Functions:

- o FUNCTION get_chan_country_sales – CUBE
- o FUNCTION get_sales_gender – Customer Analysis ROLLUP
- o FUNCTION get_sales_gender_y – Customer Analysis ROLLUP

5.7.2.1 FUNCTION get_chan_country_sales -CUBE

Create a function that takes channel, country and month as input parameters and parses and handles the null parameters then ouput correspondent SQL query statement. Note that PL/SQL and dynamic SQL is used to make the function generic.

Note: Generally, I would recommend that you not use null parameter, use a dummy parameter such as 'All' instead.

```
CREATE OR REPLACE FUNCTION get_chan_country_sales
(p_channel_desc IN VARCHAR2 DEFAULT NULL,
 p_country_id IN VARCHAR2 DEFAULT NULL,
 p_month IN VARCHAR2 DEFAULT NULL)
 RETURN VARCHAR2 IS
q_string1 VARCHAR2(4000);  -- set this to 32767
iswhr VARCHAR2(200):= NULL;
whr VARCHAR2(2000):= NULL;

BEGIN
q_string1:= 'SELECT channel_desc, co.country_iso_code,
     TO_NUMBER(TO_CHAR(SUM(sum_amount_sold),
''999999999999'')) SUM_AMOUNT_SOLD
 FROM sum_sales_month_mv s, customers c, channels ch,
countries co ';
Whr:= ' WHERE 1=1 AND ';
IF p_channel_desc IS NOT NULL THEN
 Whr:= Whr||' ch.channel_desc IN ( '||p_channel_desc||' )
AND ';
END IF;
IF p_month IS NOT NULL THEN
 Whr:= Whr||' s.calendar_month_desc IN ( '||p_month||' ) AND
';
END IF;

 IF p_country_id IS NOT NULL THEN
  Whr:= Whr||' co.country_id IN ( '|| p_country_id||') AND ';
 END IF;
 Whr:= Whr||' s.cust_id=c.cust_id AND s.channel_id=
 ch.channel_id and c.country_id=co.country_id';
 q_string1:=   q_string1 ||whr ||' GROUP BY
 CUBE(channel_desc, co.country_iso_code) ';
 RETURN q_string1;
 END;
 /
```

Call function with null parameters

Call the function with following parameters including null, set channel_desc to null (include all channels):

```
select GET_CHAN_COUNTRY_SALES
(null, '52790,52779', '''2000-08'',''2000-09''') FROM DUAL;
```

It returns the following sql statement:

```
SELECT channel_desc, co.country_iso_code,
  TO_NUMBER(TO_CHAR(SUM(sum_amount_sold), '999999999999'))
SUM_AMOUNT_SOLD
 FROM sum_sales_month_mv s, customers c, channels ch,
countries co WHERE 1=1 AND s.calendar_month_desc IN
( '2000-08','2000-09' ) AND co.country_id IN ( 52790,52779)
AND s.cust_id=c.cust_id AND s.channel_id= ch.channel_id and
c.country_id=co.country_id
GROUP BY CUBE(channel_desc, co.country_iso_code)
```

CHANNEL_DESC	COUNTRY_ISO_CODE	SUM_AMOUNT_SOLD
		2506064
	FR	162139
	US	2343924
Internet		261735
Internet	FR	14002
Internet	US	247733
Partners		823827
Partners	FR	49349
Partners	US	774478
Direct Sales		1420502
Direct Sales	FR	98789
Direct Sales	US	1321713

Call the function with the following parameters, set calendar_month_desc to null (with no limit on this field):

```
select GET_CHAN_COUNTRY_SALES('''Direct Sales'',
''Internet''', '52790,52779', null) FROM DUAL;

SELECT channel_desc, co.country_iso_code,
  TO_NUMBER(TO_CHAR(SUM(sum_amount_sold), '999999999999'))
SUM_AMOUNT_SOLD
 FROM sum_sales_month_mv s, customers c, channels ch,
countries co WHERE 1=1 AND ch.channel_desc IN ( 'Direct
Sales', 'Internet' ) AND co.country_id IN ( 52790,52779) AND
s.cust_id=c.cust_id AND s.channel_id= ch.channel_id and
c.country_id=co.country_id
GROUP BY CUBE(channel_desc, co.country_iso_code)
```

CHANNEL_DESC	COUNTRY_ISO_CODE	SUM_AMOUNT_SOLD
		18920357
	FR	1330149
	US	17590209
Internet		2529508
Internet	FR	107654
Internet	US	2421854
Direct Sales		16390849
Direct Sales	FR	1222495
Direct Sales	US	15168354

Following PL/SQL Call the function and get result in XML format:

```
DECLARE
result CLOB; vRowTag VARCHAR2(30); q_string VARCHAR2(4000);
p_channel_desc VARCHAR2(100); p_country_id VARCHAR2(100);
p_month VARCHAR2(100); vprog errlog.PROG%TYPE:=
'chan_country_sales';
err_msg errlog.ERR_MSG%TYPE; err_num errlog.ERR_NUM%TYPE;
BEGIN
-- use double quote and a single quote to enclose the list
p_channel_desc:='''Direct Sales'', ''Internet''';
p_country_id:= '52790,52779';
p_month:= '''2000-08'',''2000-09''';
vRowTag:='chan_country_sales';
q_string:=get_chan_country_sales(p_channel_desc,p_country
```

```
_id,p_month);
result:=GET_QUERY_XML_withRowTag(q_string, vRowTag);
err_num := SQLCODE;
     err_msg:= q_string;
    INSERT INTO errlog (prog,err_num,err_msg,err_day,cnt)
    VALUES (vprog, err_num, err_msg,SYSDATE,0);
INSERT INTO clob_tmp VALUES(result);
COMMIT;
END;
```

5.7.2.2 FUNCTION get_sales_gender – Customer analysis ROLLUP

Create a function passing channel, country id, month as input and returns a SQL string.

```
CREATE OR REPLACE FUNCTION get_sales_gender
(p_channel_desc IN VARCHAR2 DEFAULT NULL,
 p_country_id IN VARCHAR2 DEFAULT NULL,
 p_month IN VARCHAR2 DEFAULT NULL
 )
 RETURN VARCHAR2 IS
q_string1 VARCHAR2(4000);


whr VARCHAR2(2000):= NULL;
BEGIN
q_string1:= 'SELECT s.calendar_month_desc
cal_month,co.country_iso_code, c.CUST_GENDER,
      TO_NUMBER(TO_CHAR(SUM(sum_amount_sold),
''999999999999'')) SUM_AMOUNT_SOLD
 FROM sum_sales_month_mv s, customers c, channels ch,
countries co ';
Whr:= ' WHERE 1=1 AND ';
IF p_channel_desc IS NOT NULL THEN
 Whr:= Whr||' ch.channel_desc IN ( '||p_channel_desc||' )
AND ';
END IF;
IF p_month IS NOT NULL THEN
 Whr:=Whr||' s.calendar_month_desc IN ( '||p_month||' ) AND
';
END IF;
```

```
IF p_month IS NOT NULL THEN
 Whr:= Whr||' s.calendar_month_desc IN ( '||p_month||' ) AND
';
END IF;
IF p_country_id IS NOT NULL THEN
 Whr:= Whr||' co.country_id IN ( '|| p_country_id||') AND ';
END IF;
Whr:= Whr||' s.cust_id=c.cust_id AND s.channel_id=
ch.channel_id AND c.country_id = co.country_id ';
q_string1:= q_string1||whr||' GROUP BY
s.calendar_month_desc ,co.country_iso_code, c.CUST_GENDER
';
RETURN q_string1;
END;
/
```

Call the function with following parameters including null:

```
SELECT
GET _SALES _GENDER(null,'52790,52779','''2000-08'',''2000-09''')
FROM DUAL;
```

CAL_MONTH	COUNTRY_ISO_CODE	CUST_GENDER	SUM_AMOUNT_SOLD
2000-08	FR	F	26543
2000-08	FR	M	34768
2000-08	US	F	427120
2000-08	US	M	777566
2000-09	FR	F	28985
2000-09	FR	M	71844
2000-09	US	F	419274
2000-09	US	M	719964

Browse cube

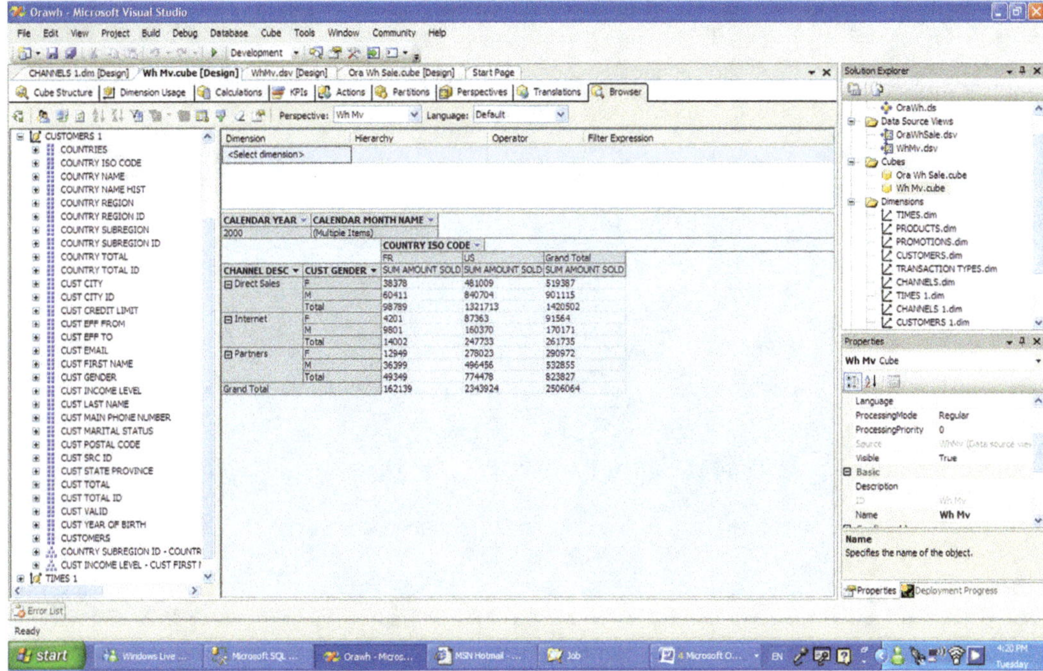

5.7.2.3 FUNCTION get_sales_gender_y – Customer analysis

Create a function passing channel, country id, year as input and returns a SQL string.

```
CREATE OR REPLACE FUNCTION get_sales_gender_y
(p_channel_desc IN VARCHAR2 DEFAULT NULL,
 p_country_id IN VARCHAR2 DEFAULT NULL,
 p_month IN VARCHAR2 DEFAULT NULL
 )
 RETURN VARCHAR2 IS
q_string1 VARCHAR2(4000);
whr VARCHAR2(2000):= NULL;
BEGIN
q_string1:= 'SELECT SUBSTR(s.calendar_month_desc,1,4)
year,co.country_iso_code, c.CUST_GENDER,
      TO_NUMBER(TO_CHAR(SUM(sum_amount_sold),
''999999999999'')) SUM_AMOUNT_SOLD
 FROM sum_sales_month_mv s, customers c, channels
ch,countries co ';
Whr:= ' WHERE 1=1 AND ';
IF p_channel_desc IS NOT NULL THEN
 Whr:= Whr||' ch.channel_desc IN ( '||p_channel_desc||' )
```

```
AND ';
END IF;
IF p_month IS NOT NULL THEN
 Whr:= Whr||' SUBSTR(s.calendar_month_desc,1,4) IN
( '||p_month||' ) AND ';
END IF;
IF p_country_id IS NOT NULL THEN
 Whr:= Whr||' co.country_id IN ( '|| p_country_id||') AND ';
END IF;
Whr:= Whr||' s.cust_id=c.cust_id AND s.channel_id=
ch.channel_id AND c.country_id = co.country_id ';

q_string1:= q_string1||whr||' GROUP BY
ROLLUP(SUBSTR(s.calendar_month_desc,1,4),
country_iso_code, c.CUST_GENDER) ';
RETURN q_string1;
END;
/
```

Call function with parameters including null:

```
SELECT  GET_SALES_GENDER_Y(null,'52779','''2000''')  FROM
DUAL;
```

YEAR	COUNTRY_ISO_CODE	CUST_GENDER	SUM_AMOUNT_SOLD
2000	FR	F	284845
2000	FR	M	601400
2000	FR		886245
2000			886245
			886245

5.7.3 Create Report Procedure Library

This section provides some complete examples of where you might use PL/SQL in a dynamic fashion to build procedure library in your applications.

PL/SQL stored procedures increase scalability by centralizing application processing on the server; they also increase manageability by serving as the powerful engine for many applications to make the global changes easier and faster.

The following procedure groups have same functionalities as function library in Section 5.7.2, the diference is that procedure using out parameter to pass resultset while function return the resultset. The procedures use PL/SQL and dynamic SQL to handle analytical requests dynamically.

PROCEDURE put_sales_statezip_cube - CUBE
PROCEDURE put_sales_roll - ROLLUP
PROCEDURE put_sales_gender – Customer analysis (Gender)
PROCEDURE put_sales_gender_y - Customer analysis (year, Gender)
PROCEDURE put_sales_trend -Trend analysis

5.7.3.1 PROCEDURE put_sales_statezip_cube - CUBE

Create a stored procedure that takes channel, country, month, postal code, postal code position as input and outputs result as SQL statement by an output parameter.

```
CREATE OR REPLACE PROCEDURE PUT_SALES_STATEZIP_CUBE
(p_channel_desc IN VARCHAR2 DEFAULT NULL,p_country_id IN
VARCHAR2 DEFAULT NULL
,p_month IN VARCHAR2 DEFAULT NULL,p_zip IN VARCHAR2 DEFAULT
NULL
,p_zip_num IN INTEGER DEFAULT NULL,q_string OUT VARCHAR2)
 IS
whr VARCHAR2(2000):= NULL;
subzip VARCHAR2(1000):=NULL;
BEGIN
q_string:=  'SELECT  channel_desc,  cust_state_province
state,
     TO_NUMBER(TO_CHAR(SUM(sum_amount_sold),
''999999999999'')) SUM_AMOUNT_SOLD FROM sum_sales_month_mv
s, customers c, channels ch ';
Whr:= ' WHERE 1=1 AND ';
IF p_channel_desc IS NOT NULL THEN
 Whr:= Whr||' ch.channel_desc IN ( '||p_channel_desc||' )
AND ';
END IF;
IF p_month IS NOT NULL THEN
 Whr:= Whr||' s.calendar_month_desc IN ( '||p_month||' ) AND
';
END IF;
```

```
IF p_country_id IS NOT NULL THEN
 Whr:= Whr||' country_id IN ( '|| p_country_id||') AND ';
END IF;
IF p_zip_num IS NOT NULL THEN
 subzip:= ' substr(cust_postal_code,1,'||p_zip_num||') ';
ELSE
 subzip:= 'cust_postal_code';
END IF;
IF p_zip IS NOT NULL THEN
 Whr:= Whr||subzip|| ' IN ( '||p_zip||' ) AND ';
END IF;
Whr:=   Whr||'   s.cust_id=c.cust_id   AND   s.channel_id=
ch.channel_id ';
q_string:= q_string||whr||' GROUP BY CUBE(channel_desc,
cust_state_province)';
  EXCEPTION
   WHEN OTHERS THEN
        Null; -- Error process
END PUT_SALES_STATEZIP_CUBE;
/
```

The procedure put_chan_country_sales can be created by similar way.
Following PL/SQL Call the procedures and get result as a correspondent SQL statement:

```
DECLARE
q_string VARCHAR2(4000);p_channel_desc varchar2(100);
p_country_id  varchar2(100);p_month  varchar2(100);p_tile
number;
vprog errlog.PROG%type:= 'put_chan_country_sales';
err_msg errlog.ERR_MSG%type;err_num errlog.ERR_NUM%type;
BEGIN
-- use double quote for list
p_channel_desc:='''Direct Sales'', ''Internet''';
p_country_id:= '52790,52779';
p_month:= '''2000-08'',''2000-09''';
p_tile:= 5;
BEGIN
put_chan_country_sales(p_channel_desc,p_country_id,p_mon
th, q_string);
```

```
--put_sales_cube(p_channel_desc,p_country_id,p_month,
q_string);
--put_sales_roll(p_channel_desc,p_country_id,p_month,
q_string);
put_sales_gender_y(p_channel_desc,p_country_id,p_month,
q_string);
END;
```

-- Do something about result in returned string q_string.

-- You may want to insert result string into error log table and review the result.

```
--EXECUTE IMMEDIATE q_string;
err_num := SQLCODE;
     err_msg:= q_string;

   INSERT INTO errlog (prog,err_num,err_msg,err_day,cnt)
   VALUES (vprog, err_num, err_msg,sysdate,0);
COMMIT;
END;
```

5.7.3.2 PROCEDURE put_sales_gender – Customer analysis (gender)

Create a stored procedure that takes channel, country, and month as input parameters and outputs a SQL string.

```
CREATE OR REPLACE PROCEDURE put_sales_gender
(p_channel_desc IN VARCHAR2 DEFAULT NULL,
 p_country_id IN VARCHAR2 DEFAULT NULL,
 p_month IN VARCHAR2 DEFAULT NULL,
 q_string OUT VARCHAR2)
 IS
whr VARCHAR2(2000):= NULL;
BEGIN
q_string:= 'SELECT s.calendar_month_desc
cal_month,country_iso_code, c.CUST_GENDER,
      TO_NUMBER(TO_CHAR(SUM(sum_amount_sold),
''999999999999'')) SUM_AMOUNT_SOLD
 FROM sum_sales_month_mv s, customers c, channels ch,
countries co ';
Whr:= ' WHERE 1=1 AND ';
IF p_channel_desc IS NOT NULL THEN
 Whr:= Whr||' ch.channel_desc IN ( '||p_channel_desc||' )
```

```
AND ';
END IF;
IF p_month IS NOT NULL THEN
 Whr:= Whr||' s.calendar_month_desc IN ( '||p_month||' ) AND
';
END IF;
IF p_country_id IS NOT NULL THEN
 Whr:= Whr||' co.country_id IN ( '|| p_country_id||') AND ';
END IF;
Whr:= Whr||' s.cust_id=c.cust_id AND s.channel_id=
ch.channel_id AND c.country_id= co.country_id ';
q_string:= q_string||whr||' GROUP BY
s.calendar_month_desc ,country_iso_code, c.CUST_GENDER ';
 END;
/
```

For calculated results, please refer to the Chapter Five <5.7.2 Create Report Functon Library>

5.7.2.2 FUNCTION get_sales_gender – Customer analysis (Gender)

5.7.3.3 PROCEDURE put_sales_gender_y – Customer analysis (year, gender)

Create a stored procedure that takes channel, country, month as input and output a SQL statement.

```
CREATE OR REPLACE PROCEDURE put_sales_gender_y
(p_channel_desc IN VARCHAR2 DEFAULT NULL,
 p_country_id IN VARCHAR2 DEFAULT NULL,
 p_month IN VARCHAR2 DEFAULT NULL,
 q_string OUT VARCHAR2)
 IS
whr VARCHAR2(2000):= NULL;
BEGIN
q_string:= 'SELECT SUBSTR(s.calendar_month_desc,1,4)
year,country_iso_code, c.CUST_GENDER,
```

```
     TO_NUMBER(TO_CHAR(SUM(sum_amount_sold),
''999999999999'')) SUM_AMOUNT_SOLD
 FROM sum_sales_month_mv s, customers c, channels ch,
countries co ';
Whr:= ' WHERE 1=1 AND ';
IF p_channel_desc IS NOT NULL THEN
 Whr:= Whr||' ch.channel_desc IN ( '||p_channel_desc||' )
AND ';
END IF;
IF p_month IS NOT NULL THEN
 Whr:= Whr||' SUBSTR(s.calendar_month_desc,1,4) IN
( '||p_month||' ) AND ';
END IF;
IF p_country_id IS NOT NULL THEN
 Whr:= Whr||' co.country_id IN ( '|| p_country_id||') AND ';
END IF;
Whr:= Whr||' s.cust_id=c.cust_id AND s.channel_id=
ch.channel_id AND c.country_id= co.country_id ';
q_string:= q_string||whr||' GROUP BY
ROLLUP(SUBSTR(s.calendar_month_desc,1,4),
country_iso_code, c.CUST_GENDER) ';
END;
/
```

For calculated results, please refer to the Chapter Five <5.7.2 Create Report Functon Library>

5.7.2.3 FUNCTION get_sales_gender_y – Customer analysis (year, gender).

5.7.3.4 PROCEDURE put_sales_trend - Trend analysis

The following SQL procedure use in-line view to get sales from different time periods.

```
CREATE OR REPLACE PROCEDURE put_sales_trend
(p_channel_desc IN VARCHAR2 DEFAULT NULL,
 p_country_id IN VARCHAR2 DEFAULT NULL,
 p_month IN VARCHAR2 DEFAULT NULL,
 q_string OUT VARCHAR2)
 IS
whr1 VARCHAR2(1000):= NULL;
whr2 VARCHAR2(1000):= NULL;
v_month_last VARCHAR2(30):=NULL;
BEGIN
v_month_last:=
substr(p_month,1,1)||to_char(to_number(substr(p_month,2,4)
- 1)) ||substr(p_month,6,5);
Whr1:= ' WHERE 1=1 AND ';
Whr2:= ' WHERE 1=1 AND ';
IF p_channel_desc IS NOT NULL THEN
 Whr1:= Whr1||' ch.channel_desc IN ( '||p_channel_desc||' )
AND ';
 Whr2:= Whr2||' ch.channel_desc IN ( '||p_channel_desc||' )
AND ';
END IF;
IF p_month IS NOT NULL THEN
 Whr1:= Whr1||' s.calendar_month_desc IN ( '||p_month||' )
AND ';
 Whr2:= Whr2||' s.calendar_month_desc IN
( '||v_month_last||' ) AND ';
END IF;
IF p_country_id IS NOT NULL THEN
 Whr1:= Whr1||' co.country_id IN ( '|| p_country_id||') AND
';
```

```
 Whr2:= Whr2||' co.country_id IN ( '|| p_country_id||') AND
';
END IF;
Whr1:= Whr1||' s.cust_id=c.cust_id AND s.channel_id=
ch.channel_id AND c.country_id= co.country_id ';
Whr2:= Whr2||' s.cust_id=c.cust_id AND s.channel_id=
ch.channel_id AND c.country_id= co.country_id ';
q_string:= 'SELECT channel_desc, country_iso_code,
      TO_NUMBER(TO_CHAR(SUM(sum_amount_sold),
''999999999999'')) SUM_AMOUNT_SOLD,
      TO_NUMBER(TO_CHAR(SUM(PAST_YEAR_SOLD),
''999999999999'')) PAST_YEAR_SOLD
FROM(
SELECT channel_desc, country_iso_code, SUM_AMOUNT_SOLD,0
PAST_YEAR_SOLD
 FROM sum_sales_month_mv s, customers c, channels ch,
countries co '||whr1||
 ' UNION ALL
SELECT channel_desc, country_iso_code, 0
SUM_AMOUNT_SOLD,SUM_AMOUNT_SOLD PAST_YEAR_SOLD
 FROM sum_sales_month_mv s, customers c, channels ch,
countries co '||whr2||
 ' ) GROUP BY channel_desc, country_iso_code';
END;
/
```

5.7.4 Reporting Frameworks and Supporting Schema

In this section, you will find a simple prototype of a reporting governing mechanism with a defined package. This allows you to generate report on which you are placing report definitions in the schema and keeping track all of reporting attempts. It can be maintained for each user. Here is the specification of this package:

Reporting Frameworks and Supporting Schema

Having built report function library and procedure library, we are now ready to move on to put everything together for a complete reporting system such as build whole report frameworks and most importantly the centralized packages to coordinate all the report components to function as a centralized report governing.

The basic purpose of the report package is to manage and to organize report components - it provides the ability to execute the needed functions or procedures in a coordinated manner. This promotes code reuse and modular design, especially in environments where the packages must to deal with the dynamic changes. By incorporating frequently used functions and procedures into packages, we can simplify modification and maintenance meanwhile gain additional functionalities, flexibilities and performance.

- ❑ Schema
- ❑ System Frame Chart
- ❑ Report Main Process Flow
- ❑ *PACAKGE DISPATCH_RPT*
- ❑ *TEST PACKAGE DISPATCH_RPT*

5.7.4.1 Schema

Using dedicated data schema to support report management has sevareal advantages:

Expandibility: instead of embedding the additional report (procedure) names into the package, report (procedure) names are stored in the tables and can be called by reading from tables thus provide the convinence in expand the reports or delete reports based on usage requirement changes.

Flexibility: report (procedure) name can be added as data not part of codes for packages, so we are able to add or delete reports without re-compile whole report packages.

Reliability: such loosely coupled structure can avoid possible risks from ruining whole system caused by few bad components; such bad reports (components) can remain isolated without causing overall impact which may cripple the whole report packages.

Here is a simple data schema to support report management:

- o Table *Rpt_Main* is a master table holding report name and proceudure name.
- o Table *Rpt_User* tie to *Rpt_Main* and holding report-user related parameters.
- o Table *Rpt_log* tie to *Table Rpt_User* and logging user report session information:
- o Table *Errlog* is used for tracking purposes.
  - ➢ Logging system-generated dynamic SQL queries for user for possible later use.
  - ➢ Logging error message.
  - ➢ Mostly for testing purposes.

5.7.4.1.1 Table *RPT_MAIN*

Holding report names and conrespondent procedure names:

```
CREATE TABLE RPT_MAIN
(
 RPT_ID     INTEGER   NOT NULL, /* report id primary key */
 CATEGORY    VARCHAR2(100),
 RPT_NAME    VARCHAR2(100) NOT NULL, /* report name */
 PROC_NAME   VARCHAR2(100) NOT NULL, /* procedure name*/
 RPT_VERSION VARCHAR2(30),   /* report version */
 STATUS     INTEGER,
 ACT_DATE    DATE,      /* activation date */
 RPT_DATE    DATE
);
```

5.7.4.1.2 TYPE OBJIECT *param_t*

Create a type first before creating table holding report parameters.

```
(param1 varchar2(100),
 param2 varchar2(100),
 param3 varchar2(100),
 param4 CLOB
);
```

5.7.4.1.3 TYPE *rpt_user_t*

Create the type to hold user information.

```
CREATE TYPE rpt_user_t AS OBJECT (
  Rpt_id         INTEGER , /* report id, link to rpt_main */
  rpt_user_id     INTEGER,    /* report-user id primary key
*/
  user_id        INTEGER ,
  param_list         PARAM_T,  /*  parameter  list  (param1,
param2, param3, param4) */
  access_level     INTEGER,
  status         INTEGER,
  act_date        DATE,     /* activation date */
  m_date         DATE      /* data manipulation date */

);
```

5.7.4.1.4 Table *RPT_USER*

```
CREATE TABLE RPT _USER OF RPT _USER _T;
```

5.7.4.1.5 Table *RPT_LOG*

Create a report log table to track report processes.

```
CREATE TABLE RPT_LOG
(
 RPT_USER_ID INTEGER  NOT NULL, /* report-user id */
 RPT_LOG_ID INTEGER NOT NULL, /* report logging id, primary
key */
 LOG_TYPE   VARCHAR2(10),
 SESSION_ID  INTEGER,
 ERR_NUM   NUMBER,          /* error number */
 LOG_MESSAGE VARCHAR2(4000), /* logging message */
 STATUS    INTEGER,
 M_DATE    DATE          /* data manipulation date */
);
```

5.7.4.1.6 Table *ERRLOG*

Create an error log table to track report errors.

```
CREATE TABLE errlog
(prog varchar(30),    /* procedure name which we intent to
tracking */
err_num number,       /* Oracle error number */
err_msg varchar2(4000), /* error message and other query
string dump */
err_day date,
cnt number);
```

5.7.4.2 System Framework Chart

Report Framework and Its Supporting Schema
And Report Main Process Flow

Figure 5-5.7-19 RPT_PACKAGE_FRAME

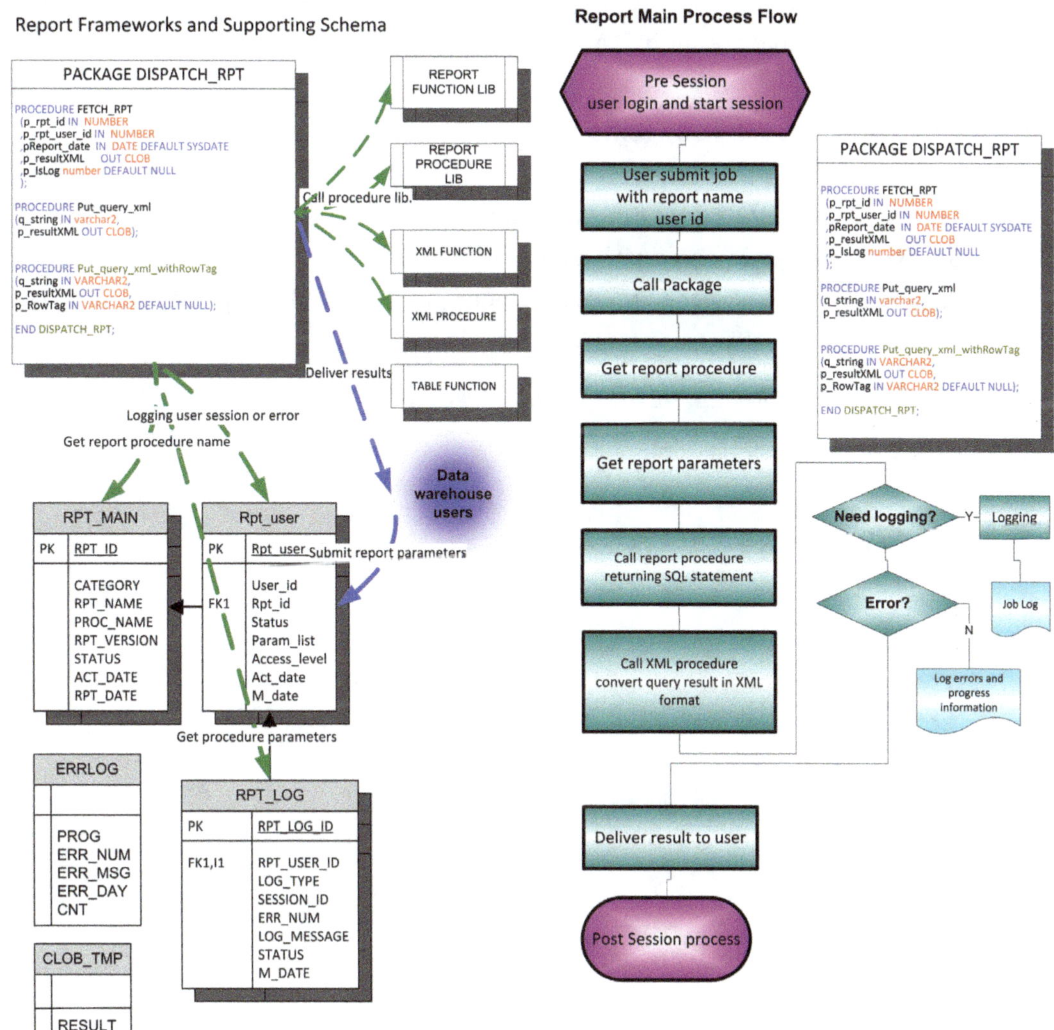

5.7.4.4 PACAKGE *DISPATCH_RPT*

Define a package with the following functionalities:

- Accept application call with parameters such as report_user_id, report_id.
- Gether the report related parameters for the user and report
- Invoke the procedure dynamically with parameters
- Compose a SQL query and return the dynamic SQL query based on parameters.
- Deliver the query result in XML format.

5.7.4.4.1 Define a package specificaton

Include three procedures,

DISPATCH_RPT - The package defines two procedures. The first procedure, FETCH_RPT, opens report using user id and report id as parameters then compose the correspondent SQL query statement. The second procedure, put_query_xml, return query result in XML format using the query string as parameter.

Put_query_xml, Put_query_xml_withRowTag - convert data into XMLformat.

Define the package specification:

```
CREATE OR REPLACE PACKAGE DISPATCH_RPT
AS
/* main procedure */
PROCEDURE FETCH_RPT
 (p_rpt_id IN NUMBER
 ,p_rpt_user_id IN NUMBER
 ,pReport_date IN DATE DEFAULT SYSDATE
 ,p_resultXML   OUT CLOB
 ,p_IsLog number DEFAULT NULL
 );
/* Accept sql query and output result in XML */
PROCEDURE Put_query_xml

 (q_string IN varchar2,
  p_resultXML OUT CLOB);
 /* Accept sql query and tag and output result in XML with tag
 */
 PROCEDURE Put_query_xml_withRowTag
 (q_string IN VARCHAR2,
 p_resultXML OUT CLOB,
 p_RowTag IN VARCHAR2 DEFAULT NULL);
 END DISPATCH_RPT;
 /
```

Here is the package body:

```
CREATE OR REPLACE PACKAGE BODY DISPATCH_RPT AS
PROCEDURE FETCH_RPT
 (p_rpt_id IN NUMBER
 ,p_rpt_user_id IN NUMBER
 ,pReport_date IN DATE DEFAULT SYSDATE
 ,p_resultXML   OUT CLOB
 ,p_IsLog number DEFAULT NULL)
AS
V_PARAM1 RPT_USER.PARAM_LIST.param1%TYPE;
V_PARAM2 RPT_USER.PARAM_LIST.param2%TYPE;
V_PARAM3 RPT_USER.PARAM_LIST.param3%TYPE;
V_PARAM4 RPT_USER.PARAM_LIST.param4%TYPE;
P_ROWTAG VARCHAR2(100):=NULL;
q_string VARCHAR2(4000);
v_procString varchar2(1000);
v_proc varchar2(100);
err_msg rpt_log.log_message%type;
err_num rpt_log.ERR_NUM%type;
null_query EXCEPTION;
CURSOR c1 (P_RPT_ID NUMBER) IS
SELECT PROC_NAME FROM RPT_MAIN WHERE RPT_ID = P_RPT_ID;
BEGIN
FOR REC1 IN C1 (P_RPT_ID) LOOP
SELECT
p.param_list.param1,p.param_list.param2,p.param_list.para
m3,
p.param_list.param4
INTO V_PARAM1,V_PARAM2,V_PARAM3,V_PARAM4
 FROM RPT_USER p WHERE RPT_USER_ID = P_RPT_USER_ID;
v_procString:='BEGIN
'||rec1.proc_name||'(:1,:2,:3,:4)'||'; END;';
-- Dynamiclly invoke procedure with parameters
EXECUTE IMMEDIATE v_procString
USING IN V_PARAM1,IN V_PARAM2,IN V_PARAM3,OUT Q_STRING;
END LOOP; -- C1
IF Q_STRING IS NOT NULL THEN
 Put_query_xml(q_string,p_resultXML);
```

```
ELSE
RAISE NULL_QUERY;
END IF;
 -- logging user's query string for repeated call
 IF p_IsLog IS NOT NULL AND p_IsLog =1 THEN
  err_num := SQLCODE;
   err_msg:= q_string;
   INSERT                  INTO                   rpt_log
(rpt_user_id,err_num,log_message,status,m_date)
   VALUES (p_rpt_user_id,err_num, err_msg,0,sysdate);
END IF;
-- logging user's error message
 EXCEPTION
  WHEN NULL_QUERY  THEN
   err_num := SQLCODE;
   err_msg := SUBSTR('Nothing generated! ', -1, 400) ;
  INSERT                  INTO                    rpt_log
(rpt_user_id,err_num,log_message,status,m_date)
   VALUES (p_rpt_user_id,err_num, err_msg,-1,sysdate);
  WHEN OTHERS  THEN
   err_num := SQLCODE;
   err_msg := SUBSTR(SQLERRM, 1, 400) ;
  INSERT                  INTO                    rpt_log
(rpt_user_id,err_num,log_message,status,m_date)
   VALUES (p_rpt_user_id,err_num, err_msg,-1,sysdate);
COMMIT;
END;


PROCEDURE Put_query_xml
(q_string IN varchar2,p_resultXML OUT CLOB)
IS
qryCtx DBMS_XMLGEN.ctxHandle;
BEGIN
qryCtx := dbms_xmlgen.newContext(q_string);
DBMS_XMLGEN.setRowTag(qryCtx, 'REPORT');
p_resultXML := DBMS_XMLGEN.getXML(qryCtx);
DBMS_XMLGEN.closeContext(qryCtx);
END;
```

```
PROCEDURE Put_query_xml_withRowTag
(q_string IN VARCHAR2,p_resultXML OUT CLOB,p_RowTag IN
VARCHAR2 DEFAULT NULL)
IS
qryCtx DBMS_XMLGEN.ctxHandle;
BEGIN
qryCtx := dbms_xmlgen.newContext(q_string);
IF NOT(p_RowTag IS NULL) THEN
DBMS_XMLGEN.setRowTag(qryCtx, p_RowTag);
END IF;
p_resultXML := DBMS_XMLGEN.getXML(qryCtx);
DBMS_XMLGEN.closeContext(qryCtx);
END;
END DISPATCH_RPT;
/
```

5.7.4.5 TEST PACKAGE *DISPATCH_RPT*

With this package in place, following PL/SQL call the package and get result in XML format: The following example illustrates a PL/SQL that you can test (the package).

```
DECLARE
PXMLCLOB CLOB;
v_IsLog Number:= 1; -- null: no logging; 1: logging
v_tespar number:= 5;
BEGIN
--DISPATCH_RPT(90,190,NULL,PXMLCLOB);
--DISPATCH_RPT.fetch_rpt(60,160,NULL,PXMLCLOB);
--fetch_rpt(60,160,NULL,PXMLCLOB);
--DISPATCH_RPT.fetch_rpt(90,190,NULL,PXMLCLOB);
DISPATCH_RPT.fetch_rpt(20,120,NULL,PXMLCLOB,v_IsLog);
INSERT INTO CLOB_TMP
VALUES(PXMLCLOB);
COMMIT;
END;
```

Note: In the following statement call package DISPATCH_RPT,

```
DISPATCH_RPT.fetch_rpt(20,120,NULL,PXMLCLOB,v_IsLog);
```

Using parameters: (report id, report-user id, null parameter, output parameter, logging)

5.7.4.5.2 List SQL query from user-report logging table:

```
SELECT LOG_MESSAGE FROM RPT_LOG WHERE RPT_USER_ID= 120 AND
RPT_LOG_ID = 80;

SELECT calendar_month_desc AS CAL_MONTH,
      TO_NUMBER(TO_CHAR(SUM(sum_amount_sold),
'999999999999')) SUM_AMOUNT_SOLD,
      NTILE(TO_NUMBER(4)) OVER (ORDER BY
SUM(sum_amount_sold)) AS TILEX
 FROM SUM_SALES_MONTH_MV s, CUSTOMERS c, CHANNELS ch
 WHERE 1=1
 AND SUBSTR(s.calendar_month_desc,1,4) IN ( '2000')
 AND country_id IN ( 52790,52779) AND s.cust_id=c.cust_id
 GROUP BY calendar_month_desc
```

5.7.4.5.3 Run the SQL query:

CAL _MONTH	SUM _AMOUNT _SOLD	TILEX
2000-04	5073466	1
2000-06	5078269	1
2000-07	5533772	1
2000-05	5611805	2
2000-01	5625050	2
2000-03	5658982	2
2000-12	5975794	3
2000-11	6086859	3
2000-09	6200331	3
2000-02	6305525	4
2000-08	6329987	4
2000-10	6554355	4

5.7.4.5.4 Get result in XML format:

```
SQL> select * from clob_tmp
```


```
<?xml version="1.0"?>
<ROWSET>
<REPORT>
<CAL_MONTH>2000-07</CAL_MONTH>
<SUM_AMOUNT_SOLD>41401495</SUM_AMOUNT_SOLD>
<TILEX>1</TILEX>
</REPORT>
<REPORT>
<CAL_MONTH>2000-06</CAL_MONTH>
<SUM_AMOUNT_SOLD>41592124</SUM_AMOUNT_SOLD>
<TILEX>1</TILEX>
</REPORT>
<REPORT>
<CAL_MONTH>2000-08</CAL_MONTH>
<SUM_AMOUNT_SOLD>42334916</SUM_AMOUNT_SOLD>
<TILEX>1</TILEX>
</REPORT>
<REPORT>
<CAL_MONTH>2000-09</CAL_MONTH>
<SUM_AMOUNT_SOLD>43216789</SUM_AMOUNT_SOLD>
<TILEX>2</TILEX>
</REPORT>
<REPORT>
<CAL_MONTH>2000-02</CAL_MONTH>
<SUM_AMOUNT_SOLD>45296002</SUM_AMOUNT_SOLD>
<TILEX>2</TILEX>
</REPORT>
<REPORT>
<CAL_MONTH>2000-03</CAL_MONTH>
<SUM_AMOUNT_SOLD>45384829</SUM_AMOUNT_SOLD>
<TILEX>2</TILEX>
</REPORT>
...
...
</ROWSET>
```

GLOSSARY

3DA	Dynamic Data Driven Approach
3DETL	Dynamic Data Driven ETL
3DP	Dynamic Data Driven Procedure
BI	Business Intelligence/Business Insight
DW	Data warehouse
EDW	Enterprise Data warehouse
ETL	Extraction, Transformation, Loading
MLMS	Multi-layer Multi-Segment
MVIEW	Materialized view/Indexed view
ODS	Operational Data Source
OLAP	Online Analytical Processing
OLTP	Online Transaction Processing
ROI	Return On Investment

Sun zi
Accent Chinese military strategist, dating from the late Spring and Autumn Period (770-476 B.C.).

His work - The Art of War is the earliest and most valuable Chinese treatise on military science.

REFERENCE

1. Introduction_to_evolution. (n.d.). In *Wikipedia*. Retrieved October 10, 2011, from http://en.wikipedia.org/wiki/Introduction_to_evolution

2. W. H. Inmon, *Building the Data Warehouse* 1991.

3. Ralph Kimball, The Data Warehouse Toolkit : Practical Techniques for Building Dimensional Data Warehouses, John Wiley & Sons, 1996.

4. W. H. Inmon, The DSS Environment - Data Warehouse, Data Marts, And Data Mining A Glimpse At The Past, A Peek at The Future

5. Sunzi

   The Art of War is the earliest and most valuable Chinese treatise on military science extant, dating from the late Spring and Autumn Period (770-476 B.C.). The book is a condensation of the experience of warfare in that historical era, with the emphasis on precautionary and intelligence strategy. By revealing the nature and important rules of warfare, Sunzi: The Art of War has had a tremendous influence on military, political and philosophical thought in China. Down the ages it has been called a "military genius." This work, now over 2,000 years old, has been translated into various languages since the 17th century, and even today has a profound influence all over the world.

   His work still been unearthed from China, the recent discovery (1972) from a tom of Han dynasty found that his book was inscribed on bamboo slips bundled with strings even before paper was invented.

AUTHOR'S BIO

Taiwei Chi is an Information Technology consultant working in the areas of Data warehouse/Business Intelligence, reporting systems designs and developments. As a battle hardened veteran architect over many years in his fields, he has gained rich knowledge and wisdom from his real life experiences.

Living in the Pacific Northwest, Taiwei loves beautiful nature as well as innovative ideas. Walking on the forest trails, breathing mountain mist, listening to the creek roaring while thinking about his works that was how this book was hatched. He can be reached at taihangshanwei@gmail.com.

www.ingramcontent.com/pod-product-compliance
Lightning Source LLC
LaVergne TN
LVHW081449060526
838201LV00050BA/1746

* 9 7 9 8 8 8 6 4 0 9 4 7 5 *